India's
Democracy

General Editor: Max Beloff
Gladstone Professor of Government and Public Administration,
University of Oxford

COMPARATIVE MODERN GOVERNMENTS

India's Democracy

A. H. HANSON
Late Professor of Politics, University of Leeds

JANET DOUGLAS
*Senior Lecturer in Contemporary Studies,
Leeds Polytechnic*

W · W · NORTON & COMPANY · INC ·
NEW YORK

Copyright © 1972 BY JOAN M. HANSON AND JANET DOUGLAS

Library of Congress Cataloging in Publication Data

Hanson, Albert Henry.
   India's democracy.

   (Comparative modern governments series)
   Bibliography: p.
   1. India—Politics and government—1947-
I. Douglas, Janet, joint author. II. Title.
JQ215 1972.H 3   320.9'54'04   77-152679
ISBN 0-393-05469-1
ISBN 0-393-09908-3 (pbk.)

PRINTED IN THE UNITED STATES OF AMERICA

1 2 3 4 5 6 7 8 9 0

Contents

Editor's Introduction

The series of which this is the first volume is intended as a contribution to the study of contemporary political institutions in a number of countries both in Europe and in the rest of the world, selected either for their intrinsic importance or because of the particular interest attaching to their form of government and the manner of its working. Although we expect that most readers of such a series will be students of politics in universities or other institutions of higher or further education, the approach is not wholly that of what is now technically styled 'political science'. Our aims have been at once more modest and more practical.

All study of government must be comparative, in that the questions one asks about one system will usually arise from one's knowledge of another, and although we hope that anyone who has read a number of these volumes will derive some valuable general ideas about political institutions, the notion that politics is a suitable subject for generalization and prediction is alien to the empirical spirit that animates the series.

The authors are concerned with government as an important practical activity which now impinges upon the life of the citizen in almost every sphere. They seek in each individual country to ask such questions as how laws are made and how enforced, who determines and in what manner the basic domestic and foreign policies of the country. They seek to estimate the role not only of elected persons, presidents, ministers, members of parliament and of lesser assemblies but also of the officials and members of the armed forces who play a vital role in different ways in the different societies.

But government is not something carried out for its own sake; ultimately the criterion of success and failure is to be found in its impact upon the lives of individual citizens. And here two further questions need to be asked : how does government conduct itself in regard to the citizen and what protection has he through the courts or in other ways against arbitrary action or mal-administration? The second question is how the citizen can in fact make his influence felt upon the course of government, since most of the countries that will be discussed in these volumes claim to be democratic in the broadest sense. And this inquiry leads on to a discussion of political parties and the various interest-groups or pressure-groups which in modern states form the normal vehicles for self-expression by citizens sharing a common interest or common opinions. To understand their working, some knowledge of the role of the press and other mass-media is clearly essential.

The study of such aspects of politics has recently been very fashionable and is sometimes styled the behavioural approach or the investigation of a political culture. But our authors have kept in mind the fact that while the nature of a country's formal institutions may be explained as the product of its political culture, the informal aspects of politics can only be understood if the legal and institutional framework is clearly kept in mind. In the end the decisions are made, except where anarchy or chaos prevails, by constituted authority.

We would like to feel that anyone suddenly required for official or business or cultural purposes to go to one of these countries hitherto unknown to him would find the relevant volume of immediate use in enabling him to find his way about its governmental structure and to understand the way in which it might impinge upon his own concerns. There is a great deal to be said for a guide-book even in politics.

Nevertheless no attempt has been made to impose uniformity of treatment upon these volumes. Each writer is an authority for his particular country or group of countries and will have a different set of priorities; none would wish to treat in the same way an old-established and highly integrated polity such as that of France or the United Kingdom and a vast and heterogeneous political society still searching for stable forms such as India.

The editor wishes to thank Miss J. F. Maitland-Jones, the deputy editor, for much help in the planning of the series as a whole and in the presentation of the individual volumes.

Preface

Events now move so fast in India that we cannot expect this little book on the country's government and politics to be up-to-date. It was completed in March 1971 and does its best to take into account the results of the elections of that month. There has been no opportunity, however, to attempt a balanced assessment of the significance of Mrs Gandhi's victory, and we fully expect that, by the time the book appears, some of our judgments will seem rather dated.

For help in planning this work, our warmest thanks are due to Professor Max Beloff, the editor of the series. We are equally grateful to Miss J. F. Maitland-Jones and Mr Neville Maxwell for reading it in typescript and making valuable suggestions for its improvement. Both opinions and errors are, of course, entirely our own.

Leeds 1971   A.H.H.
                                                    J.D.

Professor A. H. Hanson

Professor Hanson died shortly after completing the manuscript of this book. As a former student of his I should like to express on behalf of myself and countless other students, our appreciation of the teacher we all knew and respected. To have a distinguished scholar as a teacher is a great privilege but we were additionally fortunate in that Professor Hanson remained a man totally without arrogance. His door was ever open to his students and we were always welcomed with a kindliness and consideration which put even the most apprehensive at ease. To his classes, Professor Hanson brought not only his skills as a teacher and the width and depth of his knowledge but also a sense of humour, three qualities which made learning a pleasure and stimulated students to further study and thought.

It is perhaps fitting that Professor Hanson's last written work should concern India. Certainly some will disagree with the views expressed in this book, and he would have expected and welcomed such debate, but no one can doubt the deep concern that Professor Hanson felt for India and her peoples. If this study in some way helps to kindle further interest in this much neglected area of the world, then I am sure he would have been well pleased.

June 1971   J.D.

India's
Democracy

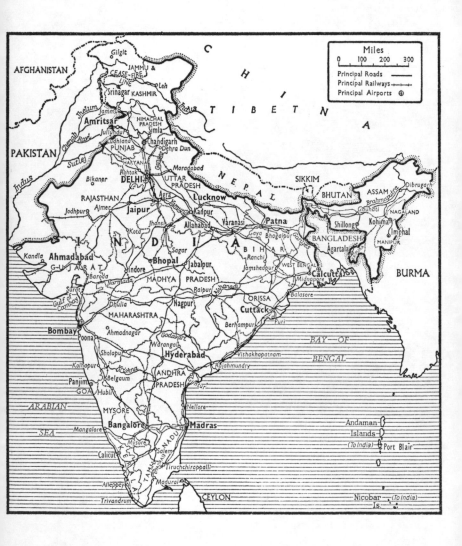

1 Introduction

In this book our main purpose is to describe a set of political institutions and to throw some light on the way in which they work. This may seem to be a comparatively modest undertaking and might even be criticised as an old-fashioned one. At present, institutional study is not as highly regarded as it used to be. For modern political scientists, the analysis of the behaviour of the participants in the governmental process and the delineation of political 'styles' seem to be of much greater importance. We ourselves believe that this change of emphasis is healthy. It has certainly given political studies a depth which in former days they all too frequently lacked. Nevertheless, we are firmly of the opinion that unless the student of a political system is thoroughly familiar with its institutional framework and has understood something of the way in which institutions have developed over the years, he lacks the points of reference that are essential for the guidance of his further and perhaps more profound investigations. Such is our justification for the approach we have here adopted.

It is precisely because of the limitations of this approach that the predominantly descriptive chapters that follow need to be prefaced by a brief discussion of some of the salient characteristics of the society with whose political institutions we are concerned; otherwise the reader might be tempted to make misleading comparisons between Indian political institutions and those of other countries to which they bear a formal resemblance. To compare political systems is certainly one of the functions of the political scientist, but we would strongly emphasise the inappropriateness of any *direct* use of the material contained in this book in aid of a far-flung comparative exercise. For if comparison is to be fruitful, it must be preceded by an examination in depth of the specific and in some cases unique features of the evolving social order of which each political system is a part. As we have neither adequate knowledge nor adequate space to undertake such an examination of India's social order, we shall have to remain content with making a few broad generalisations about 'the condition of India', in the context of which what is to be said about her political institutions should be read.

The familiar points about size and diversity are the first that must be made. With a population approaching 570 million, India is the second largest political unit in the modern world. Her diversity, as is well known, finds most spectacular expression in her multiplicity of languages. According to census data, there are over one thousand of these, including dialects, and fifteen (including, admittedly, the dead language of Sanskrit) are important enough to be specified in the 8th Schedule of the Constitution, viz.: Assamese, Bengali, Gujerati, Hindi, Kannada, Kashmiri, Malayalam, Marathi, Oriya, Punjabi, Sanskrit, Sindhi, Tamil, Telugu and Urdu. The importance of this linguistic diversity as an obstacle to nation-wide political communication hardly requires emphasis. Even Hindi, the most widely-used of India's languages, and the Constitution's designated *lingua franca,* is spoken by no more than about thirty per cent of Indians. Urdu, Punjabi, Hindustani, Bihari and Rajasthani are admittedly closely related to it (and are, therefore, sometimes included in the 'Hindi' group to produce a total of some forty-three per cent 'Hindi speakers') but they are not close enough to facilitate more than very elementary forms of inter-communication, particularly as Urdu and Punjabi have their own distinctive scripts. As for English, although it is used in all parts of the country, it remains, and is likely to remain, the second language of a small educated minority.

Differences of religious belief, particularly when they coincide with differences of social organisation and custom, constitute another divisive factor, of greater political importance than language in those areas where people of dissimilar faiths are living side by side. Although Hinduism, of one variety or another, is the religion of the vast majority, a very substantial minority of Muslims (representing over 10 per cent of the total population) was left on the Indian side of the border after the creation of Pakistan. Indeed, of the countries of the world only Indonesia and Pakistan herself contain more Muslim inhabitants than does India. If to the Muslims are added the comparatively small communities of Sikhs, Jains, Parsees, Buddhists and Christians, together with the tribal 'animists', one arrives at a figure for non-Hindus amounting to rather more than one-fifth of the total population.

The predominance of Hinduism, with its characteristic caste system, certainly means that a majority of the Indian people have something in the nature of common beliefs and analogous social structures. However, as an amorphous and syncretistic religion, without any recognised 'establishment', Hinduism itself shows immense diversities, both as between different beliefs and as between different regions. The schematic division of the Hindu population into the familiar *varnas, viz.* Brahmin (priest), Kshatriya (warrior), Vaisya (merchant), and Sudra (worker), is almost useless as a means of interpreting the endless and baffling complexity of local caste divisions; and one must never forget that there are still many millions of Indian citizens whose 'untouchable' status puts them right outside the *varna* system and subjects them to forms of discrimination which, although forbidden by law, are still very widely practised. Moreover, there is nothing that can be described as a 'typical' Indian community. Transported to a village in Uttar Pradesh, a man from rural Kerala would feel as much of a foreigner as would – say – a French peasant sent to live in the south of Italy. Even in Uttar Pradesh itself, there are immense differences of social organisation and culture between the 'ordinary' villagers and the tribal peoples – and it must be remembered that there are substantial tribal minorities in every state of the Indian Union.

Perhaps the biggest of all differences in life-styles are those that separate rural India, where some 70 per cent of the people live, from urban India. To some extent, admittedly, these are brought together by the phenomenon of rural-urban migration, particularly when the emigrant, as is often the case, retains ties with his native village; but the 'spread effect' of urban civilisation is still weak. Poor and ill-provided as they are in comparison with European or American urban centres, the Indian towns offer amenities and facilities – particularly for their better-off inhabitants – which are totally unknown in the countryside. More importantly in the present context, the town-dweller rapidly acquires 'western' habits and tastes which

3

penetrate the countryside only very slowly and unevenly. In particular, he becomes much more rapidly politicised. As India is ruled from the towns, this imparts something of an urban bias to political life and policies. Indeed, there is a sense in which the rural areas may be regarded as the towns' colonies – although it should be noted that, with the rise of an enterprising rural middle class, this situation is changing, particularly in the more prosperous agricultural areas.

All this means that attempts to generalise about the working of Indian political institutions, once one leaves the confines of New Delhi, are very hazardous indeed. As one would expect, institutions with the same formal structures operate very differently and even serve dissimilar purposes from one part of the country to another. One may even ask whether India, as such, can be described as having a common political culture, as distinct from a common political structure. The answer to this question, however, is by no means simple, for to some extent the institutions themselves create the culture, since the consequences for political attitudes of a certain type of institutional experience, particularly when this is prolonged, are by no means negligible. Moreover, the prevalence of Hindu modes of life and thought, the existence of modern means of communication (from railways to radio), and the memories (now fading) of common subjection to a foreign conqueror are all forces, of varying strength, that contribute to an all-India sense of 'the public interest'. How important they are, in comparison with the divisive forces, is difficult to say, but it may be significant that a consciousness of being Indian, as distinct from Bengali or Maharashtrian or Madrassi, rises to the surface only when activated by a foreign 'threat', whether from Pakistan or from China, or by some external blow to India's national pride. As soon as more-or-less normal foreign relations are restored, the brief surge of all-India patriotism quickly fades away, to be replaced by a renewed consciousness of the importance of those issues which divide Indian from Indian. Such consciousness, as might be expected, is particularly strong among groups such as the tribal peoples, the southerners, and the Untouchables, who feel that the political decision-takers persistently discriminate against them. Particularism tends to be the norm; universalism the exception. The political unity of India, therefore, is fragile. No government can take it for granted; every government has to do whatever is possible to cultivate it. Historically, it has been achieved only as a result of foreign conquest, and there are some who would argue that it is incompatible with independence and democracy. Such an argument, however, goes well beyond the evidence on the subject that is available to us, which can only be described as highly ambiguous in its implications.

As we have suggested, one of the elements of unity among the diversity – although not one that stimulates a sense of common interest – is *caste*. This is India's 'peculiar institution', and no analysis of Indian politics that neglects it can be worth very much. In the past it has provided a principle of social cohesion, particularly at the local level. The caste system defines and delimits a person's hereditary rights and duties with a thoroughness, comprehensiveness and rigidity unparalleled by any other system of social organisation. It represents perhaps the most complete and uncompromising of all denials of the principle of human equality, since it places certain groups of human beings, vis-à-vis other groups, in a 'polluting' category. As Louis Dumont has shown, it is the apothesis of the idea of *homo hierarchicus* as against that of *homo aequalis*. Although, over the years, it has undergone many changes, and although the conditions of modern life, particularly in the towns, have lessened its impact and significance, it nevertheless remains a social, psychological and political phenomenon of massive importance.

Historically, caste institutions have provided a peculiar – and probably unique – means of adjusting social relations in a comparatively static and overwhelmingly agrarian society. As the society becomes more dynamic and less agrarian, such institutions might be expected to wither away. With increasing social mobility and enhanced individualism, it might be supposed that behaviour would diverge more and more from the norms fixed by caste status, and that the whole system of fixed rights and duties which is of the essence of caste institutions would suffer erosion. In the long run, it may be that this is precisely what will happen; indeed, it is already happening, although very patchily. But the long run can be very long indeed, and one now feels less confidence than one formerly felt in predictions that caste is about to collapse before the joint assaults of monetisation, urbanisation, the improvement in communications and the development of secular education. Its roots run very deep, and it has shown a remarkable and unforeseen capacity to adapt itself to changing human needs.

Indeed, there are some respects in which caste has become more rather than less important to Indians than it was before. In a society where change is tending to blot out so many of the traditional landmarks, the caste can provide the individual with a focus of loyalty and a point of reference from which he derives a much-needed psychological satisfaction. For the present, no official organisation nor voluntary organisation can offer an acceptable substitute. It is for this reason, more than any other, that caste has acquired a new political significance, one that has been underlined by the constitution-makers' decision to give special privileges to so-called scheduled (i.e. backward or disadvantaged) castes. From its various local homes, it has moved out into the wider arena of state politics. In almost every Indian state, there are now 'caste associations' which act, in the manner of pressure groups, on behalf of their members. Here we see a fascinating interpenetration of the new with the old – the adaptation of a traditional institution to the demands of modern public life. Equally important is the fact that caste divisions, which originally reflected hereditary ritual status, have now become related, in the most complex, uneven and regionally variable way, to class divisions, which of course are oriented towards economic status. Indeed, what appears to be caste competition is often a more-or-less distorted reflection of a class struggle, in which groups of people enjoying comparable economic advantages or suffering comparable economic disadvantages engage in battle for access to the rights and privileges (e.g. education, jobs, contracts) that governmental and private agencies have to offer. Yet this is not always so, for caste status and economic status are as often divergent as coincident and economic differentation within the caste itself is a marked feature of modern Indian society. Moreover, class struggles themselves vary in intensity from area to area. In tribal areas, they hardly exist; in Calcutta, they often dominate (and indeed disrupt) the life of the city. It is not our purpose here to sort out these complexities, but simply to point to their existence. The point to remember is that caste is a political factor of the highest importance, and that it is likely to remain so for a long time.

It is even more important, in reading the following pages, to remain conscious of the most basic of all facts about India: her extreme poverty. For those who have never visited the country, 'Asiatic poverty' is difficult to imagine in human terms, although of recent years television has lifted a corner of the curtain of distance that conceals it from the affluent West. Even among the countries of South and South-East Asia, India is one of the poorest. For the period 1954–6, Myrdal has estimated her income per head at Rs 260. Only Pakistan, with an income of Rs 210 per head, occupied a lower position in the league. Indonesia (Rs 300), Burma (Rs 300), South Vietnam (Rs 350), Philippines (Rs 380), and Thailand (Rs 400) all surpassed India, while Ceylon (Rs 460) was almost twice as well off, and Malaya (Rs 780) fully three times. Since then, there have been some rather ill-documented changes in relative positions. Pakistan, for instance, has equalled and perhaps exceeded the Indian figure, but this only means that India, although she has registered an improvement in absolute terms, is now at the bottom. Corresponding figures, also in Indian rupees, for some of the more developed countries, are: Italy Rs 1,700, United Kingdom Rs 4,067, Sweden Rs 5,293, and the United States Rs 9,258. Such statistics, as is generally admitted, may well exaggerate the contrast, but they do at least provide some general quantitative idea of the depth of India's poverty, as seen from the vantage point of the 'West'.

Such poverty inevitably implies malnutrition, low housing standards, ill-health, poor work-capacity, lack of occupational adaptability, and an inadequate level of savings. Consequently, by the operation of a whole series of familiar vicious circles, it means that the achievable rate of economic development is very low in relation to the country's human needs. Poverty, in fact, breeds poverty.

Here we are solely concerned with poverty's political consequences. These are by no means as simple as is sometimes imagined. 'If I were an Indian peasant, I would go thoroughly bolshie', is a not uncommon reaction from those who encounter Indian poverty for the first time. Extreme poverty does not in itself, however, breed political radicalism, particularly if it is

7

combined – as it usually is in India – with illiteracy, which is the condition of the majority (76 per cent at the 1961 census). Undernourished, sick and ignorant people do not have the energy or the knowledge to concern themselves, more than intermittently, with political matters; they are far too occupied with keeping body and soul together. Among the poor, the general level of political participation is low. Even when, on occasion, they are moved to express their frustrations by rioting or by 'non-cooperating', they are driven more by despair than by hope, and are often led by demagogues whose aim is to enlist mass violence in the service of a religious community or political faction. Despite the comparatively high voting figures in Indian elections, the apathy of the masses of rural Indians is proverbial. Indeed, it may well be one of the reasons for the degree of political stability that India has so far enjoyed.

But it is equally well known that as soon as the poor begin, as a result of the national and international 'demonstration effect', to question the necessity of their own poverty, and as soon as the process of economic development starts to shift them, or at least some of them, from a condition of absolute destitution to one of relative deprivation, they increasingly resort to political action, often of a violent kind, for the purpose of improving their economic well-being. Subjectively, their poverty ceases to be an accepted condition and becomes a *grievance,* responsibility for which is laid at the door of 'the authorities'. The question is then how far the political system is able to remedy this grievance or to arrange for its alleviation. Current developments, both in the towns and in the country-side, suggest that India is moving into this phase where the poverty of the masses ceases to be tolerable to them, although the extent of the 'radicalisation' of the poor differs very conspicuously as between one area and another. What is certain is that the wealthier classes are now feeling a hot breath down their necks.

In India as elsewhere, extremes of poverty have their counterpart in extremes of wealth. According to the figures produced by the Reserve Bank of India in 1960, households in the top tenth income bracket received 36 per cent of all pre-tax income, while households in the bottom tenth had to be content with one per cent. Contrasts in life-styles between those at the top and those at the bottom are particularly obvious, because the wealthy engage in conspicuous consumption and show little solicitude for the welfare of their poorer compatriots. As long as the 'rich man in his castle, poor man at his gate' philosophy is generally accepted, these rampant and all-too-visible inequalities are quite compatible with political stability. Only in a very slowly changing society, however, does such a philosophy win widespread support. As soon as an element of flexibility and dynamism is injected into the social order, resentment at 'unjustified' inequalities makes rapid headway and becomes a political factor of the first importance.

Indian governments have realised the politically explosive potentialities both of the demonstration effect and of a consciousness of relative deprivation. It is for this reason, as well as for reasons of human solidarity and of national pride, that they have embarked on a series of plans to develop the economy and to make greater abundance available to all. But unfortunately, as is usually the case, acceptance by a government of responsibility for the 'condition of the people' raises expectations to a level where it is difficult simultaneously to satisfy all or even most of them. In the long run, government-promoted economic development may well give the politician more room in which to manoeuvre, but in the short run it has built-in destabilising effects, particularly as its benefits are unevenly distributed as between both classes and regions. In India these contradictions are exacerbated by the fact that the government, while persistently preaching an egalitarian *credo*, has chosen a developmental pattern which tends to increase rather than to decrease inequalities of the more visible and hurtful kind. Of these, inequalities between the employed and the unemployed (who increase in number every year) are just as important as those between the rich and the poor.

Poverty, therefore, tends to become one of the most crucial and least tractable of political issues, compelling the attention even of those who have become hardened to the spectacle – as most better-off Indians are compelled, in psychological self-defence, to become – and who do not regard it as a national disgrace. Its impact on political life, however, remains anything but straightforward. Although it may express itself in support for parties and groups that preach class warfare and attempt to organise the poor for revolutionary action, it may equally well find more indirect expression in movements of a regionalist and communalist kind. These complexities of poverty-inspired politics have as yet been insufficiently studied. In the pages that follow we shall be referring to them no more than incidentally; but what must always be remembered is that poverty on the Indian scale, as soon as it ceases to be accepted by its victims as an irremediable condition, the product of a religiously-sanctified social order that gives each man his appropriate status, can stimulate an extremely fierce kind of political activity.

These are some of the considerations that students of Indian politics must constantly bear in mind. Most of them would appear to militate against the success of the democratic experiment, since a viable democratic system would seem to demand a measure of consensus which in India is conspicuously and perhaps increasingly lacking. The extraordinary thing is that, despite everything, India's democracy has had twenty years of vigorous life, at a time when countries with comparable (and, indeed, in some cases much less serious) problems have abandoned democracy for more authoritarian forms of rule. It is our object in this book not only to describe India's democracy but, to the extent that we are able, to account for the degree of success which it has achieved and to form at least a tentative view about its continued viability.

2 The British Legacy

To draw up a balance-sheet of imperialism is notoriously difficult, whether for India or for any other country that has undergone a prolonged period of foreign rule. In India's case, discussion has tended to concentrate on the impact of British domination on the pattern of economic development. Early in the present century, the Indian economic historian R. C. Dutt argued vigorously that Britain had drained India of her resources, and this view has subsequently been developed by many socialist writers, of whom one of the most recent and persuasive is Frederick Clairemont. Others, of whom Maurice and Taya Zinkin are current examples, have attacked this thesis with equal vigour and have even argued that Britain lost rather than gained economically by the maintenance of her Indian rule.

What cannot be denied is that the economic consequences for India of imperialism, whether in the long run advantageous or disadvantageous, were sometimes spectacularly cruel, particularly in the early days of the British raj. One cannot forget, for instance, the deliberate and callous destruction of Indian textile handicrafts, as a result of their virtual exclusion from the British market, combined with free entry into the Indian market of the products of the Lancashire cotton mills. Contemplating the results of this policy, Lord Bentinck in 1834 made his famous remark about 'the bones of the cotton-weavers bleaching on the plains of India'. A longer-term if less spectacular consequence of treating India as a market wide open to British goods was the creation of an excessive dependence on agriculture as a means of Indians' livelihood. Nehru himself stressed this 'hopeless' dependence when, writing shortly before the Second World War, he pointed out that the proportion of agriculturalists to the total occupied population had increased to 74 per cent from 55 per cent in the mid-nineteenth century.

If there had been more positive development of agriculture, this growing disproportion might not have been as damaging as it was; but the contribution made by the British in the form of irrigation works (particularly in the Punjab) was largely offset by the discouragement of the cultivator through the inequities and disincentives built into the land-tax system. Writing of the severe famines that afflicted parts of India in the late nineteenth century, Sir Henry Cotton, a prominent Indian civil servant, expressed the opinion that Britain's 'rigid and revolutionary methods of exacting land revenue' had 'reduced the peasantry to the lowest extremes of poverty and wretchedness', and underlined the irony of the fact that the statute book was 'swollen with measures for the relief of victims' whom the British land administration had 'impoverished'.

To pretend that this represents the whole story would be foolish; but it was certainly the aspect of the story that made the strongest impact on the minds of the Indians themselves, as they awoke to political self-consciousness. If any generalisation is possible, perhaps the most accurate one is that provided by Barbara Ward, who writes that the British in India 'launched but did not complete the process of economic development', largely as a consequence of their devotion, until very late in the day, to *laissez-faire* doctrines; but even this judgment would be regarded by many Indians as erring on the side of charity.

Equally disputable and disputed is the total impact of British rule on the development of Indian society. Widely accepted by Marxists and most clearly expressed by the Indian Communist leader, Hiren Mukerjee, is the view that in the eighteenth century, when Britain took imperialistic advantage of the disintegration of the Mughal Empire, India was on the eve of a 'bourgeois revolution', and that this was prevented by the British conquest from working its transformatory effect on the traditional society. Nehru expressed a similar view when he alleged that in the eighteenth century India was 'as advanced industrially, commercially and financially as any country prior to the Industrial Revolution', and that most of her contemporary problems were due to 'arrested growth and the prevention by British authority of normal adjustment taking place'. His presentation of the issue, however, is by no means free from ambiguity, as in the same context he not only describes the Mughal government as 'despotic and feudal' and the people as 'apathetic and servile', but suggests, with good reason, that the 'middle class' was not strong enough to seize power. As the processes of history are irreversible, the 'hold-up' theory can be neither proved nor disproved. All one can say is that an objective examination of conditions in eighteenth century India suggests its implausibility, and that it savours of a mechanistic, 'four-stages' type of Marxism which Marxist scholars are now tending to abandon. How India would have developed if she had been left free to work out her own destiny must remain purely speculative. Indeed, it is extremely unlikely that she *could* have enjoyed such freedom; for her political condition was such as to make her 'opening up', in one form or another, virtually inevitable.

In specifically political terms, the balance sheet is equally difficult to draw up, unless one accepts the point of view that loss of national independence is always bad. The balancing operation, moreover, is inherently ambiguous, since almost every positive item is simultaneously a negative one. For instance, the statement that Britain promoted India's political modernisation (which, at least in the long run, is true) immediately provokes the question of how much that was valuable in the traditional society she destroyed in the process. Tilak, Ghose and the other neo-traditionalist revolutionaries of the early twentieth century said 'Too much', and there are many distinguished Indians to-day, such as Jayaprakash Narayan and Vinoba Bhave, who would echo this sentiment. It is also pertinent to ask whether modernisation, as conceived by the British, was the right kind for India, and whether, on the assumption that it *was* right, it was bought at an unnecessary and avoidable human cost. Britons have displayed more than a little complacency on this subject, and even 'native' modernisers, such as Jawaharlal Nehru, have approached it in a spirit of profound ambivalence.

One puts these questions only to emphasise their unanswerability, and to direct attention to the questions to which an answer *can* be attempted. Of these, two would seem to be of direct importance for the understanding of India's post-independence problems, with which we are here mainly concerned. How did the British see themselves as rulers of India? And how did the Indians see them?

The British view of themselves evokes the conception of 'trusteeship' – a word that has given rise to a formidable tangle of emotion and misunderstanding. It achieved wide popularity immediately after the First World War, when 'mandated' territories were being created under the aegis of the League of Nations and when Britain, for the first time, stated that self-government within the empire was her ultimate political aim for India. To show that this was something more than a pious hope, the British government promulgated the Montagu-Chelmsford Reforms of 1919 under which authority was decentralised with a division of power between the Centre and provincial governments. At the Centre, there was little substantive change but in the provinces a system of dyarchy was introduced whereby a range of 'transferred' subjects such as local self-government, health, education, agriculture and industry were entrusted to ministers responsible to a legislature elected on a restricted franchise. Provincial Governors retained authority over certain 'reserved' subjects, largely in areas of law and order and revenue. This instalment was greeted with enthusiasm by the moderates (subsequently to organise themselves as the Liberals) among the Indian politicians, and did indeed prove to be the beginning of a constitutional advance which, both in pace and scope, would have been inconceivable to an earlier generation of imperialists and was alarming to many of the Conservative leaders of the 1920s and 1930s, such as Winston Churchill. It was this new line, as the Russians might have termed it, that by a process of backward projection created a popular illusion that Britain had always regarded herself as holding India 'on trust' and that the Montagu-Chelmsford Reforms and the Government of India Act of 1935 represented the fulfilment of a long-standing, self-assumed obligation; the penultimate stages of a history of preparation for self-government, beginning with the Indian Councils Act of 1861 and wending its way through the Ripon Reforms of the 1880s and the Morley-Minto Reforms of 1909. The Indian Councils Act of 1861 had restored legislative powers to the provinces and provided for three Indians to be appointed to the advisory Legislative Council at the Centre. As 'a measure of popular and political education', Lord Ripon had established a network of rural district boards and municipal committees, with half or more of their membership elected, and enjoying powers over health, sanitation, public works, education and certain levies. The principle of election at provincial and central level was recognised in the Morley-Minto Reforms. The central Legislative Council was expanded and twenty-seven of its sixty members were to be elected by provincial assemblies. In the provincial legislatives themselves, non-official majorities were introduced though the franchise was limited to municipal and district boards, universities, chambers of commerce and certain categories of landowners. Some degree of representation had been conceded but the reforms did not entrust executive responsibility to the assemblies. This series of reforms was certainly not seen by the British at the time of their introduction as part of a process leading ultimately to self-government. Later attempts to present them in this light necessarily generated a massive scepticism among the main body of India's national leaders as to Britain's real intentions, a scepticism which persisted right up to the eve of Independence in 1947.

Admittedly, some of the early nineteenth century Liberals, such as Macaulay, Ross and Trevelyan, 'had looked on the task of modernisation as a cooperative enterprise to be increasingly trusted to Indian hands', and 'did not shrink from proclaiming that in the last resort the process must lead to self-government'; but this was little more than a 'gratuitous form of liberalism so distant was it from practical reality' (Eric Stokes). Speaking in the Commons in 1833, Macaulay himself quoted without criticism the view of James Mill (later also accepted, *de facto,* by his more celebrated son) that any form of representative government was totally unsuited to India. Nor is the very tenuous re-emergence of the 'liberal tradition' in the 1870s of much significance. Trevelyan then suggested to the House of Commons Committee on Indian Finance that quasi-representative provincial and local bodies 'would be a school of self-government for the whole of India, the largest step yet taken towards teaching its 200,000,000 people to govern themselves, which is the end and object of our connection with that country'. Trevelyan's was a voice mewing, rather than crying, in the wilderness; for more typical of British opinion, both then and later, was Sir John Strachey's robust declaration of 1888:

> ... let there be no hypocrisy about our intention to keep in the hands of our own people those executive posts – and there are not very many of them—on which, and on our military and political power, our actual hold of the country depends. Our governors of provinces, the chief officers of our army, our magistrates of districts and their principal executive subordinates ought to be Englishmen under all circumstances that we can foresee.

Right up to 1918 Britain's view of her role in India was predominantly and unashamedly 'paternalistic'. Britain ruled India, and would continue to rule it as far into the future as the eye of man could discern, both for her own good and for India's good. Usually no distinction was made between the two 'goods'; they naturally coincided, just as that of General Motors, in the view of an American Secretary of the Treasury, coincided with that of the United States. Indians were regarded as inherently unfitted for self-government or for representative government, which in those days were treated as synonymous. Liberal Secretaries of State for India, such as the Gladstonian John Morley, held this opinion as firmly as Conservative Viceroys, such as Lord Curzon. 'A fantastic and ludicrous dream' was Morley's characterisation of the suggestion that India might be given the benefit of British-type political institutions. The men on the spot, of course, were even more categorical. Forbes, a member of the Governor's Executive Council in Madras, wrote in 1906 that

> administration in India will only be good administration so long as it is essentially British; that no intellectual or educational attainments will ever endow the Indian with the qualifications necessary to govern wisely and well – qualifications of which the Englishman in India has shown himself to be possessed; and that the Indian will fail in *character*, however brilliant he may be in intelligence and erudition.

Only a few socialist and maverick radical intellectuals made any serious attempt to argue with views of this kind.

At least up to the Montagu-Chelmsford Reforms of 1919 (which signified different things for different British politicians) 'reforms' were intended to *strengthen* British rule by associating with it the 'sounder' elements in Indian society. Princes, zamindars,* university administrators and leaders of religious communities were drawn into central and provincial conciliar bodies, first by co-option, later through election by their peers. The extremely gradual opening up to Indians of the higher ranks of the Indian Civil Service was similarly inspired. Up to the early years of the present century, moreover, the basic rightness of this policy was accepted even by those Indians who wished to see it pursued more vigorously. Congress itself was originally a gathering of Indian 'gentlemen' who thought in terms of participation, not of independence, and who could be positively effusive in their expressions of appreciation of the benefits that British rule had brought. One prominent member, Sir Phirozeshah Mehta, in making 'the confession of faith of a devout and irreclaimable Congressman', went so far as to say that he accepted British rule 'as a dispensation so wonderful ... that it would be folly not to accept it as a declaration of God's will'.

This does not mean, however, either that the British had a single self-image or that all Indians looked at them in the same way. Throughout the nineteenth century, and even beyond, there was a broad and fluctuating distinction among British administrators in India between the utilitarians and the traditionalists. The former saw their role as one of rationally-inspired social engineering. They were impatient with the back-wardness of 'native' manners and customs, in much the same manner as the missionaries were horrified with their wickedness. Believing in the 'principles of political economy' almost as fervently as the missionaries believed in the dispensations of Providence, they regarded themselves as bringers of western enlightenment. Bentinck and Macaulay are generally regarded as typifying this approach to Indian affairs, but to find it in its purest form one has to turn to lesser figures, such as Pringle of Bombay, who, in the words of Dr Ravinder Kumar, combined with a 'vision of society as composed of individuals rather than of social groups a conviction of the effectiveness of rational action' — such action, in his view, being the reform of the

* i.e. landowners recognised and used by the government as tax-collecting agents.

traditional system of land revenue in accordance with the principles of Ricardian economics. Others, such as Elphinstone, were acutely aware of the political dangers of such dogmatism and emphasised the need for 'moderation'; but it was not until the assault on traditional institutions had provoked the Mutiny of 1857 that the moderates were able to establish their case. Even when, under the impact of this shock, the greatest that British imperialism in India ever experienced, non-disturbance of established social institutions had become the new orthodoxy, the utilitarian-traditionalist controversy continued, *sotto voce*. Indeed, the Deccan Riots of 1875 may be regarded, in a sense, as one of utilitarianism's later products, in so far as they were provoked by the Bombay government's determination to apply free market principles to landed property.

Not until comparatively late in the nineteenth century did the administrators of British India, the Indian Civil Service, develop the equivalent of a clear 'departmental policy', as a result of the accumulation of experience and the crystallisation of routines. It was then that the struggle between traditionalists and utilitarians finally subsided. The firm establishment of British rule, on a basis of passive acceptance by a majority of the population, also meant that in Britain interest in Indian affairs became fitful and sporadic, depending more on the current evaluation of the 'Russian menace' than on the condition of India itself. Nevertheless, the Conservative self-image in matters Indian always differed marginally from the Liberal. Tories became the sponsors of an unyielding paternalism, whereas Liberals tended to favour the development, although a very slow development, of 'partnership'. This difference was sufficient to make life difficult for a reforming Liberal Viceroy, such as Lord Ripon, since the vast majority of the men on the spot favoured, and indeed actively sustained, the Conservative view – as when Ripon, through the so-called 'Ilbert' Bill, attempted to make British residents subject to the jurisdiction of 'native' magistrates. To the extent that utilitarianism retained any influence, it became absorbed in the concept of efficiency, which became the watchword of those who saw danger to British rule in the increasingly routine-bound character of the administration. The most powerful and, for the time being, effective exponent of the 'efficiency' doctrine was Lord Curzon,

Viceroy from 1898 to 1905, whose attempts to tone up the ICS made him almost as unpopular with the British in India as his lordly disregard of nascent Indian aspirations made him with the Congress-wallahs.

Until Gandhi appeared on the scene towards the end of the First World War, the masses of Indians accepted British rule with characteristic resignation. After all, India was not without experience of foreign conquerors. The British, of course, could not be 'absorbed', like the previous ones, but they could be regarded as a kind of caste with ruling prerogatives and its own peculiar and incomprehensible way of life (dharma). Even if they were unable to prevent periodical famines, they preserved internal peace and dispensed even-handed and uncorrupt justice at least between Indian and Indian. Devotees of the traditional social order suffered little disturbance, while the more modern-minded could take advantage of the western type of education provided by a limited number of British-established and British-run schools and colleges, which produced a flow of native recruits for subordinate positions in the public services and for the independent professions, such as law and medicine. Efforts to promote economic development, admittedly, were very limited, but so were expectations of government action in this field. The building of railways, the extension of irrigation works and the establishment of plantations helped to develop a market economy which brought advantage to the Indian mercantile community as well as to British businessmen; but the 'principles of political economy', together with a prudent fear of the social consequences of rapid economic change, inhibited the government from taking more direct and positive steps to improve the system of production. India was regarded as the 'brightest jewel in the British crown', and a jewel neither has nor is expected to have dynamic characteristics. Peace, order and military splendour were its refulgent properties. They pleased the British and, for the time, it seemed that they satisfied the Indians – or, at least, those Indians who 'counted'.

Yet all the time, and with increasing speed towards the end of the nineteenth century and at the beginning of the twentieth, British imperialism was creating its own gravediggers. This process of creation was both uneven and complicated. Its first manifestation was a growing sense of unease and dissatisfaction among the more educated inhabitants of the great cities. Those who were affected by it, as might be expected, were Indians who had been able to take advantage of educational opportunities to qualify themselves for the government service or the professions.

These potential leaders of opposition to British rule were divided into two broad groups, although the distinction between them was anything but clear. The first, which may be called the 'modernisers', were men who had eagerly accepted the offerings of western culture, but who were becoming increasingly dissatisfied with available job-opportunities, frustrated by the lack of any effective 'partnership', and offended by their contemptuous relegation to an inferior status. Among the most important of their demands were greater access to the top jobs in the public service and a more serious effort to extend the principle of political consultation. The second group may be called, for want of a better word, the 'neo-traditionalists'. Among these, subjection to western education had induced a revulsion against 'alien' values. With the help of western scholars, such as Max Müller, they were in the process of rediscovering the allegedly original and pure traditions of Hinduism, which seemed to them superior, as well as more consonant with the dignity of Indians, than the meretricious cultural offerings that the British had brought with them. Grossly to over-simplify, it might be said that whereas the modernisers swore by John Stuart Mill, the neo-traditionalists found their inspiration in the Hindu holy books, the Vedas and the Gita. This distinction, however, is fuzzy (and not merely at the edges), since the modernisers could not escape from their own traditions, nor could the neo-traditionalists accept those traditions in their entirety; but it was real enough to create a schism in the nascent nationalist movement, which gave rise to an organisational split at the Congress session at Surat in 1908, and which has never been completely healed.

At this stage, the modernising-traditionalist dichotomy broadly coincided with the growing controversy between revolutionaries and reformists. Gokhale, the widely respected Congress leader, was a westernised intellectual whose moderation predisposed him to co-operate to the utmost limit with the British authorities, if only they could be persuaded to introduce significant advances towards representative government. His revolutionary-minded opponents, who thrived on the lack of success that attended his persuasive efforts, were Tilak, the admirer of the eighteenth-century Maharashtrian military hero, Shivaji, and Aurobindo Ghose, the devotee of the Bengali goddess of destruction, Kali. Disputes between the two factions facilitated the pursuit, by the British, of a 'divide and rule' policy, and as a result the decade that began in 1908 was a comparatively easy one for the raj, with the revolutionaries suppressed and the reformists disoriented. Not until Gandhi returned from South Africa in 1916 and a frightened imperial government played into his hands by combining an ambiguous promise of self-government with a series of repressive actions culminating in the Amritsar Massacre of 1919* did the situation fundamentally change. In retrospect, perhaps the most significant event of those years, or at least the most symptomatic one, was the conversion to the policy of non-cooperation of Motilal Nehru, Jawaharlal's father, one of the most westernised of Indians, a *bon viveur* and a highly successful lawyer.

The advent of Gandhi, of course, transformed relations between Britain and India. It was not only that India acquired an immensely respected leader with a style of politics after her own heart – what Professor Morris-Jones has termed the 'saintly' style, in the tradition of the Indian *sadhu*, or holy man. More importantly in the present context, he brought about a precarious yet effective reconciliation between the modernist and traditionalist elements in the national movement. His simultaneous appeal to the sophisticated Motilal Nehru and to the simple peasant is evidence enough of that. He also created, through the technique of *satyagraha* (non-violent resistance) a strangely powerful amalgam of reformism and revolutionism, ideally suited to undermine the self-confidence of English gentlemen who were already beginning to have doubts about the exact nature of their mission in India. Adopting as his instrument a western form of political organisation, the Indian National Congress, and working in close relationship with some of the most highly westernised elements in Indian society,

---

* When British troops killed hundreds and wounded thousands by firing into a peaceful and unarmed crowd.

such as the businessman Birla, he himself remained a traditionalist in his approach to social problems. Together with a determination to bring about the establishment of *swaraj*, or national
independence, went a profound belief in the virtues of rural
simplicity and emphasis on self-denying service as the essential
constituent of the Good Life. Together with a mastery of modern
political techniques went an acceptance of caste institutions (but
not of untouchability) and a profound respect for the Hindu
scriptures and a particular veneration for the *Gita*. In his own
person he embodied the contradictory values of an Indian
society that had been deeply affected by a long period of alien
rule; yet he brought together these contradictions in an
integrated amalgam. Amid the tumult of a society under stress,
he alone was calmly confident that he knew the path ahead, and
he alone had the almost mystical power to persuade both the
classes and the masses that it was the path that must be
followed.

Yet this reconciliation of tradition and modernity in the
person of Gandhi was, as we have emphasised, tenuous and
fragile. Even his powerful charisma maintained it only with
difficulty, and he found himself frequently disillusioned with
the behaviour of the less spiritually-minded members of the
nationalist movement. The latter, on their side, often found
Gandhi incomprehensible or even downright reactionary. The
Communists, as might be expected, regarded him – at least for
most of the time – as an agent of the Indian bourgeoisie or
even as a covert defender of British imperialism. Many of the
Bengalis, who had their own tradition of terrorist political
activity dating back to the early years of the century, found
both his non-violent strategies and his *sadhu*-like attitudes quite
unacceptable. Even Jawaharlal Nehru, with whom he had a
strangely profound affinity, was frequently angered or saddened
by what seemed to be Gandhi's self-defeating tactics, as when the
Mahatma called off the first Civil Disobedience Movement
because of the bloodthirsty violence displayed by the enraged
people of Chauri-Chaura, or brought the second movement to
an end on the basis of a vague and ambiguously-worded 'pact'
with the Viceroy, Lord Irwin.

Today, with Gandhi long dead, the symbiosis of modernity
and tradition remains, but the kind of reconciliation between

them that he envisaged has all but disappeared from view, although there are a few, such as Jayaprakash Narayan, who still strive valiantly to maintain it. There is certainly an inter-penetration of the two elements, as illustrated by the creation of modern-type associations to defend and promote traditional caste interests; but there is also tension, as illustrated by the recent violent agitation to persuade the government to ban the slaughter of cows – a tension that expresses itself not only in political manifestations but in the divided minds of so many educated, middle-class Indians. Both the interpenetration and the tension are, to a large extent, the product of one hundred and fifty years of British rule.

This has here been emphasised because it is one of the most subtle and pervasive yet least understood legacies of the Indo-British relationship. The other legacies, both positive and negative, being comparatively well-known, require no more than brief catalogue and comment.

The legacy of which Britain remains most proud, and in which Indians themselves have learned to take a certain pride, is the administrative one. The Indian Civil Service was without doubt the most valuable of the British bequests to independent India. It consisted of a small administrative aristocracy (fewer than 2,000), largely Indianised by 1947, 'generalist' and non-technical in character, highly educated and carefully selected by a difficult competitive examination, remarkably adaptable, almost entirely free from corruption, exceptionally devoted to duty, imbued with an intense *esprit de corps,* and, perhaps most important of all, pan-*Indian* rather than regional or provincial in its loyalties. The process whereby this administrative elite transferred its allegiance to a new regime represented a major effort of adaptation which many thought was foredoomed to failure. From being the virtual master of India, the ICS had to become its servant. By many of the indigenous politicians who acquired office after 1947 it was regarded, initially, as imperialism's Trojan Horse. The more extreme of them demanded its abolition; but Nehru and Patel, who had learned to appreciate its efficiency and integrity, wisely decided that, administratively, continuity was the best policy. Without the ICS, orderly administration might have collapsed and regional separatism triumphed. With it and its successor, the Indian

Administrative Service, independent India still had a 'steel frame' and an instrument through which political decisions could be put into effect – often, it must be admitted, woodenly and unimaginatively, but always with some degree of systematic competence.

Yet even here there were elements of ambiguity in the legacy. The *esprit de corps*, detachment and exclusiveness of the service conferred on it some of the characteristics of a caste, and tended to isolate it and, in some measure, to alienate it from the mainstream of Indian social and political life. Moreover, its traditional orientation towards the maintenance of law and order and the collection of revenue made it less than an ideal administrative instrument for the tasks of social and economic development which the new government wished to pursue with such vigour. Its smallness together with the great gap of intelligence and ability that separated it from the middle and lower ranks of the public service, were also serious disadvantages. They involved the imposition on it of an exceptionally heavy burden of miscellaneous duties, and exacerbated an already excessive degree of centralisation in the administrative process. The direction of a multitude of routine-minded pen-pushers by a tiny elite corps constituted a style of administration better suited to the maintenance of imperialist domination than to the building of a new nation and the development of its human and material resources.

Nevertheless, one only has to compare the Indian Administrative Service with the bureaucracies of so many of the other 'new nations' to realise how valuable it is. Of all the legacies of British rule, this was perhaps the *least* ambiguous.

Equally important, although of more controversial significance, was the experience of self-government that, in its latter days, the British raj gave to its Indian subjects. At the time, very few Indians appreciated its value – nor could they have been expected to do so. The Montagu-Chelmsford Reforms of 1919, which established a 'dyarchy' in the provinces, with indigenous ministers responsible to provincial assemblies for 'nation-building' subjects, such as education, health and agriculture, were rejected by most Congressmen and accepted by the 'swarajist' wing of Congress only as a means of exposing the fraudulence of British pretensions to be advancing the cause of self-rule. Even participation in the more complete type of provincial self-government introduced by the Government of India Act, 1935, was agreed to by Congress only with many reservations, in the face of opposition from a powerful left wing. Yet from 1921 to 1937 'dyarchy' limped along, providing many prominent Indians with experience of the techniques of parliamentary debate and ministerial responsibility, while the victory won by Congress in eight of the eleven provinces in the elections of 1937 inaugurated a far more important, if much briefer, course in the arts of self-government. Experience at the local levels was, perhaps, less useful – for the district boards and municipal councils never played a very important role – but it was by no means insignificant.

The resignation of the Congress ministries, as a protest against Britain's declaration of war on India's behalf in 1939, and the subsequent 'Quit India' campaign, which resulted in the imprisonment of all the more important Congress leaders, interrupted this experience. Nevertheless, by 1946, when the 'Interim' government was formed with Jawaharlal Nehru as Vice-President of the Viceroy's Executive Council, both Congressmen and members of other parties had acquired a considerable knowledge of and, what was more important, a *respect for* parliamentary procedures and conventions. This was unusual, if not unique, for a country in the process of emerging from imperial tutelage, and its effect was certainly to facilitate the transition from subjection to independence. In many respects, as we shall see, the 1950 Constitution was the 1935 Constitution writ large, and the men who had acquired experience of operating the 'slave' Constitution were by no means tyros when they undertook the task of operating the 'free' one.

Yet doubts about the appropriateness of the legacy were expressed and even now have not been laid to rest. That parliamentarism should be so closely allied with imperialism raised doubts about its value, and not only in the minds of the extreme revolutionaries, such as the Communists, who were anti-parliamentary by ideology and conviction. Gandhi himself, although a democrat of sorts, was no enthusiast for parliamentary institutions; both he and his disciples envisaged the creation of a 'pyramidal' political system, operating through consensus, with the 'village republic' as its base. These ideas, which were never very clearly formulated, may perhaps be dismissed as romantic utopianism; in any case, as soon as Nehru and Patel acquired political power, they never had a chance. It is still legitimate to ask, however, whether parliamentary democracy was really the most appropriate political framework for independent India, and in the present confused and ominous political situation one may expect that this question will be posed more and more insistently. All one can safely say is that neither in 1947 nor subsequently was there any coherent or generally acceptable alternative. Irrespective of ideological leanings and political predispositions, the main body of Congress leaders and supporters were at one with their fragmented rivals (including even the Communists after 1958) in accepting a multi-party parliamentarism, based on universal suffrage, as the only practicable political system. And although 'parliamentary cretinism', as Lenin once rudely described it, has abounded, there can be no doubt that, over the twenty years that have elapsed since the Constitution came into force, a genuine respect and even love for democratic institutions has developed, which has been to some extent reinforced by their extension to the 'grass roots', through the establishment of the system of *panchayati raj* (democratic decentralisation) in the rural areas. What is perhaps even more remarkable is the extent to which specifically British democratic procedures have been consciously imitated, particularly at the parliamentary level. The democratic institutions of the United Kingdom, introduced with such caution and received with such suspicion during the latter days of the British raj, have indeed cast a long shadow.

Perhaps the greatest legacy of all, but also the most ambiguous and tenuous, is the unity of India. It is great because, throughout her long history, India has rarely enjoyed a unity other than that imposed upon her by a foreign conqueror. It is ambiguous because the unity that the country now possesses is the product of one of the most bloody and unanaesthetised political amputations of modern times. It is tenuous because it is perpetually assaulted by centrifugal forces, regional, linguistic and communal, which are currently tending to increase rather than decrease in strength.

In 1947, the British raj found itself in a situation of profound historical irony. Having, at the cost of much effort, given India a political unity apparently more firm and extensive than the country had ever had before, it was compelled, by force of circumstances only partly of its own making, to preside over the division of the sub-continent, through the creation of Pakistan, one of the least viable-looking 'splinter' states that the world has ever seen. Whether this operation was historically inevitable will long continue to be a matter of controversy, and historians will also continue to dispute over the question of the precise moment when the die was cast. Indian nationalists still attribute most if not all the blame to a 'divide and rule' policy deliberately pursued by Britain from the period of the Mutiny onwards. For this attribution there is indeed much justification. Imperialist powers quite naturally try to consolidate their rule by exacerbating the disputes that divide one group of their subjects from another, particularly when confronted by the menace of a united nationalist movement. In the Indian case, the existence of a Muslim minority, formerly dominant and possessing a distinct religious culture, made the pursuit of such a policy all too easy. On the other hand, Britain did not *create* this dichotomy in the body politic; moreover, although she had done much to exacerbate it, she began to find it increasingly embarrassing as the day of Independence approached.

'Divide and rule', to the extent that it was pursued, became possible because the Muslims were a comparatively backward community, economically and educationally, whose leading men tended to live on the memories of past glories rather than adapt themselves, by a process of partial assimilation, to the new British-dominated regime. As the nationalist movement developed, largely under Hindu auspices (despite its theoretical secularism), they naturally looked to the British for the protection of their distinctive economic, social and religious interests; for, in their eyes, a British raj was a lesser evil than a Hindu one. Only between 1916 and 1922 did the two communities come together in an alliance, and even then it was much more an alliance of leaders than of the rank-and-file. By the Lucknow Pact of 1916, Congress accepted the basic Muslim demand for separate electorates, and during the immediate post-war period Gandhi's civil disobedience campaign acquired somewhat unnatural allies among those Muslims who, in the so-called 'Khilafat' movement, were demanding the restoration of the old caliphate, one of the casualties of Britain's defeat of the Ottoman Empire in the First World War. With the calling off of civil disobedience and the exhaustion of the Khilafat agitation, however, Hindu-Muslim relations sharply deteriorated, and the late 1920s were a period of serious communal riots.

Britain's contribution to the rift was obvious enough, both before and after the Hindu-Muslim 'honeymoon' period. In the first decade of the twentieth century, the British government was only too ready to accede to the demand of the Muslim notables, first specifically advanced by a deputation to Lord Minto in 1906, for separate communal representation. This was embodied in the Morley-Minto reforms of 1909, which some historians have chosen to regard as the germ from which Pakistan grew. Later, and particularly in the 1930s, Britain used Mohammed Ali Jinnah and his Muslim League, before either had become politically significant enough to have real bargaining power, as one of her standing justifications for refusing to treat the claims for self-government, as presented by the leaders of Congress, as acceptable or even seriously negotiable. But Jinnah willingly supplied the necessary intransigence, which soon raised him to the status of a hero figure in his own community, while the Congress leaders contributed materially to the growth of communal antagonisms by their persistent failure to see any element of justice in the League's demands or of reality in the Muslims' fears. Even Gandhi, who was prepared to 'fast unto death' on behalf of communal harmony, was unmistakably a Hindu leader with a predominantly Hindu appeal, despite the syncretism of his personal religious beliefs; while Nehru, the out-and-out secularist who regarded religious disputes as a mere symptom of the 'backwardness' he was impatient to overcome, could hardly conceal the manner and outlook of a Kashmiri Brahmin. Both were inhibited, by their profound belief in the unity of India, from correctly judging the drift of Muslim opinion, while among their followers were to be found a large body of specifically *Hindu* nationalists. These paid little more than lip-service to the secularism that was supposed to be part of the essence of the Congress creed. When Congress, called to office by the provincial electorates in 1937, had the opportunity to demonstrate its alleged neutrality as between the two main religious communities into which Indians were divided, it failed to convince the mass of Muslim opinion that it was anything but an essentially Hindu organisation. Experience of Congress rule, in fact, transformed the Muslim League from a gathering of notables into a mass party and enabled Jinnah, at Lucknow in 1940, to commit it to the demand for Pakistan. Yet even at the eleventh hour, when the League had fully demonstrated the extent of its disruptive power, the Congress leaders were still reluctant to treat it as a fully legitimate political force with a genuine mass basis; and by that time, of course, the British had completely lost control of the divisive communalist party towards whose growth they had so significantly contributed.

Yet, although deprived of its sub-continental coverage by the creation of Pakistan, the unity that Britain had created was by no means entirely lost. Ironically enough, in that part of the sub-continent which retained the name 'India' it acquired a strength which, had there been no partition, it would certainly not have possessed. For the new India had a political cohesiveness that could never have characterised an India which included the areas now allotted to Pakistan. If, by some miracle, the Cabinet Mission's plan of 1946 had won acceptance by both Congress and League, the resultant political entity would have taken the form of a loose federation in which the Centre would have enjoyed few powers except over currency, communications, foreign policy and defence – and even these could hardly have failed to become the subjects of persistent and acrimonious dispute. By contrast, the India that remained after partition was able to give herself, as we shall see, a much more unified form of government with a much stronger Centre – a government which (if one has to continue to use such terms) was quasi-federal rather than federal in character. A further irony was that the Constitution which provided this government with its legal and conventional framework was based, in the main, on the 'slave' Constitution of 1935 which Congress had denounced. Hence Britain, in a very real sense, remains the progenitor of whatever measure of unity India now possesses – which, despite the growth of fissiparous tendencies, remains considerable. For not only did Britain, in 1935, sketch the outlines of the political instrument through which that unity found expression; she established the predominance of New Delhi over the provincial (subsequently state) capitals, and was instrumental in the creation of a sense of 'Indianness' stronger than that which Indians had felt under any previous regime.

Admittedly, that sense was not, for the most part, a deliberate British creation. To some extent it was the spontaneous product of British-promoted improvements in transport and communications. Even more, it was the consequence of the way in which the people, under Gandhi's leadership, reacted towards what they came to regard as a denial of their political rights as *Indians*, and not merely as Bengalis, Madrassis, Maharashtrians, Punjabis, etc., or as members of particular classes, castes or groups. Congress itself, which united Indians, albeit sometimes very tenuously, for the fight for freedom, and which held them together, at least to the required degree, during the crucial years that followed Independence, was the illegitimate child of the British raj. That it was created partly as a result of the efforts of a British 'civilian', Allan Octavian Hume, was of course a historical accident. The point is that it grew, became militant and acquired organisational cohesion and an experienced leadership as a result of the prolonged struggle which the British forced it to wage for the acquisition of national independence. More than any other 'national front' movement of recent times, it developed an 'interest-aggregating' capacity which stood it in good stead when it was called upon to form a government. Twenty years had to pass before its electoral majorities began to crumble, and more than twenty years before the factions into which it was divided acquired sufficient intransigence to cause an open split in its ranks. That Indians should feel positively grateful for this unintended achievement of the British raj can hardly be expected. Nevertheless, even though the achievement was wished upon Britain by the unpredictable processes of history, it remains of cardinal importance.

In this chapter we have persistently emphasised what we have termed the ambiguousness of the British legacy, and we have deliberately refrained from any attempt to draw up a 'balance-sheet'. It must be said, however, that when all criticisms have been made the legacy was a better one than that left by Britain to most of her other colonial possessions, and much better than that left by other colonial powers to most of theirs. That its favourable features were not lost is at least partly due to the skill with which, at the end, the 'independence' operation was mounted, and particularly to the excellent understanding that was achieved between Mountbatten, the last British Viceroy, and Nehru, the first Indian Prime Minister – an understanding well documented by H. V. Hodson's account of the operation in *The Great Divide*. To say that Britain and India 'parted friends' sounds insufferably sentimental, but there is some reality behind the phrase. Even the Russians eventually came to understand that the break was clean, and no mere cover for the replacement of an open colonialist relationship by an insidious neo-colonialist one.

Yet at the very parting of the ways, ambiguity persisted; for the terrible massacres and enforced emigrations that stained the accompanying partition cannot simply be dismissed as having nothing to do with the character of British rule or the development of British policy. To the end, the raj remained janus-faced.

3 The Constitution

The political life of India takes place within the framework of a Constitution devised between the years 1947 and 1950. The devising body was a Constituent Assembly, elected by a system of proportional representation from the provincial legislatives, which had themselves been elected, on a restricted franchise, in December 1945.

Originally, the Assembly had been intended as a Constitution-making body for the whole sub-continent, but this was not to be. Even before partition, the Muslim League boycotted the Assembly, and after partition, the lifting of the boycott in the new, truncated India gave the League's 'rump' a representation of only 28 in a body of 298 members. As Congress, in the elections of 1945, had obtained an overwhelming majority outside the area destined to become Pakistan, the Assembly became, to all intents and purposes, 'a one-party body in an essentially one-party country', to quote the words of Granville Austin, the author of the standard work on the making of India's Constitution. Of the 298 seats, Congress occupied 208. Congress, therefore, was in a commanding position.

The circumstances in which it was performing its constitution-building role were anything but easy. It was a time when the great bloodbath that accompanied Partition was followed by undeclared war between India and Pakistan over Kashmir; when the whole sub-continent was nearly overwhelmed by economic crisis; when the Communists were unleashing peasant revolt in Telengana; and when Sardar Patel, with the assistance of his ICS *alter ego*, V. P. Menon, was engaged in the delicate and dangerous operation of 'integrating' the princely states. The socio-political background to the framing of the Constitution could hardly have been less propitious. It is rather extraordinary, therefore, that the whole process, although lengthy, was also very smooth.

This was partly a consequence of the domination of the Assembly by Congress, and of the domination of Congress by a handful of hero-figures of the national liberation movement, such as Nehru, Patel and Azad. But it was also due to the fact that the Assembly was not building on a *tabula rasa*. Its 'model' was the 'slave' Constitution of 1935, and many of its labours were devoted to the elimination from this Constitution of its 'slavish' features. Other models, as we shall see, were not without influence, but the British constitutional legacy exerted a persistent and ironical fascination, with the result that the ultimate product bore a greater resemblance to that of the previous exercise than most Indians, at the time, were prepared to admit.

That the British had bowed themselves out meant that the most grievous badges of 'slavery' were automatically eliminated. British-appointed Viceroy and governors, with their reserve powers and emergency powers, had gone. To consolidate these gains, and to ensure that the new regime should not possess comparable powers of oppression, it was decided to write into the Constitution certain Fundamental Rights: the Right of Equality, the Right of Freedom, the Right against Exploitation, the Right to Freedom of Religion, Cultural and Educational Rights, the Right to Property, and the Right to Constitutional Remedies. As usual, the question arose as to the limitations that might be imposed on such rights in the 'public interest', and the Indian constitution-makers, like so many of their predecessors in other countries, found some difficulty in agreeing on an answer. Decision was not made easier by their determination to include in the Constitution – although without benefit of legal protection – certain Directive Principles of a 'positive' kind which might easily come into conflict with the familiar 'negative' liberties. Among the former were the promotion of the Welfare State, the distribution and control of material resources so as best to subserve the common good, the prevention of such concentration of wealth and means of production as would be detrimental to popular welfare, the right to equal pay for equal work, to a decent standard of life, to education and to public assistance, and the protection of the interests of the so-called backward classes. All these found their origin in a series of Congress policy decisions during the pre-Independence period, and particularly in the Nehru Report of 1928 and the Karachi Resolution of 1931. They also, as we shall see, derived inspiration from the provisions of certain European constitutions.

One of the most hotly-debated questions was about the extent of the application of the concept of 'due process'. Two major issues were here involved: the compulsory acquisition of property by the state and the preventive detention of persons regarded as a potential menace to public order. The first was given immediacy by the intention of Congress to put an end to the *Zamindari* and *jagirdari* systems of landholding. Should the right to compensation be justiciable? The Assembly eventually decided that it should not, but since the constitutional provision covered only the acquisition and not the *redistribution* of property by the state, the government soon found itself in legal difficulties, which had to be overcome by constitutional amendments. The second was even more urgent, since the Assembly, as we have seen, was meeting at a time when the Communists had adopted a policy of fomenting rebellion, particularly in the rural areas. Under such circumstances, it was inevitable that preventive detention should be permitted and that the courts should be forbidden to inquire into the necessity of detention orders. Under this provision the first Preventive Detention Act, of February 1950, was passed – to be used, in the words of Sardar Patel, against those 'whose avowed object was to create disruption, dislocation, and tamper with communications, to suborn loyalty and make it impossible for normal government based on law to function'. Its constitutionality was tested and confirmed by the Supreme Court, and it was subsequently extended on eleven occasions. On these two important issues necessity of state triumphed over due process. One should immediately add, however, that neither these powers nor the President's emergency powers, about to be discussed, have been used by the government to create a police state. As Granville Austin has said, in India 'it is the denial of rights, not their existence, which makes news'.

As the Constituent Assembly was meeting in disturbed circumstances, it was almost inevitable that the President should receive powers to suspend constitutional guarantees and indeed the normal operation of the constitution itself. There were those, particularly on the left, who saw ominous parallels between such powers and the hated 'reserve powers' and 'safeguards' placed at the disposal of the Viceroy under the 1935 Constitution; but parallels were rather superficial. The new executive was not, like the Viceroy, given dictatorial control of foreign affairs and defence, nor was it empowered to 'certify' bills rejected by the legislature or (in practice) to disallow bills that had been duly passed. For the new Constitution embodied the conception of a responsible executive, in which the President acted in accordance with the advice of a Prime Minister and Cabinet responsible to a democratically-elected Parliament. Nevertheless, the powers actually granted were drastic enough. If the President was satisfied that security was threatened by external aggression or internal disturbance, he might declare a state of 'general' emergency, applicable to the whole Union. Under these conditions, both the Fundamental Rights and the powers granted by the federal provisions of the Constitution to the governments of the states could be suspended. The President was also empowered, if satisfied that the government of a state could not be carried on in accordance with the constitutional provisions, to issue a proclamation suspending the normal constitutional arrangements in the state, to assume the functions of the state's executive and to declare that the powers of its legislature should be 'exercisable by or under the authority of' the central Parliament. This is what is generally known as a proclamation of 'Presidential Rule'. Thirdly, the President might issue a proclamation of 'financial emergency' in a situation threatening to financial stability. For its duration, the finances of a state became subject to central control and all money bills were reserved for presidential assent.

These emergency provisions have by no means been dead letters. A national state of emergency was declared when the conflict with China broke out in 1962, and Parliament proceeded to pass a Defence of India Act, to remain operative until six months after the proclamation was rescinded. In the 1950s, five States, Punjab, PEPSU,* Andhra Pradesh, Kerala and Madhya Pradesh came successively under the emergency

* Patiala and East Punjab States Union, which ceased to have separate existence as a result of the reorganisation of the states in the mid-1950s.

provisions relating to constitutional breakdown, and since 1967 these have been used so frequently and extensively that any count now becomes rapidly out of date.

However, the Constitution embodied safeguards against their abuse – although certain recent cases have raised the question of how effective these really are (see below p. 47). A general emergency required, within two months of its promulgation, a confirmatory resolution of both Houses of Parliament. A 'state' emergency needed to be similarly confirmed; it automatically expired at the end of six months unless reconfirmed by fresh resolutions; and it could not remain in force, by dint of successive reconfirmations, for more than three years.

As constitution-makers, the Indians displayed their originality in little more than the size of the document that they produced, which is one of the longest constitutions the world has ever seen. Those parts of it not adopted or adapted from the 1935 Constitution were the product of an eclectic process of borrowing from other democratic and federal constitutions. As a member of the Drafting Committee put it, the policy was one of 'pick and choose ... to see what would suit the genius of the nation best' – a policy that was facilitated by the visits paid by another member, B. N. Rau, to England, Eire, Canada and the United States. In formulating Fundamental Rights and discussing 'due process' the Assembly turned to the example of the American Constitution. The Directive Principles were at least partly inspired by the constitution of the Republic of Ireland – the country, in the opinion of Nehru, 'where the conditions obtaining before the treaty were the nearest approach to those we have in India'. Even the enshrinement of Roman Catholicism in the Irish Constitution was paralleled by the clause about cow-protection in the Indian. From Australia, with its Grants Commission, came the idea of the Finance Commission; and the Australian example was also influential in persuading the Assembly to introduce a 'concurrent' list of powers and to permit the central Parliament to regulate matters normally reserved to the 'lower tier' federal units, should this be requested by two or more of them. From Canada came the conception that the central government should have overriding powers to secure 'peace, order and good government'. England contributed, among other things, the relegation of the

President to the status of a 'constitutional monarch' and the central idea of cabinet government. Such lack of originality, of course, was inevitable, given the educational background and political experience of the constitution-makers. Even if they had had different backgrounds and different experiences, true originality would still have been difficult; for democracy, of one familiar kind or another, could hardly have been denied to the Indian people, while some kind of federalism was clearly indicated by the size and heterogeneity of the new state. The only question, therefore, was where the emphasis should be placed, how the well-known elements of any liberal form of government should be combined to produce an instrument which would accommodate India's political traditions and offer a framework for the solution of her political problems. As Austin has well said, the words used by Carl von Doren to describe the mood of the constitution-makers in Philadelphia in 1787 were equally applicable to that of the constitution-makers in New Delhi in 1947:

Over the whole convention still hung the dread of future tyranny as well as of immediate anarchy. The delegates were sure that unless anarchy could be avoided, an early despot was certain to appear, as in the classic pattern of republican failure. They believed that anarchy could be at least postponed by the establishment of an adequate central government, but they could only guess what powers would make it neither too weak for security nor too strong for liberty.

In the India of 1947, a serious approach to these basic issues demanded dedication and ingenuity rather than originality. Such qualities, fortunately, were to be found among those who led the Assembly's deliberations.

The only real conflict of principle within the Assembly was that which divided the westernisers from the traditionalists – and even this was rather muted. As the westernisers had come to dominate the Congress leadership, it was inevitable that they should win on all the major issues and that such concessions as they chose to make to their critics should be marginal. Gandhi, whose ideal constitution differed radically from the one eventually adopted, was removed from the scene by murder in 1948, but even if he had lived it is unlikely that his influence on its actual provisions would have been very great. Old, fatigued and considerably disillusioned, he had retired from active politics to devote himself to moral uplift and social service. Moreover, his proposals for a *panchayat*-based, decentralised constitution seemed to the political realists who made up the majority of the Assembly as impracticable and dangerous as his suggestion that Congress should be transformed from 'a propaganda vehicle and a parliamentary machine' into a non-political social service agency. Much as they respected the Mahatma as the Father of the Nation, the great men of 1947-50, Nehru, Patel, Azad and Ambedkar, would have nothing to do with what they privately regarded as the political fantasies of his old age.

In the event, Gandhian influence on the final constitutional document was almost entirely confined to certain of the Directive Principles, such as the injunctions to discourage the consumption of intoxicating liquors and to encourage the organisation of village *panchayats*. As these items, like the rest of the Directive Principles, were not justiciable, they carried only moral force and their implementation remained at the discretion of the government. It would be an exaggeration, however, to suggest that Gandhi's ideas had already ceased to command respect; for the Directive Principles were not regarded by those who framed them as mere idealistic addenda to the Constitution. It was expected that Indian governments would treat them seriously, on pain of forfeiting popular confidence. Even today, the fact that they have been placed at the very beginning of the Constitution means that no government can afford to openly disregard them, unless it feels able to give very good reasons for doing so. The legislative record of independent India, moreover, shows that they have in fact been treated seriously. The system of local self-government known as *panchayati raj* has become, as we shall see, one of the most characteristic features of Indian democracy. As for prohibition, this has been widely but not quite universally enforced, since its enforcement has depended on the discretion of the governments of the individual states, not all of whom have considered its advantages to outweigh its disadvantages; but no foreign visitor to India could go away with the impression that the consumption of alcoholic drinks is anywhere regarded with official favour or even neutrality. One might add that another and far more important Directive Principle, that which enjoins the authorities to promote the 'distribution of ownership and control of natural resources to subserve the common good and to ensure that the operation of the economic system does not result in undue concentration of wealth and means of production', has become embodied in the terms of reference of the Planning Commission. Although this is not exclusively Gandhian, Gandhi would certainly have approved of it.

Nevertheless, it was parliamentary, representative democracy, which Gandhi and his most faithful disciples regarded as a harmful foreign importation, that provided the essential basis of the constitution, both at the Centre and in the states. The westernisers, therefore, had emerged victorious. There was never any serious doubt that they would do so.

Turning to the major provisions of the Constitution, designed to provide India with its normal form of government, we must first note that at the Centre formal executive power is vested in a President and Vice-President: the former elected by a 'college' consisting of the elected members of both Houses of the Union Parliament and the elected members of the states' legislative assemblies; the latter by the members of both Houses of the Union Parliament assembled in joint meeting. Actual executive power lies with a Council of Ministers selected by a Prime Minister called to office by the President as possessing, or likely to possess, a majority in the Lower House, the Lok Sabha.

In terms of parliamentary sovereignty, the Lok Sabha is where the power resides at the Centre. Elected by universal franchise, it consists of not more than five hundred members representing constituencies in the States, together with not more than twenty-five representing the Union Territories*. It has a maximum life of five years, and is subject to dissolution. The upper House, or Rajya Sabha, consists of not more than two hundred and fifty members, of whom twelve are nominated by the President (i.e. by the government) and the remainder elected, on a system of proportional representation, by the elected members of the state legislatures. Although legislation requires the consent of both Houses, financial control, via

* i.e. territories for which the Central Government has the ultimate administrative responsibility.

taxation and appropriation, lies exclusively with the Lok Sabha. The Rajya Sabha is not subject to dissolution; its members have a six-year period of office and one-third of them retire every second year.

Arrangements in the states, now eighteen in number, are not dissimilar – at least in those states that operate a bicameral system. Here the President's role is performed by the Governor, who, however, is not elected either directly or indirectly but appointed by the President himself (after 'consultation', of course, with the Union government). *De facto* executive power lies with a Council of Ministers under a Chief Minister, except to the extent that the Governor is endowed with discretionary powers in the exercise of which he does not need to take 'advice'. Among these are powers to 'reserve' certain types of bill for consideration by the President, to keep the President informed about the administration of any Scheduled Areas* the state may contain, and to report to the President his view, if such it be, that the government of the state can no longer be carried on in accordance with the normal constitutional provisions.

The Chief Minister and the Council of Ministers are collectively responsible to the state legislature. Bicameralism or unicameralism in the states is partly at the discretion of the Union Parliament, which can create or abolish legislative councils with the consent of the relevant legislative assemblies. In those states that have adopted the bicameral principle, the lower House, or Legislative Assembly, has the same kind of predominance that the Lok Sabha enjoys at the Centre. Consisting of not more than five hundred nor less than sixty members, and elected by universal franchise from territorial constituencies, it makes and unmakes governments and wields exclusive powers in matters of finance. The Legislative Council, which also has upper and lower size limits, is partly nominated by the Governor and partly elected by 'colleges' consisting of members of the Legislative Assembly and of representatives of municipalities, teachers and graduates. Like the Rajya Sabha, it is not subject to dissolution but to biennial renewal of one-third of its members, who have a six-year period of office.

Most of the above arrangements are simply adaptations (duly written out in the Constitution) of the familiar British

* i.e. principally tribal areas.

system of parliamentary and cabinet government. It is the manner in which they work, rather than their formal structure, that presents features of real interest, which will be dealt with in subsequent chapters. From a structural point of view, far greater interest attaches to the federal aspects of the system, which were the product of the Founding Fathers' determination to permit adequate regional autonomy in a country of great size and diversity yet to retain a strong and, in the last resort, authoritative central government.

As in all federal constitutions or federal-type governmental arrangements, there is a formal division of legislative powers between the central unit and the regional units. These powers are arranged in three lists, Union, state and concurrent. The Union list, which specifies the powers reserved to the central government, contains ninety-seven entries and includes defence, foreign affairs, communications, currency and coinage, banking and insurance, and customs duties. The state list of sixty-six entries includes law and order, local government, public health, education and agriculture. The forty-seven entries in the concurrent list include the legal system, trade and industry and economic and social planning. In respect of 'concurrent' items the laws passed by the central Parliament prevail over those passed by the parliaments of the states.

To enable Centre and state to perform their respective duties, each is endowed with specific powers of taxation. By the Seventh Schedule of the Constitution, the Union was given authority to impose taxes on income other than agricultural income, most customs and excises, a corporation tax, capital taxes, taxes on property other than agricultural property, taxes on succession, other than succession to agricultural land, taxes on railway freights and fares, taxes on stock exchange transactions, certain stamp duties, and taxes on newspapers and advertisements. To the states it assigned land revenue, taxes on agricultural income, succession and estate duties on agricultural land, excises on land, buildings and mineral rights, taxes on the entry of consumption goods into the local area, taxes on the consumption or sale of electricity, sales taxes, advertisement taxes other than those on advertisements in newspapers, vehicle taxes, taxes on animals and boats, tolls, taxes on professions, trades, callings and employments, capitation taxes, luxury taxes, and stamp duties other than those specified in the Union list. It is not expected, however, that the states shall be financially independent. Provision is made for the assignment to the use of the states of the proceeds of several Union taxes, of which the most important are property taxes, succession taxes and taxes on railway fares and freights, and for the sharing between the Union and the states of the yield of the income tax, according to 'such percentage as may be prescribed . . . and in such manner and from such time as may be prescribed' by the President. As for the Union-levied excises, these must go to the states in whole or in part 'in accordance with such principles of distribution as may be formulated . . . by law'. The Constitution also empowers the extension of grants-in-aid by the Union to 'such states as Parliament may determine to be in need of assistance', and an even wider aid-granting power is authorised by Article 282, which enables the Union (and incidentally the states as well) to 'make any grants for any public purpose, notwithstanding that the purpose is not one with respect to which Parliament or the legislature of the states, as the case may be, may make laws'. This last article, as we shall see, has proved of much greater importance than the Founding Fathers imagined it would be. To advise about the distribution and allocation of shared taxes and the principles governing grants-in-aid (other than those dependent on Article 282), there is a quasi-judicial Finance Commission, appointed at five yearly intervals. So far, four such commissions have met and presented their reports, which, as may be imagined, are awaited with considerable interest and sometimes trepidation by both Union and states.

Borrowing powers are given by the Constitution to both Union and states. A state may borrow from the Union as well as from other sources, but so long as it remains indebted to the Union it has to obtain the Union's permission for the raising of other loans. As the Union has advanced large sums to the states, the practical effect of this provision has been to make loan-raising an exclusive Union prerogative.

As in other federations, the provision of financial resources by the upper tier to the lower tiers has proved an important instrument of political and administrative centralisation. This was not foreseen by the constitution-makers, who established the Finance Commission to ensure that the states would obtain their tax-shares and grants-in-aid as of right, without strings attached. It was also assumed that most grants-in-aid would fall within the commission's jurisdiction and contribute no more than marginally to a state's income. Neither expectation has been realised. Not only have grants-in-aid become essential components of the states' finances; the bulk of them have fallen outside the purview of the commission and been made (at least in theory) conditional upon the state's agreeing to carry out certain centrally-formulated schemes and projects.

Nevertheless, the constitution-makers, although not envisaging this vigorous use of the financial weapon to bring the states into line with centrally-devised policies, were anxious enough to ensure that the Union government should have at its disposal adequate means of combatting centrifugal forces. Indeed, they embodied in the Constitution certain provisions which, if frequently operated, would have the effect of reducing the governments of the states to mere agencies of the Union government.

In some respects, their 'agency' status is a normal and continuing one. By the Constitution, states are enjoined to secure compliance, within their borders, with centrally-promulgated laws and to refrain from impeding the exercise by the central government of its executive powers. Over and above this, however, there is a wide variety of constitutional provisions designed to ensure that, in the last resort, the Centre's will shall prevail. The Central Parliament, for instance, may make provisions for the adjudication of inter-state disputes about the use, control and distribution of river-waters. By a two-thirds majority, the Council of States can give the Central Parliament the right, for a period of one year, to make laws on any matters contained in the states' lists. The governor of a state (who is appointed by the President) may withhold consent to a bill passed by its legislature, or may 'reserve' certain classes of bills for consideration by the President. Moreover, under the 'emergency' provisions the President, with the approval of the Central Parliament, can give directions to the states as to the manner in which they shall exercise their authority, or, if he is satisfied that normal constitutional arrangements in a particular state have broken down, himself assume any or all of the state government's functions. Even more extraordinary, in a political entity that purports to embody the principle of federalism, is the fact that neither the territorial integrity nor even the existence of any state is constitutionally guaranteed. By a simple majority, on the recommendation of the President, the Central Parliament can establish new states and alter the areas, boundaries and names of the existing states. This power, moreover, is no dead letter; it was used in the mid-1950s to reorganise the states along linguistic lines and has been subsequently employed to divide the former Punjab state into Punjab and Haryana and to bring into existence the new state of Nagaland. In theory, there is nothing to prevent a ruling party at the centre from using its majorities in the Lok Sabha and Rajya Sabha to effect an amalgamation of all the states, thus creating, *de facto*, a unitary form of government. When to all this is added the fact that the states are very considerably dependent, for their top administrative talent, on 'all-India' services, centrally recruited and organised it would appear that, constitutionally, India is something less – or something more – than a 'true' federation, if true federalism implied a co-equal relationship between two tiers of government. To avoid the ambiguities involved in the use of the term 'quasi-federation', it could be described, alternatively, as a federal government with very strong unitary features. Rajendra Prasad, the Founding Father who subsequently became President of the Indian Union, was clearly of the opinion that such categorisations were of no importance. 'Personally', he said, 'I do not attach any importance to the label which may be attached to it – whether you call it a Federal Constitution or a Unitary Constitution or by any other name. It makes no difference so long as the Constitution serves our purpose.'

The question, however, is precisely *whose* purpose the Constitution is to serve, and it is in the light of the various answers that can be given that the emphasis may be placed on one section of the constitutional provisions rather than another. The really interesting issue, of course, is not what the Constitution formally provides but how it works in practice; for the *political* relationships between the two governmental tiers cannot be prescribed but only influenced by legal provisions, however firmly entrenched. As is well known, one needs to make a distinction between federalism as a constitutional device and federalism as a system of government. How far India is federal in the latter sense will be discussed below in Chapter 5.

What is clear is that, at those points where there was a real choice to be made, the Founding Fathers were at pains to emphasise the *unity* of the truncated country with which Partition had presented them. It was for this reason that the 1935 Government of India Act had much to offer them whereas the Cabinet Mission's plan, which envisaged the loosest of loose federations, had nothing. In addition to the features that we have already catalogued, their centralising policy is seen in the retention of a single, unified judicial system for the whole country, headed by the Supreme Court. Nevertheless, the inescapable fact of diversity necessarily involved them in some rather queer exercises in the art of compromise, which may be illustrated by the complicated provisions, difficult to justify on strictly rational grounds, for constitutional amendment. The most vital of all types of amendment, that affecting the size, shape and number of the constituent states, was, as we have seen, made subject to simple majority vote in the Central Parliament. Most others require a majority of not less than two-thirds of those present and voting. However, amendments relating to the manner of electing the President, the organisation of the judiciary, the distribution of legislative power between Centre and states, the representation of the states in the Central Parliament and the procedure for amending the Constitution itself, require the consent of at least half the state legislatures. Thus the states, although dependent on the goodwill of the Central Parliament for their very existence, possess, so long as they continue to exist, certain rights which may be legitimately described as half-entrenched. 'The extraordinary diversity in the amending process', writes Dr Alexandrowicz, a leading authority on Indian constitutional law, 'provides for flexible solutions. . .'. So it does – but it hardly makes for constitutional intelligibility.

Actual amendments to the Constitution have been variable in importance. Comparatively trivial are those which have made marginal changes in the three lists of powers, Union, State and Concurrent. More serious are those that limit the right of free speech in the interests of preserving friendly relations with foreign powers and preventing defamation or incitement to commit offences. Of fundamental importance, too, is the Seventh Amendment (1956), which brought to an end the original division of the states into 'Parts A, B and C' and created certain centrally administered territories. But the most crucial of all the amendments are those relating to property rights, which exempt from judicial process the determination of compensation for property redistributed under the Land Reform Legislation and render immune from challenge in the courts, on the grounds of inconsistency with Fundamental Rights, a whole range of regulatory and property-extinguishing powers regarded as necessary by Governments for the pursuit of their economic objectives.

We apply the word 'crucial' to these amendments for two reasons; first, because without them the government of India would not have been able to give effect to some of the most important of its policies; secondly, because their effectiveness, for the purpose for which they were designed, has recently become subject to judicial challenge.

Since the elections of 1967 many things have changed, and one of them is the importance of the Supreme Court, which was previously rarely overburdened with cases involving constitutional interpretation. Today, as a consequence of one of its own decisions, it seems likely to become inundated with 'constitutional' business. The decision that made the difference was that promulgated in the Bank Nationalisation case, when the court struck down an Act on the grounds that it involved an abridgement of Fundamental Rights. This represented a reversal of its previous decisions to the effect that the First, Fourth and Seventeenth Amendments, which had restricted property rights in the interests of land reform, were not incompatible with the 'entrenched' Article 31 of the Constitution, which guarantees 'the right to property'. The new decision would appear to imply, among other things, that compensation payable under a law for the acquisition of any property has become justiciable. If this is so, and if Parliament (as in Golaknath's case the Supreme Court decided by six votes to five) cannot abridge Fundamental Rights, any measure involving acquisition with compensation will become the subject of endless and crippling litigation. As a commentator has said, Parliament consequently becomes 'really helpless and stuck with a rigid situation'. The only solution would appear to be a further amendment of the Constitution – which the results of the 1971 elections would seem to make possible.

Clearly the court, as guardian of the Constitution, has here become involved in an issue of major political importance. No less significant is its decision against the government in the much-publicised case about the constitutionality of the presidential order depriving the former princes of their purses and privileges. If Mrs Gandhi had been successful in her original intention, which was to effect this deprivation by constitutional amendment, which required a two-thirds majority in both Houses, there would have been no difficulty. But having failed to make the grade in the Rajya Sabha by one vote, she had recourse to a presidential order which appeared to owe what validity it possessed to a somewhat strained interpretation of the President's constitutional powers. It was the striking down of this order by the Supreme Court that provided the Prime Minister with one of her major election issues.

The use of the President of his 'emergency' powers may also become subject to judicial action, although it has not done so as yet. President Giri's declaration of an emergency in Uttar Pradesh (1970) took place under unusual circumstances. Political conditions in the State were not – by post-1967 standards – abnormally disorderly, but the Chief Minister, during a parliamentary recess, had lost his majority, as a result of defections. It would have seemed *de rigueur* to allow him time to meet the Assembly, in order to discover whether, with support from other quarters, he could carry on the government. However, President Giri, on Mrs Gandhi's instigation, declared Presidential Rule, which lasted fourteen days. Accusations of the misuse of this presidential power were both immediate and angry, and although no-one chose to question the constitutionality of his action before the Supreme Court, there was talk of impeaching him.

Does all this mean, it may be asked, that the government is now straining at the constitutional leash, or that there is general dissatisfaction with the work of the Founding Fathers? To the first question the answer is 'Yes', for there can be no doubt that the Constitution now seems less adaptable to governmental purposes than it formerly did. To the second, one may give the provisional answer that the Constitution no longer commands the respect that it once commanded. Even the accusation of 'unconstitutionality' is nowadays less an expression of affection for the constitution than a cry of rage against unacceptable political decisions.

This change in opinion has taken place fairly suddenly. Writing in 1965, Mr Granville Austin could plausibly congratulate the Indian people on the extent to which they had accepted the work of the Founding Fathers, who had 'expressed the aspirations of the nation' by bringing to their task the 'two wholly Indian concepts' of 'consensus and accommodation'. Up to that time, indeed, the constitution had not become the recipient of violent abuse, which was commonly reserved for the politicians. Even the extreme left-wing parties, such as the Communists, had decided to take advantage of the opportunities that it provided rather than attempt its overthrow, and the same might be said of right wing groups such as the Hindu Mahasabha and Jan Sangh. Certainly, there was the DMK's demand for an independent 'Dravidistan' in the south, which would have involved the dissolution of the Indian Union, but this party was already having second thoughts, and was about to settle for a policy of greater states' rights, which would not necessarily involve even constitutional amendment. Only a Gandhian rearguard had produced considered proposals for fundamental constitutional change. These, embodied in Jayaprakash Narayan's 'Proposals for the Reorganisation of the Indian Polity', were received with respect rather than enthusiasm. Most educated Indians regarded them as impracticable.

Today, the situation has changed. It is not merely that political violence has alarmingly increased. It is that organised bodies of political opinion, right, left and centre, no longer accept the Constitution as imposing on them rules which, however inhibiting they may seem, ought to be obeyed in the interests of orderly government and peaceful change. The immediate threat to constitutional government of course, comes from the extreme left. E. M. S. Namboodiripad's and Jyoti Basu's Marxists, although prepared to work within the Constitution to the extent of contesting elections and participating in coalition governments, make no secret of their determination to establish, when opportunity offers, a 'dictatorship of the proletariat', and certainly are not prepared to limit themselves to the use of democratic methods. The Marxist-Leninists, who are threatening the Marxists from an even more extreme position, overtly and indeed contemptuously reject constitutional politics and work for the violent overthrow of the present form of government. Meanwhile, on the right, among the Hindu communalist groups, the cause of constitutionalism is hardly faring better. Here the attack is on the secularism which provides the Constitution with one of its essential foundations. But possibly even more ominous, although less spectacular, is the growing tendency of Mrs Gandhi's government to treat the Constitution as something that can be, and ought to be, manipulated for party-political advantage, rather than as a set of rules which all must obey.

In these circumstances, and with the ever-increasing defiance of the rules of democratic process by angry and frustrated people at all levels of political life, the question is not only whether the Constitution of 1950 can be preserved, but whether constitutional government itself can be maintained. Military revolution, although difficult in a country of India's size and diversity, is not impossible, and it is also conceivable that a state or group of states might decide to opt out of the Union and set up an independent government. But perhaps more likely than either of these possibilities is a transformation of political practice, within the formal framework of the Constitution itself, so radical as to subvert the conventions and customs that have hitherto been accepted and operated. A breakdown of cabinet government at the Centre, for instance, might open the way to an assumption by the President himself of those powers now exercised 'on his behalf' by the Prime Minister and Council of Ministers. This would almost certainly require, in the first instance, the proclamation of an emergency, which could not last for more than two months without parliamentary sanction. Thereafter, a continuation of presidential rule, within the framework of the Constitution, would presumably depend on the willingness of Parliament to surrender to the President its legislative and financial prerogatives or alternatively to exercise them in accordance with his wishes. This would undoubtedly raise constitutional difficulties, but it might not be unworkable, given a compliant Supreme Court and a populace sufficiently disillusioned with parliamentary democracy to welcome strong presidential government as the only way of maintaining order and stability.

Such a possibility was certainly being discussed, if only *sotto voce,* when Indira Gandhi decided to pit her personal presidential choice, successfully, against the official Congress nominee; and if India were ever to cease to be a parliamentary democracy, the stepping down by the President from his present supra-political eminence is perhaps the most likely way in which it might occur. The fact that President Rajendra Prasad, in the early 1950s, showed himself rather less than contented with the role of figure-head suggests that, given the 'right' President, a presidential *coup d'état,* preserving the simulacrum of constitutionalism, is no mere fantasy. Nevertheless, it is hardly likely that, in such circumstances, the constitutional fig-leaf could for long be kept in position; for the simultaneous imposition of presidential rule at both levels, Centre and state, would probably demand that the President, with the help of the military, should bend the constitution to his will so violently as to destroy its letter as well as its spirit.

Speculations of this kind are unavoidable in the present situation, despite Mrs Gandhi's remarkable victory in the 1971 elections. It is still too early to say whether the apparent restoration of a dominant-party system will save Indian democracy, or whether the country is heading for a crisis in which all the familiar landmarks, including the Constitution itself, will be obliterated. It would be foolish indeed to imagine that because India has a Constitution which has worked reasonably well for twenty years she is permanently exempt from those political diseases which in other countries have brought democratic constitutions to a sudden end or distorted them out of all recognition.

When all this has been said, however, it remains true that there is still more political discussion about the *interpretation* of the Constitution than about its replacement or internal subversion. This type of discussion is particularly fierce and persistent in matters relevant to Centre-state relations. There are many who claim, for instance, that the rights which the Constitution gives the states have been arbitrarily disregarded.

The villain of this particular piece is the grant system. The practice of making large central grants, tied to particular projects and conditional (at least in theory) on satisfactory performance, has, we are told, reduced the states to an 'agency' role in respect of virtually all the important 'nation-building' subjects included in their own exclusive lists. Moreover, such grants, being made directly by the relevant central government department to the state governments, fall outside the purview of the Finance Commission, which is thereby prevented from playing its constitutional role of financial 'mediator' between Centre and states. The Planning Commission has also been condemned as an agency of 'extra-constitutional' centralisation. Although it possesses *de facto* power to approve the states' quinquennial and annual plans and has attempted to become what amounts to a second cabinet, this body is not mentioned in the Constitution and owes its existence not even to parliamentary legislation but to a mere cabinet resolution.

Accusations of this kind of 'unconstitutionality' have become the stock-in-trade of the right-wing Swatantra Party, which has sought to win political popularity by banging the states' rights drum and presenting the Planning Commission as a manifestation of the conspiracy of socialistically-minded bureaucrats to deprive the Indian people of the liberties that are their birth-right. It is only fair to add, however, that similar accusations have come from politically more neutral sources. Prominent among the defenders of the Finance Commission, for instance, is Asok Chanda, formerly Comptroller and Auditor General, while major attacks on the 'unconstitutional' pretensions of the Planning Commission have been launched by the well-known economist D. R. Gadgil (now its Deputy Chairman) and by the Estimates Committee of the Lok Sabha.

Others, on the other hand, have argued that in practice the Centre has often been unable to get its way even in matters which fall clearly within the scope of its constitutional prerogatives. Professor Marcus Franda, for instance, in his *West Bengal and the Federalising Process*, has shown how helpless is the Union government when confronted by the *non possumus* of a powerfully-entrenched state government. That such contradictory points of view are possible certainly provides evidence of the flexibility of the Indian Constitution in the field of

Centre-state relations. It deliberately provided for a 'cooperative' form of federalism, in which the actual balance of power between the two tiers could change over time and according to circumstance. Even if it had not done so, experience of other federations strongly suggests that the development of convention and the evolution of political practice would have produced a similar result, although with more difficulty and even greater controversy.

That discussion should be continuing shows that respect for the Constitution still remains strong. The sources of such respect among the more educated Indians are not difficult to discover. First, there is still a widespread conviction, not entirely confined to those who occupy a 'centrist' position in politics, that twenty years of constitutional government prove that the Founding Fathers did their work well. Secondly, Indian politicians, even of the new generation, are disciples of those who imbibed constitutionalism with their English-type education and who learned the practice of constitutional government through service in or association with the central and provincial legislatures of pre-independence days. Thirdly, even those who would like to replace the Constitution by something radically different find difficulty in suggesting a coherent and workable alternative.

As for the masses, one may guess that few of them are even aware of the existence of a Constitution, still less of the rights that it gives them and the duties that it imposes on them. The ordinary villager, it may be surmised, is merely conscious, as in the past, of the existence of a raj which manifests itself mainly in the form of official personalities who come giving orders or bearing gifts, and which accords him a periodical right, which he may or may not value, to choose between rival candidates in national, state and panchayat elections. This could conceivably be regarded as a source of stability, so long as the masses remain comparatively passive; but there is certainly no guarantee of their continued passivity, which is already being shattered in certain parts of rural India; and it is extremely unlikely, to say the least, that when they become roused they are going to pay any respect at all to the constitutional rules which are today creating controversy among their 'betters'.

Therefore, although there is still support for the Constitution, and although anti-constitutional forces have not yet acquired sufficient strength to break it, no-one can now claim, as Austin did, that 'the absence of comment about the constitutional situation in India is a mark of the Constitution's effective working'. Nor can one sustain his cheerful belief that the Constitution 'has been accepted as the basis for democracy in India in the matter-of-fact way that a family presumes the soundness of the foundations of the house in which it lives'. Even if there were an Indian 'family', in his sense, it might well be mistaken about the soundness of its house's foundations. As it is, not only are the foundations being inspected in a highly critical spirit, but some of the family's members have decided to band themselves together into a demolition squad. That there could be hard times ahead for the Indian Constitution is no matter for surprise. The surprising thing is that the work of the Founding Fathers should have withstood the storms of the last twenty years. This very fact gives them a certain uniqueness among constitution-builders in the less developed countries.

4 Elections, Parties and Pressure Groups

Elections

In 1951–2 independent India held her first general elections. Their organisation presented a mammoth task, which required the services of no fewer than one million government officials. Two hundred thousand polling stations had to be established and manned and some two and a half million ballot boxes provided. The world's largest exercise in democracy to date, it was a unique occasion.

The sheer size of the operation was not the only problem. In the remoter areas physical communications presented difficulties that sometimes verged on the fantastic. In some of these areas elephants had to be commandeered for transport and at least one election official had to cope with the experience of guarding polling booths against a marauding tiger. The registration of voters also had its complications as a result of diverse traditions about surnames. In many parts of the country separate facilities had to be provided for women voters. Above all there was the problem that a majority of the voters, among both men and women, was illiterate.

Many western observers confidentially predicted that the whole thing would degenerate into a shambles. That the elections were in fact conducted in a fair and orderly manner must be attributed at least in part to the efforts of the Central Election Commission, an independent body which set the electoral ball rolling by defining no fewer than 3,772 constituencies for central and state parliaments.

Of the voters, consisting of all men and women over the age of 21, just over 50 per cent decided to exercise the franchise. Bearing in mind that the rate of illiteracy was over 75 per cent this must be regarded as a remarkably high proportion of the one hundred and seventy-six million entitled to vote, particularly when we remember that only one-fifth of this number had any previous experience of voting. Inevitably there was some misunderstanding and confusion. Behaviour at polling stations was sometimes – to say the least – curious. Much of it, however, was nothing more than an 'eastern' version of the kind of nonsense that takes place at an election in Britain, America or any other western country. Indians, for instance, found it as natural to garland ballot boxes as Britons find it to wear rosettes. The important thing was that there was very little disorder and very little malpractice. In fact the first exposure of the mass of Indians to electoral politics passed off successfully.

Subsequent elections merit a similarly favourable verdict. In 1967 the disruption of political meetings was the main form of violence, and in only 8 per cent of the 474 reported disturbances during the sixty days preceding the poll did deaths or serious injuries occur. Since then, the use of violence for political ends has increased dramatically, and it could hardly have been expected that the 1971 election would be as peaceful as the preceding ones. In West Bengal, when political murders reached a figure of 1,200 in 1970, there was some doubt whether an election could be held at all. Nevertheless, a massive influx of troops helped to keep deaths down to a figure of 120 during the seven weeks of intensive campaigning, and to ensure that the election day itself passed off relatively peacefully. Elsewhere, violence was less extreme, although Bihar saw some bloody affrays, largely a product of caste rivalries, and both Uttar Pradesh and Gujerat had some Hindu-Muslim riots, serious enough to warrant firings by the police and the imposition of curfews. Yet despite these blots on the electoral record, no-one could seriously claim that, in the 1971 exercise, violence had reached a level where it called in doubt the validity of the verdict of the ballot-box. India is certainly becoming a more violent country, but she can still manage to hold a well-conducted general election.

Until 1967 every election confirmed the position of Congress as the dominant party. Not only was it the largest single party in the Lok Sabha; with three exceptions it maintained a leading position in the states. As a result of each of the elections of 1951–2, 1957 and 1962, 70 per cent or more of the Lok Sabha seats were won by Congressmen. Its nearest rival, the Communist

Party of India, was able to win only between sixteen and twenty-nine seats: not sufficient to give it the status of the official opposition – for this designation and the parliamentary privileges and facilities which went with it were (and are) reserved for a party which can muster at least fifty seats. It should be noted, however, that Congress was not as conspicuously successful in its efforts to dominate the state assemblies. In 1952 Congress failed to win an overall majority in PEPSU, Travancore-Cochin,* Orissa and Madras. In the first assembly of the new state of Andhra Pradesh, it gained only forty seats against the Communists' forty-one. In Kerala, in 1957, the Communist Party not only beat Congress but was able to form a government, while in Orissa a Congress government had to depend on the support of the locally-based Jharkhand Party. In both of these states mid-term elections became necessary. In Kerala, after a period of presidential rule (made necessary by the outbreak of political disorder in the state) Congress, by dint of electoral agreements with the Socialists and the Muslim League, gained a stable majority; in Orissa it had to have recourse to the formation of a coalition government with another local party, the Ganatantra Parishad. Furthermore, during the same electoral period the Congress government of Madhya Pradesh fell victim to internal factionalism, with the consequence that presidential rule had to be imposed. The third general election, which saw a drop in the total number of Assembly seats held by Congress from 68.4 per cent in 1951–2 to 61.3 per cent, was followed by similar, although rather less severe, difficulties. Congress's period of office in Kerala was short-lived and followed by a further spell of presidential rule, while in Madhya Pradesh the Congress government was dependent on the support of the Independents.

What emerges from the election results between 1951 and 1962 is that Indian politics were far more competitive at the state level than at the central, and that Congress weakness was particularly marked in certain areas of India. Nevertheless, in most of the states, Congress's position remained secure. This does not mean, however, that it ever enjoyed majority support at either level. Invariably, as a result of the 'first past the post'

* Like PEPSU, this state disappeared as such during the process of reorganisation.

system, there was a large gap between votes cast and seats won. For example, in the Lok Sabha election of 1951–2 Congress won 74.4 per cent of the seats on a popular vote of 45 per cent whilst the Socialist Party required 10.6 per cent of the popular vote to win only 2.5 per cent of the parliamentary seats.

During the period 1951–1967, therefore, Congress was a 'dominant' party which was not the first choice of the majority of the Indian electorate. This was the party's Achilles' heel, the vulnerability of which was revealed in the 1967 elections.

These elections altered the shape of Indian politics – although their long-term significance is still difficult to assess. Congress's hegemony in the states was most affected but the disaster did not stop there. In the Lok Sabha Congress lost 95 seats. True, it still held 284, while its nearest rival, the Swatantra Party, had only 44. But Congress's majority of 65 was by no means as safe as it appeared, for factionalism in the party had reached a stage where such a majority could not be relied upon. Eventually, the internal disputes produced a split (to be discussed later in this chapter) with the result that Mrs Gandhi found her majority reduced to virtually nil and could remain in power only as a result of the support which she received from parties of left-wing tendencies. But the situation for Congress was far worse in the states, where it received its greatest shock. Bihar, Punjab, West Bengal, Orissa, Madras, and Kerala were all lost. Moreover, many of the 'tallest poppies', such as Kamaraj, Atulya Ghosh and S. K. Patil, were all rejected. But although Congress's capacity to win seats had obviously declined, its capacity to attract votes was only marginally affected. On the poll it suffered a decline of 3.7 per cent in the Lok Sabha elections and one of 4.3 per cent in the State Assembly elections.

Here indeed lies one of the clues to Congress's failure in the 1967 elections. Formerly the simple majority voting system had operated in the party's favour; the fragmentation of the opposition enabled it to win seats on minority votes. By 1967 however at least some of the opposition parties had learnt the tricks of the trade. They no longer wasted their resources by spreading them over too many constituencies and they entered into electoral agreements on a hitherto unprecedented scale. Such pacts had eaten into Congress majorities in the 1962 elections; in 1967 they were sufficiently extensive to yield big dividends.

This is not however a sufficient explanation for Congress's defeats. In Madhya Pradesh and Gujerat, for instance, where there were electoral alliances between opposition parties, most Congressmen retained their seats. The main countervailing factor here seems to have been that the state Congress parties remained comparatively united; and it would seem that the loss of both votes and seats was generally correlated with a combination of powerful opposition alliances and intense internal factionalism within the state Congress parties concerned. It should be noted, however, that there is some evidence pointing to a causal connection between the solidity of an opposition alliance and the strength of factionalism within Congress; and once the opposition had gained the day many Congressmen were sorely tempted to increase its power by defecting from their party. To put the matter simply, in former days to be outside the Congress Party was to be in the political wilderness, whereas in 1967 the politically ambitious had several alternative possible homes. A further factor worth mentioning is the growth of factionalism in Congress's Central Election Committee, the body ultimately responsible for the selection of candidates. As a result there may have been some reduction of the vote-getting capabilities of the candidates chosen and perhaps a weakened sense of loyalty on the part of the elected member to the Congress organisation as a whole.

Be that as it may, Congress did best in states such as Gujerat, Madhya Pradesh, and Maharashtra, where internal factionalism was held in check by the onset of the elections. Its success in Andhra Pradesh, where factionalism was unrestrained, was probably due to the fact that the opposition parties were equally factionalised. In only three of the states where strong opposition alliances operated, viz. Rajasthan, Madhya Pradesh and Gujerat, did Congress retain its domination of the State Assemblies; even so in Rajasthan a spell of President's Rule intervened before a stable Congress ministry could be created. Opposition alliances, combined with the prevalence of 'breakaway' Congress groups, account for the party's loss of power in Kerala, Orissa, West Bengal and Punjab. In Madras, Congress's downfall was not due primarily to its own disunity or to the solidity of an oppositional alliance, but to the extraordinary progress that had been made by a strictly regional party, the Dravida Munnetra Kazhagam (DMK), which appealed to the separatist ambitions and anti-northern instincts of the Tamil population. Everywhere, however, attention has to be paid to strictly local factors if a full explanation is to be given of the sharp change in the balance of political power that the 1967 elections registered.

The major immediate outcome of the elections was the proliferation of unstable coalition governments in Northern India. Their instability was due to the diversity of their political components and to what an Indian journalist described as their 'ideological promiscuity'. Since in most cases it was only the desire for power that had brought the parties together, the creation of governments with stable parliamentary support proved extremely difficult. The habit of 'floor crossing' rendered governments impotent, with the result that Presidential rule had to be frequently imposed. Nor was the situation improved by the mid-term elections of February 1969 in Uttar Pradesh, West Bengal, Bihar and Punjab. This mini-general election, involving some two-thirds of the total Indian electorate, followed the trends of 1967. Although Congress improved its position in Uttar Pradesh (and was able to form a ministry) and maintained its position in Bihar, in the Punjab and West Bengal it sustained further losses. Public disenchantment with the performance of non-Congress coalitions redounded very little to Congress's advantage, particularly as the party had not fulfilled the oft-repeated injunction to 'pull itself together'. Indeed, later in the year it split into two organisationally separate parties, thereby placing in grave jeopardy the Congress majority in the Lok Sabha itself.

In December 1970 Mrs Gandhi, whose New Congress government depended on parliamentary support from other parties, chose the issue of the purses and privileges of the erstwhile princes as the occasion to dissolve Parliament and to go to the country – for the Lok Sabha's first mid-term election. As, in most states, the national election was not to be accompanied by elections to the State Assemblies, she was able to make a direct appeal to the people, without enlisting the help of the local and regional factions by a series of 'wheeler-dealer' compromises. Indeed, she had little alternative, as her party had been deprived of much of its grass-roots organisation by the split which she herself had engineered. It was a strategy which went against all of the accepted assumptions about the nature of Indian party politics, and many observers regarded it as a desperate gamble. There were none, even among her most optimistic supporters, who expected it to pay off so handsomely. When all the results had come in, Mrs Gandhi's Congress found itself with 350 seats in the Lok Sabha – 122 more than it held at the time of dissolution. For the opposition, both left and right, it was an electoral disaster. Of the parties that had entered into the 'grand alliance' against Mrs Gandhi, the rival Congress found itself reduced from 66 seats to 16, the Samyukta Socialists lost 20 of their 23, the Swatantra (the second largest party after the fourth general election) obtained only 6, and even the Jan Sangh, which had increased its representation in every previous election, sank from 35 to 21. Regional parties, with the outstanding exception of the DMK in Tamil Nadu and the 'mushroom' party demanding a separate state for Telengana (the Telengana Praja Samiti) were almost erased from the national political scene. The only major party to improve its position was the Marxist Communist Party, CPI(M), which took second place with 25 seats.

In two of the three state elections that were simultaneously held, Mrs Gandhi's Congress also made spectacular gains. In Orissa, previously ruled by a Swatantra-led coalition, it emerged as the largest party, with 51 seats. In West Bengal, although the CPI(M) won 111 seats (a gain of 22), Mrs Gandhi's Congress, with 105, registered an improvement of 50 on the mid-term electoral performance of the undivided Congress, with the result that it was able to take the lead in the formation of a coalition government, in partnership with the other Communist Party and two regionally-based parties (the Bangla Congress and the Forward Bloc). Only in Tamil Nadu did a regional party (the DMK) triumph in the state elections, and then only by dint of an electoral arrangement with Mrs Gandhi, whereby the DMK was given a free run for the Assembly seats in return for an undertaking not to contest Mrs Gandhi's candidates in 10 of the Lok Sabha seats.

In our concluding chapter we attempt some very general

assessment of the significance of this remarkable election, but it is far too recent to be seen in any kind of perspective – too recent for us to be able to benefit even from the evidence provided by any election study in depth. Superficially, the success of Mrs Gandhi's socialist appeal would appear to indicate the advent of a nation-wide political opinion of a radical kind, together with a return to charismatic forms of leadership which were thought to have died with Nehru. That proverbial fount of political wisdom, the New Delhi taxi-driver, is said to have summed up the situation with the words: 'Mrs Gandhi will work for the ordinary man'. Whether she will or can remains to be seen. What is certain is that ordinary men have given her an unprecedented vote of confidence.

So much for the results of the voting exercises. What of the voters themselves? Participation has been consistently high, ranging from about 50 per cent in the first elections to 61 per cent in the last ones. Does this mean that democracy can now be regarded as well established in India? Such a conclusion would be quite unwarranted. Even if we succeeded in excluding all other factors which might influence our answer, we should need to know far more than we know at present about the motivations of the participants. It would, however, be reasonable to suppose that in the vast majority of them understanding of a commitment to a democracy as such is extremely weak. Nevertheless, one must not underestimate the influence of *habit* in the adjustment of citizens to democratic forms of political life.

Such studies of voting behaviour as have been made are suggestive rather than conclusive. In support of the argument advanced by Phyllis Rolnick, that the Indian electorate is 'ineffective' as a result of its inability to conceptualise or analyse situations other than familiar personal ones, one might quote the micro-study by A. H. Somjee of a Gujerati village with a 5 per cent literacy rate. There, only 10 per cent of the voters knew the names of their candidates and only 21 per cent were familiar with the symbols used by the political parties. Even when known, the symbols are often taken too literally. In a West Bengal constituency in 1969, for instance, voters were found to be giving serious discussion to the rival merits of the plough, the symbol of the Bangla Congress, and the yoked bullocks, that of the old Congress Party. On the other hand the Indian Institute of Public Opinion found that in 1961 28.8 per cent of an urban sample of voters had attended political meetings and 27.2 per cent of a rural sample. The proportion of those who reported listening to speeches by political leaders and candidates was even higher – 31.8 per cent of the urban sample and 28.5 per cent of the rural. From its data the Institute concluded that some 40 per cent of the urban population and 34 per cent of the rural was 'interested' in political affairs. Most of those questioned, however, were not very familiar with the names of political leaders and very few indeed had any clear knowledge of the political issues about which they were being called upon to vote. Nevertheless, further studies show that at least in certain areas among certain strata of the electorate the right to vote is highly prized and used with some discrimination. It is of course a matter of no surprise that there should be a fairly high positive correlation between voting levels and levels of modernisation.

The influence of caste on voting behaviour has been considerably discussed. Selig Harrison, in his *India, the Most Dangerous Decades,* suggested that it was the dominant influence, but this suggestion has been effectively challenged. Certainly, where caste associations exist, they will attempt to bargain with the political parties in the interests of their members. Caste associations, however, are not universal, and at the village or small town level the impact of caste on voting is so various and complicated as to defy generalised description. Even some caste associations now find it impossible to 'deliver the vote' to a particular political party because of the divergencies between the economic interests of different groups of their members. In such circumstances, as well as in others, voting by class, which is usually interpreted as a sign of 'modern' political behaviour, is becoming the order of the day. Sometimes class is closely associated with caste; elsewhere there is no correspondence, or only a weak correspondence between the two. As one would expect in so large and varied a country, poised between tradition and modernity, the possible patterns of electoral politics are almost infinite. That the determinants of voting behaviour are changing, perhaps radically, would seem to be indicated by the results of the 1971 election. Indeed, some observers have rushed into print to ascribe a new maturity to the Indian electorate, and even to announce the birth of a 'new politics'. Caste politics, factional politics and 'vote banks' are said to have been swept away by Mrs Gandhi's new broom. All this is highly speculative – and highly unlikely. It is true that the politicians who relied on the well-established methods of vote-catching received a marked set-back – necessarily exaggerated by the 'first-past-the-post' system – in the 1971 elections. But it is also highly probable – and totally neglected by those who see the New Jerusalem writ large in a single election result – that Mrs Gandhi's victory depended on the support of two huge voting blocs, each with its own special interests to protect: the Untouchables and the Muslims. In so large and varied a country, occupying an ill-defined point on the spectrum that links modernity with tradition, one must expect great variations in the pattern of voting behaviour not only from place to place but from time to time. It would, therefore, be premature, at the very least, to present the 1971 election as a major breakthrough in the cause of political modernity and rationality.

Parties (1): *Congress*

Even a cursory study of election results between 1951 and 1967 confirms the dominance of the Congress Party; but it tells us very little about the actual functioning of the party system and still less about the nature of the dominant party itself. Why did Congress provide the main political leadership and why were the opposition parties so weak? These are the crucial questions when one comes to look at the Indian party system.

In conversation with Michael Brecher, Krishna Menon emphasised the one great advantage that Congress had over its competitors. 'The great strength of the Congress party', he said, 'is that they have a place in the hearts of the people. There is nothing to take its place. I mean you cannot compare it to a western political party; it's not strictly a party, it's got a mystique; it's a movement still.' Although opposition politicians often fought with the independence movement (frequently as Congress members) their parties did not form part of the hard core of this movement, and consequently did not fully share in the mystique. 'I have begun with Congress', said an old man in Moradabad rural constituency, 'have stayed with Congress and will end with Congress, because Congress is the first party. The flowers that bloom in the field, the crops that grow in the field, they are there because of Congress'. Such naiveté may not be typical but it gives expression to sentiments with which millions of Indians would have agreed.

The old man's son, however, voted for the Praja Socialists and displayed none of his father's fond memories. Here's the rub. Congress continues to remind voters of the glorious past, but memories fade and new generations come to the polls. The Congress old guard has practically disappeared and the banners in Bombay no longer read 'a vote for the pair of bullocks is a vote for Pandit Nehru'. Even among the middle-aged Congress leaders very few have 'graduated' from British jails. Here we have at least part of the explanation both of Congress's former dominance and of its more recent – but possibly temporary – loss of dominance.

A second and equally important explanation is to be found in political organisation. When a party ceases to have a charismatic leader and finds that its emotional ties with the electorate are weakening, it can often find a substitute in firm and efficient organisation. Even before Independence Congress possessed an organisational network more extensive and intensive than that possessed by almost any other national independence movement. Moreover it was far more of a national party than most of its opponents; for their strength was – and for the most part remains – confined to specific areas of India, while the strength of Congress was nationwide, not only covering British India but penetrating into the princely states. It also had unrivalled 'grass roots' in the villages. From the districts and talukas, a hierarchy of elected committees arose to the pinnacle of the All-India Congress Committee (AICC). Through this elaborate party structure Congressmen learnt many of the skills necessary for the maintenance of party support. They succeeded in tapping the resources of indigenous business interests and in recruiting and activating a wide variety of people from different classes, groups and castes. These were able to win the support, at least in the form of the casting of votes, of people who chose to remain outside the party itself – people who, although perhaps disagreeing with many specific items of Congress policy, respected it as an effective organisation capable of delivering whatever 'goods' there were to deliver. Organisational effectiveness, therefore, goes a long way to explain the former Congress dominance.

Although, as is the way with national independence movements, all these advantages proved wasting assets once Independence had been achieved, they were lost only very gradually. For over twenty years Congress was able to withstand the strains to which, as a ruling party, it was subjected and to preserve a great deal of its capacity for interest-aggregation. Here the successive stages whereby it had built itself up into a genuinely national party may be briefly recalled. Originating amongst a 'microscopic minority' of westernised professional men, at the beginning of the twentieth century it began to recruit support from the business community. Then, with the advent of Gandhi, it stretched out towards the masses. Although it rarely reached the lowest ranks of Indian society, it achieved widespread popularity among the middle strata such as peasant proprietors, petty tradesmen and skilled artisans. Moreover, its advent to office as a governing party enabled it to appeal to even more diverse socio-economic groups, who tended to regard it as the only political vehicle through which their aspirations might be realised. Congress itself, of course, was very anxious to draw every possible group into its net, if only for the purpose of increasing the number of its votes. The High Command therefore strove vigorously to maintain its catch-all nature, so that Nehru's slogan of 1953, 'the Congress is the country and the country is Congress' might be realised. Such a broad-based party fitted in very well with certain concepts of the Hindu religion and moreover could be justified on the grounds that unity was necessary to solve the problems of national integration, political legitimacy, and economic development.

But easy as it may be for a national leadership in these circumstances to think in terms of aggregation and accommodation, it is much more difficult for a local leadership to do so. The locals are faced with the choice of preserving their own leadership by discouraging recruitment, or winning additional votes by bringing into the organisation new elements which may subsequently displace them. Admittedly, this difficulty has been considerably eased by the expansion of the amount of political power available to anyone with the will and capacity to seize it. Even before Independence this was so. For instance, at a time when the elite composition of Congress was becoming more diversified, the 1935 Government of India Act, by extending the powers of the provincial assemblies, considerably increased the range of effective participation. Since Independence, of course, opportunities for participation have grown very rapidly. New units of the party have been developed, state governments have been created and – perhaps most important of all – the introduction of panchayati raj has provided new outlets for the satisfaction of political ambitions both by groups and by individuals. Moreover where the local Congress leadership is factionalised the rival leaders will willingly accept newcomers as a means of strengthening their own positions. In some parts of India even the participation of former princes and zamindars has been welcomed. On balance, despite the misgivings of many sections of the local leadership, this integrative and aggregative tendency of the party prevailed over countervailing forces during the first twenty years of Independence. But its significance, as we shall see, changed. Before Independence, it was undoubtedly a source of strength; after Independence, it gradually became transformed into a source of weakness.

At this stage, it will be useful to look in rather greater detail at the membership of the party and at the manner in which it is 'socialised' and organised. The number of members varies widely from time to time. For fairly obvious reasons it tends to become inflated in election years and deflated in non-election years. Nevertheless it is always in the region of several millions. There has been no overall study of the composition of Congress membership but sample studies done in three States, West Bengal, Gujerat and Maharashtra, show a predominance of agriculturists, followed by service workers, business men and professional men in that order. The caste composition of the membership varies from area to area, but it is clear that outside the towns most of the leaders are from the middle castes. These elements, first involved in Congress politics in the 1920s and 1930s, now tend to dominate the organisation at the district and state levels, and are rapidly moving upwards to the area of central parliamentary politics.

The recruitment of Congress members from a wide spectrum of caste and interest groups has tended to reinforce the factionalism which is characteristic of all Indian organisations and associations. The factions are like miniature parties within the broad party. Although their numbers and relative strengths vary perpetually and confusingly, one can agree with Paul Brass that 'organisationally, Congress is a collection of district factions and state factions forming alliances and developing hostilities in a constant struggle for positions of power and status in Congress-controlled institutions'. One should immediately add, however, that this is truer of Uttar Pradesh, the area that Brass studied, than of many other parts of India. Actual factions are not entirely chaotic or anomic in their mode of operation; indeed one can detect certain rules which are generally regarded as appropriate for the regulation of factional activity – rules which in normal circumstances will be enforced by higher party authority. It has even been alleged that factionalism within the Congress party serves some useful purposes. Factions, for instance, are alleged to be the agents of political recruitment, and indeed there is some evidence in some parts of India of a direct positive relationship between the intensity of factional conflict and the size of party membership. They are also said to widen the basis for grass roots political participation and to keep the party responsive to the perpetual changes in its political environment. What is certain is that conflicts which might otherwise have provided a basis for inter-party competition have become internalised in Congress, thereby keeping the opposition parties weak and giving the Congress leadership a sufficient diversity of base to keep it in political power. These advantages of factionalism are – or at least were – real, but there is obviously a debit side to the phenomenon. Not only does it make the process of decision-taking difficult and lengthy; it may result in the total paralysis of a leadership which becomes increasingly preoccupied with the maintenance of internal unity to the exclusion of every other objective. Even more importantly, to quote the words of Baldev Raj Nayar, 'the spectacle of constant bickering amongst Congressmen, the public display of inner party controversies and the open defiance of party discipline make not only for the denigration of the Congress Party, but also lead to a contempt for the political system and politics itself'.

The minimum degree of party unity necessary for coherence is supposed to be promoted by the 'steel frame' of its formal organisation; but the larger the party has become, and the more diversified its membership, the greater has been the difficulty in reconciling organisational form with political content. The advent of Independence naturally exacerbated this problem, with which the leadership attempted to cope by accompanying its demand for a change of attitude on the part of Congress members (from fighting the government to collaborating with it) with the introduction of new patterns of recruitment and organisation. In the hope of creating a hard core of disciplined activists, new emphasis was given to the already-existing division between primary and active members. There were differing subscriptions, varying qualifications for membership, and unequal voting rights. To link rank and file members, both new and old, primary and active, to the higher echelons of the party, new Mandal Committees were created, each covering an area of roughly 20,000 people and composed of at least twenty-five primary Members. These were to be the basic units from which the higher committees would be elected; they were also to prove a field organisation for political education and for the implementation of Congress's constructive programme. In fact, they were not very effective in performing either of these tasks, for they tended to fall between two stools : they were too large and too remote to effect any thorough penetration of the villages but too small to be able to play any effective part in rural development schemes. In 1964 the Mandal was replaced by a new basic unit, the Block Congress Committee, the area of which coincided with that of one of the most important political-administrative units of the new panchayati raj. This proved more successful, at least to the extent of gearing Congress political activities in the rural areas to the task of winning the elections in the new local bodies. In the same year membership requirements were once again subjected to scrutiny. The ubiquitous practice of creating bogus members for purposes of internal party elections had adulterated the whole meaning of primary membership. It was suggested therefore that primary members should be deprived of their voting rights. This was naturally opposed and eventually a compromise was arrived at whereby primary members' rights were confined to the election of active members to the Block Congress Committees; active members alone would have the right of voting in elections to higher party bodies. Obviously the application of this new rule would not put an end to bogus enlistment; nor did it. The dichotomy between size and purity remains, and is likely to remain, unsolved.

The 'intermediate' organs of Congress, the District and Provincial Committees, present rather less serious problems since they have more clearly defined roles to play. The three hundred and ninety-one District Committees, elected by the Block Committees, have the duties of recommending candidates for the State Assembly and the Lok Sabha, of acting as Election headquarters, of providing a focus for the auxiliary groups of Congress, and perhaps most important of all, of electing the Provincial Congress Committees. The PCC is the top Congress body in the state, and as such plays a crucial role in state parliamentary politics. At the national apex of Congress organisation there are two bodies both of considerable size: the Annual Session and the All-India Congress Committee. The former consists of five thousand delegates elected by the whole membership of Congress; the latter consists, in addition to the Congress President and a number of co-opted members, of one-eighth of the membership of each PCC, elected by the members of the PCC itself. A permanent executive, designed to give strong and continuous direction to Congress activities throughout the country, is provided by the Working Committee, two-thirds of which is appointed by the President, the remainder being elected by the AICC. Constitutionally, as Nehru said, 'the basic policy of the party is laid down by the Annual Session, it is interpreted and implemented by the AICC and it is carried out by the Working Committee'. In practice, as is usual with most large political parties, these relationships have been almost exactly reversed. The Annual Session is no more than a large and amorphous consultative body, while the AICC, although sometimes restive, normally accepts the policies laid down by the Working Committee. It was during one of these periods of restiveness that the AICC insisted on appointing one-third of the membership of the Working Committee, which formerly was entirely nominated by the President. During the same period of controversy the AICC also secured the right to elect the Parliamentary Board, one of the most important central organs of the party. As might be expected, during the period leading up towards the split in the party, debates in the AICC increased in liveliness; non-official resolutions were introduced, many of them highly critical of the leadership, and special meetings were held to consider specific issues.

As with all parties whose origins are extra-parliamentary, Congress has had great difficulty in integrating its legislative and organisational wings. This problem was exacerbated after Independence, when, through the adoption of the British model of parliamentary government, councils of ministers became responsible to parliaments and through parliaments to the people. Nehru and the other top leaders fully accepted this constitutional doctrine, which involved a reduction in the influence of the party as such and its relegation to the role of taking broad programmatic decisions and organising its members for electoral and 'constructive' work. The practical difficulties of effecting this type of 'separation of powers' are well known, and there were not a few powerful men among the Congress leaders who bitterly complained that intraparty democracy was being jettisoned.

At the centre, the Prime Minister and the Congress President tended to regard each other at best with suspicion and at worst with outright hostility. Kripalani, who succeeded Nehru in the Congress presidency when the latter became Prime Minister, tried to insist that political decisions should be made in consultation with the Working Committee, a body which he tried to insulate from governmental influence by limiting the number of ministers among its members to one-third of the total. Nehru and Patel fought him vigorously, with the result that, within two months of Independence, Kripalani, tired of the struggle, resigned from the Congress presidency and, soon after, from the party. A later President, Tandon, was equally hostile to the governmental leadership. He, too, was forced to resign, and Nehru, to prevent any repetition of such a situation, himself assumed the office of President, which he occupied for a period of five years. According to Frank Moraes, this victory for the parliamentary wing created a 'Congress habit of mind . . . which led the overwhelming bulk of the party to look to the Prime Minister and not to the President of Congress for political guidance'. Although Nehru relinquished the presidency in 1955, elections to this office remained firmly under his control until his death in 1964. It seemed, as is usual in conflicts of this sort, that the parliamentary wing had won; but in the 1960s the relationships between the two wings became much more fluid again. Nehru himself was partly responsible for these developments, in so far as through the so-called Kamaraj Plan he virtually ordered the resignation from office and return to organisational work of six central ministers and an equal number of chief ministers of states. Within a year Kamaraj, one of the most powerful figures in Congress, was elected to the presidency. As a member of the small group known as the Syndicate, Kamaraj was responsible for engineering the succession of Shastri to the prime ministership; but although he played almost an equally prominent role in securing the prime ministership for Mrs Gandhi after Shastri's untimely death, he then lost control, partly but not entirely as a result of the defeat which he suffered in the 1967 elections in his home State of Madras, where for many years before his translation to the Congress presidency he had been a very powerful Chief Minister. Rather surprisingly, Mrs Gandhi showed a determination to be independent of those responsible for her elevation, and for a time it seemed that the balance between the organisational and parliamentary wings had swung back decisively in favour of the latter. Indeed in his book *The Congress Party of India,* Stanley Kochanek assumed that the conflict had been decided, and that the Prime Minister had, at least in normal times, become the '*de facto* leader of both party and government'. But the times were not normal, and the relationships between the two wings turned so sour that party unity could no longer be maintained. In bringing about the eventual split, the new Congress President, Nijalingappa, played a leading role.

In state politics, this conflict was even sharper. Its pattern had varied from state to state. In Maharashtra, for instance, Y. B. Chavan, formerly Chief Minister, succeeded in keeping the organisational wing firmly under his control, but in West

Bengal it was the organisational leader, Atulya Ghosh, who achieved dominance. Elsewhere the fortunes of battle rocked to and fro with varying results. Where the battle has been most severe, as in Uttar Pradesh, it has on several occasions resulted in the overthrow of ministries. Attempts by the central leadership to mitigate the conflict by arranging regular meetings between the two wings have met with only partial success. In many of the states, the two wings are virtually two independent parties, the PCC or some section of it acting in the manner of an opposition, with its supporters in the Assembly tabling motions critical of the government and using question time as an opportunity to publicise its discontent and to embarrass the Chief Minister.

Since Independence, the changing relationship between Centre and states has also proved a source of embarrassment to Congress. In theory decisions of the AICC and the Working Committee are binding throughout the party; in practice, the central organs have rarely dared to behave monolithically vis-à-vis their state counterparts. The mere giving of orders has been clearly recognised as incapable of maintaining that modicum of unity which the party requires. Hence every effort has been made to improve opportunities for two-way communication between Centre and state leaders. Itinerant central officials tour the states; a regional balance has been carefully preserved on many of the Central Party Committees; and the enlargement of the Working Committee has ensured that every state is represented on it. These organisational innovations reflect the downward diffusion of power within the party's hierarchical structure. Particularly since the creation of the 'linguistic' States in the 1950s, a new type of politician has risen to prominence, the ambitious regional leader. Very different in background and outlook from the westernised elite which still tended to predominate at the Centre, this rough-hewn type of man gave his first loyalty to the state which provided him with support. Comparatively distant and potentially hostile, the Centre was for him a forum where advantageous bargains might be struck, rather than a source of orders and guidance. If sufficiently successful, of course, he might himself become the incumbent of a central ministry or a Central Party post, but when he did so he took with him all his local prejudices and local loyalties. Consequently the 'bargaining' relationship between the various personalities and groups in New Delhi received powerful reinforcement. More and more the party's central policies reflected a series of elaborate compromises between regional particularisms. This recognition of the strength of regional forces did not necessarily weaken the party but it certainly changed the nature of Congress's total political impact.

What *did* weaken the party in the long run, although it temporarily seemed a source of strength, was the close association between factionalism and patronage. The distribution of favours was, of course, the most important of the weapons that a dominant faction could wield. If used judiciously it could be the means of bringing together a whole state organisation in a precarious unity. One of its most successful practitioners, Kairon, the leader of the dominant faction in the Punjabi Party from 1956 to 64, managed his unruly followers by what he described as 'the American technique' – everyone had his price. Another successful practitioner, Atulya Ghosh of West Bengal, once admitted that under his leadership the PCC had become 'a place for spoils and favours' – a situation which he justified on the grounds that the alternative was mobocracy, which indeed it seems to have been. A rough measure of the extent of patronage may be found in the size of state cabinets; often these have been swollen to as many as fifty members as a result of the splitting of ministries in order to find suitable places for exigeant factional leaders. Fortunately for the state bosses, government intervention in the economy, through 'the licence, permit, and quota raj', and the expansion of government activities in the rural areas have greatly increased the amount of patronage at their disposal. As a result of these new opportunities, party managers today tend to have less recourse to the techniques of mere arbitration between factions than was the case in the past.

Where, however, the party organisation in a state lacks a dominant faction, with the result that sheer chaos is just around the corner, arbitration from the Centre can be of great importance. Many disputes have been brought to the attention of the Working Committee, to be referred to one of the sub-committees charged with supervising the affairs of state party organisations. Of these, the Parliamentary Board and the

Central Election Committee, both composed of major party leaders, are the most important. In the past, the board developed techniques whereby it could measure the strength of the competing factions and 'recommend' arrangements whereby they might all receive some satisfaction. In both Uttar Pradesh and Madhya Pradesh, where factions abounded, the board on several occasions scored outstanding successes. However, by no means all of its efforts have paid off. For instance, even when Nehru himself ordered fresh elections for the West Bengal PCC, the local boss Atulya Ghosh, with the backing of the majority of his party, refused to obey. Normally, the Parliamentary Board has not attempted to intervene in states where a particular faction has enjoyed long-term dominance, since the most likely result of such intervention is to cause defection. It should be added that since about 1965 the board has rarely been in a position to use its arbitral powers effectively.

Elections have provided the supreme test for the party's central conciliation machinery. Here the role of the Central Election Committee can be crucial. In the first three elections the CEC played a dominant role in the selection process, drawing up the final elections list in such a way as to conciliate all the more important interests within the Party. Prominent national leaders have played an important and time-consuming role in this process. In 1957, for instance, Morarji Desai personally interviewed all four thousand would-be candidates in Bihar. The principle generally applied is that 'sitting tenants' should retain a majority but rival interests receive a degree of representation that they will not regard as outrageously unfair. These techniques, however, fell to pieces in the fourth general election, since the CEC itself had become factionalised.

So far, we have presented Congress as an 'aggregative' party, consisting of diverse groups, interests and factions between which compromise, although difficult, proved possible until very recently. It nevertheless presents itself to the public as an 'ideological' party, devoted to the achievement of socialism and equality. That most outside observers do not attach much importance to this ideology is perhaps partly the fault of Congress itself. The Avadi Resolution of 1954, which proclaimed the objective of establishing a 'socialistic pattern of society', was at the time of its passing described by one newspaper as 'brilliantly vague', and it is well known that 'socialism', as interpreted by Congress, can mean if not all things to all men, at least most things to most. A cynic, indeed, might describe it as a flexible philosophy which has sought to appeal to the urge for change among the have-nots and a desire for security among the haves. Indeed, if this were not the case the party would be inhibited from performing the 'aggregative' function which we have so strongly emphasised.

Thus, although the Congress Party, in its original form, survived twenty-two years of Independence, it always displayed certain weaknesses which threatened not only its dominance but its very existence. Indeed, its failure to win a clear majority of the total votes cast in elections meant that, in a sense, it always existed on sufferance, i.e. so long as its rivals were incapable of presenting a series of united fronts. In 1967, as a result of their newfound capacity to do so, this basic weakness stood fully revealed. The question was then whether, faced with a really massive electoral setback, the party would prove capable of uniting to fight back and re-win lost ground. For some parties, such an external threat might have brought about a closing of the ranks; but not for Congress. Groups which had previously supported Congress had done so to achieve purposes which the party could satisfy only if it remained in power. As soon as it was defeated or seriously weakened, such groups felt no qualms about defecting. Indeed, coming events cast their shadow before them, in so far as disunity at the centre made Congress, even before the elections, look a much less viable political force than it had looked in the past. The failure of the CEC to play its accustomed role meant that over a thousand ex-congressmen were standing against the official candidates. For the same reason, state bosses had been left free to construct their own election lists, with the result that minority groups, deprived of the chances they normally enjoyed, were sufficiently alienated to form or join one of the innumerable Jan ('People's') Congresses.

This breakdown at the centre had no one single cause, but the removal in 1964 of Nehru's unifying presence was undoubtedly a very important factor. Through the exercise of his unrivalled authority, Nehru had been able to insure that the Party Central Command had been virtually faction free. His death left a vacuum in New Delhi which was never filled. Significantly, the most notorious and long-lasting of the central factions, the so-called Syndicate, came into being during his last illness. An alliance of non-Hindi state leaders, its original purpose was to prevent the election of Morarji Desai to the Party Presidency. Although it played a useful role in securing the unopposed election of Shastri as Prime Minister, the virtually unconcealed factionalism it introduced into the central councils of the party had wrought havoc by the time of the 1967 elections. A rival faction, which supported Morarji Desai for the prime ministership, as against Mrs Gandhi, was less powerful and united, but hardly less damaging. Thus even before the elections of 1967, the stage was set for the subsequent party split. That the split actually occurred when it did, however, must be attributed to various 'accidents', of which Mrs Gandhi's personality and ambitions were among the more important.

The onset of the actual crisis, in the summer of 1969, arose from a dispute about candidates for the Indian presidency. Under the influence of the Syndicate, which was still capable of mobilising significant support, the CEC deliberately selected a candidate, Sanjiva Reddi of Andhra Pradesh, of whom Mrs Gandhi disapproved. One of Mrs Gandhi's supporters, Giri, then announced his decision to stand as an Independent. Mrs Gandhi threw down the gauntlet not only by openly supporting Giri (who was subsequently elected) but by pushing through the Working Committee a decision to nationalise the commercial banks, a measure which, although part of Congress's official policy, she knew would be little to the taste of the Syndicate and its right-wing supporters. This not only proved her commitment to socialism, it gave her an opportunity to demote the equally right-wing Morarji Desai who held the Finance portfolio, on the grounds that he could not possibly be sympathetic to the 'new line'. After a speaking tour in which she was received with considerable enthusiasm, her next move was to allow the circulation of a resolution which sought to bring to a premature end the Congress presidency of another of her leading rivals, Nijalingappa of Mysore. The reply of the so-called right wing was to mobilise its parliamentary supporters to challenge Mrs Gandhi in the Lok Sabha when it re-assembled in November. In the meantime, Nijalingappa contrived to exclude two of Mrs Gandhi's henchmen from the Working Committee. In reply, she boycotted the Working Committee and set up a so-called Steering Committee at her own residence. Now entirely in the hands of the Prime Minister's opponents, the Working Committee launched an unprecedented attack on her and finally, on 12th November 1969, expelled her from the party for her 'constant denigration of the organisation ... acts of indiscipline' and 'a basic and overriding desire to concentrate all power in her own hands'.

Thus the party split into a 'new' Congress under Mrs Gandhi and an 'old' Congress under Nijalingappa. As we have suggested, the split was primarily the product of a factional struggle; but inevitably it has been given ideological colouration. Mrs Gandhi, who has to rely upon the support of non-Congress left-wing groups in the Lok Sabha, presents herself as a true socialist and her opponents as right-wing opportunists. This is not an entire falsification of the situation, as policy differences of the kind suggested do indeed separate the two groups – although how important they are still remains to be seen. In some ways these critical events resemble those of 1950, when Tandon, the Congress President, challenged Prime Minister Nehru. On that occasion too the Prime Minister won; but there was no split. Tandon's supporters remained in the party because by leaving it they would have committed political suicide. The great differences between the first episode and the second was that in the autumn of 1969 Congress, deeply riven by factions, had no leader of Nehru's prestige to impose a solution. Although the deadlock between the rival groups might have been broken by some act of compromise, a sufficiently prestigious arbitrator was nowhere to be found. Moreover the new fluidity of the political situation meant that neither group believed that its chances of winning the next series of elections would be prejudiced by splitting the party. For the so-called 'dominant party system' it was the end of the road – or seemed to be so until Mrs Gandhi led her New Congress to overwhelming victory in the 1971 elections.

Parties (2): *others*

As we have seen, one of the essential features of Congress's dominance was the fragmentation of the opposition. Over the

period of the four elections, literally hundreds of parties have
come into and gone out of existence; for example, since 1951–2
in West Bengal alone some fifty-six parties have put up
candidates. Throughout India, an average of four political
parties have competed for each parliamentary seat, and there
are some constituencies in which the electorate has been confronted with no fewer than nine candidates. The result has
been to enable Congress, as often as not, to snatch victories on
a minority vote.

This situation could only prevail so long as the non-Congress
parties were unable to combine in alliances. The question is why
they did not do so, on any significant scale, until 1967. Part of
the answer is that the presence of an aggregative party at the
centre of the political spectrum left the other parties to occupy
peripheral positions. Many of them, both right and left, found
that they had more in common with Congress itself than with
their potential allies. Each party, moreover, tended to stimulate
among its members a sense of almost caste-like exclusiveness,
which precluded the formation of stable alliances with other
parties. To this must be added a desire, to some extent characteristically Indian, to maintain unimpaired the doctrinal purity
of the party, and the fact that there are some parties – for
instance, the Communists – which do not regard the winning
of elections as the most important aspect of their activities. These
parties, in particular, provided a secure ideological home for
those alienated groups and individuals who are produced in
such large numbers in any society involved in the complicated
process of transition from the traditional to the modern. For
them, cooperating with other parties was almost equivalent to
breaking down the walls of the house. When all this is taken
into account, the fragmentation of the opposition to Congress
is by no means difficult to explain.

Multiplicity and diversity make any attempt to classify Indian
political parties a very hazardous undertaking. The Election
Commission makes a simple distinction between all-India parties
and regional ones; but this is not very useful, since there are so-
called all-India parties whose strength is almost exclusively concentrated in certain regions. The distinction between traditional
and modernist parties also requires careful handling, since in
India traditionalism and modernity are so confusingly inter-

meshed. Indeed, however modernist a party may be at the level of its national leadership, it always becomes less so as one moves down towards the grass roots. Neither is the conventional distinction between 'right' and 'left' by any means satisfactory; since these classifications, always ambiguous, often become ambiguous to the point of sheer incomprehensibility in the Indian context. Nevertheless, bearing in mind these difficulties and limitations, one may be justified in attempting a provisional classification of Indian political parties, other than Congress, into (1) parties of the left, (2) parties of the right, (3) traditional parties, (4) regional parties, and (5) minor parties, based on specific and parochial groups and issues.

On the left there are the Socialists and the Communists, at present both divided. By origin, the Socialists were defectors from Congress. In 1948, when it became no longer possible for socialists to organise themselves within Congress as a Congress Socialist Party, a number of members of this Party defected from Congress to form an independent Socialist Party. Within a few years, they were joined by another group of defectors, Gandhian in inspiration, calling themselves the Kisan Mazdoor Praja Party, to form the Praja Socialist Party. By 1955, however, disagreements within the new party about its relationships with Congress and the Communists resulted in a split, from which two organisations emerged: the Praja Socialist Party, under Asoka Mehta, and the Socialist Party, under Dr Lohia. Subsequent political manoeuvrings, which involved the return of Asoka Mehta to the Congress fold, led to an attempted unification of the Socialist forces, under Dr Lohia, as the Samyukta Socialist Party. However, Lohia's extreme militancy, together with his aggressive championing of Hindi as the national language, soon led to the re-emergence of the PSP as a separate organisation. The cause of socialism in India has suffered severely from these complicated and ever-changing disagreements about policy and ideology among the top leadership, which has always tended to have a prima donna quality. The socialist parties have built up their main strength in the north, but in those areas of South India where the balance of power between Congress and the Communist Party is a delicate one, they have played a political role greater than their numbers and electoral strength would otherwise warrant. If the two parties had been united in 1967, they could have formed the largest opposition in the Lok Sabha. One of their major difficulties has been to find a clear-cut political position somewhere between Congress and the Communists. In 1971 the Samyukta Socialists won only three seats in the Lok Sabha and the Praja Socialists only two. Both parties also did very badly in the three state elections.

Until the split of 1962, the Communist Party of India was the most tightly-disciplined of Indian parties – although its discipline was poor by the standards of Communist parties elsewhere. The largest of the opposition parties, its main strength lay in the non-Hindi areas. After a highly varied political past, which involved support for the war effort between 1941 and 1945 and a vigorously revolutionary and terroristic episode between 1948 and 1952, it committed itself to the 'parliamentary road to socialism' at its Amritsar Conference of 1958. This involved important organisational changes, of which the most important was the replacement of the work-place cell as the basic unit by the residence-based branch. These changes, both ideological and organisational, were never fully accepted by the party's leftists.

The subsequent split in the party was closely connected, although in a rather complicated way, with the outbreak of hostilities between India and China in 1962. It is also partly to be explained by the death of the CPI's most prominent leader, Ajoy Ghosh, and by the alleged scandals that were discovered in the political record of his successor, Dange. Dange's leading opponents, E. M. S. Namboodiripad and Jyoti Basu, leaders of the Party in the two States where the CPI was best entrenched, Kerala and West Bengal, were responsible for the split, which resulted in the creation of the new Communist Party (Marxist), which originally appeared to be Peking-oriented rather than Moscow-oriented. Taking advantage of the rank and file's suspicion of the CPI's comparative respectability, the CPI(M) established itself as the major Communist Party in both West Bengal and Kerala, where it became the dominant party in the United Front governments which emerged from the 1967 elections. Subsequently, it received set-backs in both states. Although still electorally the most powerful party in West Bengal, it is now strongly challenged by Mrs Gandhi's Congress. In Kerala, it was forced to yield office to a CPI-led government, enjoying New Congress support, and in the 1971 elections secured only two of Kerala's nineteen Lok Sabha seats. To-day, moreover, the CPI(M) is in danger of being outflanked by a third and even more revolutionary communist party, the Communist Party (Marxist-Leninist), which was formed in the summer of 1967. This new party is closely associated with the so-called Naxalites, violent direct-action revolutionaries who take their name from the place in North Bengal which was the original scene of their anti-landlord activities. With a membership of roughly twenty thousand, the CPI(ML) excludes electoral activities and pursues policies of mass action and terrorism which have the full approval of Peking. The leaders of this third Communist Party are far younger than those of its parent parties, whose top men were recruited from the middle class intelligentsia of the 1930s. They and their followers are most active in those areas where the CPI(M) is strongest. The CPI(ML) has found in West Bengal, with its deep urban poverty, terrorist traditions, and acute class struggle, a happy hunting ground; and it is also influential in Andhra Pradesh, where it has succeeded, to some extent, in reviving the Telengana peasant struggles of 1948 to 1952. The Andhra group, however, by no means sees eye to eye with the Bengal group, and there is at least a possibility that it may split away from the CPI(ML) to form yet a fourth Communist Party. As a result of the growing complexities of the political situation, together with the disappearance of a single centre of leadership for the international Communist movement, it would seem that the Indian Communists have become as subject as the Indian Socialists to amoeba-like splits. Ideological controversies combine with personal rivalries to make Communist unity a thing of the past.

Most of the Communist successes, electorally and otherwise, have been achieved in areas with high literacy rates and high voting turnouts. The educated unemployed would appear to provide them with a high proportion of their most consistent supporters. Like other Indian parties, however, they have marked caste affiliations in certain areas. Oddly enough, their caste supporters are by no means invariably at the bottom of the social scale; in Andhra, for instance, they formerly had the support of the Kammas, a caste which included many substantial landowners.

The situation among the parties of the right is almost equally complicated. For instance, although the non-traditional right would appear to be represented by the Swatantra Party, formed in 1959, there is more than a little doubt about the genuineness of this party's modernism. For one of its most prominent founders, Minoo Masani, the Swatantra is essentially a bourgeois party, devoted to 'the protection of the individual against the increasing trespasses of the state'; but it also includes among its leaders both Hindu traditionalists and old Gandhians, such as Rajagopalachari, formerly Governor General of India and Chief Minister of Madras. Furthermore it has attracted the support of a number of ex-princes, including the colourful Maharani of Jaipur. Despite the ability of its leadership, its penchant for adopting unpopular causes, such as a dialogue with Pakistan and the retention of English as a national language, tends to limit its appeal. In Andhra Pradesh it has some support among the more prosperous peasantry, but its main strength lies in the North, in Orissa, Rajasthan, Bihar and Gujerat, where it tends to be dominated by ex-princes and landowners.

Probably of greater importance is the traditionalist 'right', consisting of the Hindu communal parties. Of these, the real 'Messiah of backwardness' is the Ram Rajya Parishad. It not only defends caste institutions but goes to the extent of suggesting that Untouchables, by virtue of their association with 'impure' or 'polluting' occupations, should be given the management of the sanitary departments and of the leather and hide trades. Politically it is far less influential than the oldest of the Hindu parties, the Hindu Mahasabha, which was founded in 1907 and before Independence concentrated its attention on fighting the demands of the Muslim League. Since 1947 opposition to westernisation has been the keynote of its policies and activities.

Also on the traditionalist 'right' is the Rashtriya Swayamsevak Sangh (RSS). This, however, is not a normal political party, but an authoritarian-type youth organisation much given to para-military activity. The ban placed upon it after the assassination of Gandhi convinced many of its adherents that they needed parliamentary representatives to protect their interests, particularly as their friend and protector, Shyama Prasa Mookerjee, had resigned from Nehru's cabinet. For this purpose they created the Bharatiya Jan Sangh, the Indian People's Party, which subsequently became the most powerful of the traditional parties. Oddly enough, the Sangh objects to being tarred with the brush of communalism and points proudly to the fact that it has non-Hindus among its members and even among its parliamentary candidates. Officially its policy is based on nationalism and culture, not on religion – 'one country, one culture, one nation, and the Dharma Raj (Rule of Law)'; but in fact the party continues to be linked with the RSS. At first it devoted much of its attention to opposing government measures regarded as hostile to the interests of Hinduism, but more recently it has diversified its areas of interest. While remaining socially conservative, it has put forward economic policies radical enough to enable it to take part in merger negotiations with the PSP. As a result, this once well-disciplined party suffers from internal divisions; for the party's old-timers are naturally suspicious of its new and more radical members, while the latter are divided between socialists and anti-socialists. For the same reasons its relationship with the RSS is considerably less happy than in former days.

The Hindu communal parties were formerly strong in areas such as Punjab and West Bengal, with large Muslim minorities. To-day their greatest strength lies in those regions of northern India where a traditionally-minded but dissatisfied middle class, both rural and urban, plays a prominent political role. The Jan Sangh is influential throughout the Hindi heartland, and in 1967 it became the main opposition party in Haryana, Madhya Pradesh and Uttar Pradesh, and won control of the two local government bodies in Delhi, the Municipal Corporation and the Metropolitan Council. Subsequently, the Sangh formed a coalition with the Sikh Party, the Akali Dal, to form a coalition government in Punjab. As we have noted, it suffered a set-back in the 1971 elections, the most serious feature of which was the defeat of all seven of its parliamentary candidates in New Delhi, which it had come to regard as its own electoral preserve.

The Muslim League must be numbered among the traditionalist and communal parties, although its 'rightism' is as doubtful as that of the Jan Sangh. Left as a rump by the partition of India, it has its main strength among the Malabar Muslim community which makes up one fifth of the population of the State of Kerala. There it is a minor but occasionally significant participant in state politics. Under predominantly conservative leadership, it proclaims that although it is socialist it does not believe 'in tampering with private property'. Recently is has showed signs of revival among the Muslims of Northern India, particularly in those areas where they have suffered in communal disturbances.

The growth of regional loyalties has not only presented problems for the national parties; inevitably, it has created a sizeable crop of regionally-based parties. In 1957 these regional parties actually occupied more seats in the state assemblies than all other parties, apart from Congress. Some, like the Samyukta Maharashtra Samiti, were like miniature independence movements, bringing together many political parties in an alliance to demand the creation of a linguistic state; but once this purpose was achieved they broke up into their original component parts. One of the most important of contemporary regional parties, the Akali Dal, is peculiarly resistant to neat categorisation. Located in the Punjab, the party is the political arm of a religious group, the Sikhs, who, accepting no division between the religious and the secular, have made their temples, the Gurdwaras, into party headquarters. The mass appeal of the Sikh leader, Master Tara Singh, who for thirty years 'bestrode the Sikh political world like a colossus', welded the Akali Dal into a strong organisation, well financed by Sikh businessmen as well as from temple funds. Originally somewhat ambiguous in purpose, the party found its 'soul' when it put forward the demand for a separate linguistic state, originally known as Punjabi Subha. Through the division of the old Punjab into Punjab and Haryana in 1965 this demand was granted, and the Akali Dal is now the largest single party in the new Punjab State. Not unexpectedly, however, it has fallen prey to factionalism, partly as a result of religious divisions among its Sikh supporters. There is also the usual struggle between left and right in the party, as the dominant business interests which originally gave its economic policies a strongly conservative flavour are now under attack.

The other state now under the control of a regional party is Madras (now renamed Tamil Nadu) where the Dravida Munnetra Kazhagam (DMK) has had complete charge of the government since 1967. Heir to the anti-Brahmin and anti-northern movements which have played so prominent a part in Madrassi politics, the DMK is the successor of the now-defunct Justice Party, from which it is distinguished by the greater breadth of its popular appeal. Led, like most other Indian political parties, by members of the intelligentsia, it has been particularly successful in its use of the mass-media. Originally secessionist, proclaiming the need for independent Dravidistan, it adopted socialist policies largely by way of reaction to alleged northern 'imperialism'. Although secessionism has now been dropped from its programme, it still fosters and draws strength from anti-northern sentiments among the Tamils. As a governing party, the DMK has not been an unqualified success, and it suffered a severe blow in 1969 through the death of its leader, Annadurai. Its dominant position in regional political life, however, has given Madras a firm and coherent administration which might well be the envy of those states suffering from coalitions.

Regionalism in India is an extremely complicated phenomenon; for within every region, however defined, there are sub-regions. These have given birth to political parties more parochial in their affiliations than the state-wide parties we have hitherto been discussing. These parties sometimes play a crucial role. In Orissa, for instance, Congress has twice been dependent upon the support of such parties: first on the Jharkhand Party, representing the tribal peoples, and then on the Ganatantra Parishad, representing the highland areas and dominated by their former princely rulers. Such minor parties rarely have long lives. The Ganatantra Parishad, for instance, has merged with the Swatantra. On the other hand, the Jharkhand Party, which once merged with Congress, has recently resumed independent existence.

It might be expected in Indian conditions that caste would form the ideal base for a political party, but in fact very few parties with exclusive caste affiliations have appeared. The sheer complexity of caste divisions and caste antagonisms has virtually compelled caste leaders to operate through established political parties rather than attempt to create vehicles on their own. Although formerly the CPI in Andhra Pradesh was virtually the political machine of the Kamma caste and the PSP in Kerala that of the Nair Service Society, the only major party that now remains clearly related to the traditional divisions of Hindu society is the Republican Party, the successor of the Scheduled Castes Federation, created to represent the interests of the Untouchables, or Harijans.

Until recently, the ruling party's superiority both in organisation and in aggregative capacity has limited the opportunities of the opposition parties to become genuinely mass-based. A major source of their recruitment has been groups feeling themselves seriously threatened by the social changes which Congress wished (or said it wished) to promote. In the rural areas, for instance, there has been some recruitment to the right-wing and traditionalist parties among the ex-princely families and the landowning classes. Being free from governmental responsibilities, opposition parties have often been better placed than Congress to exploit local grievances, frequently by adjusting their policies to the conditions prevalent in the region or locality. Resultant inconsistencies and contradictions have never bothered them very much. Thus, in 1969, when the political future of the town of Chandigarh was in dispute, the Jan Sangh of the Punjab urged that it should become the Punjabi capital, whilst the Jan Sangh in neighbouring Haryana demanded that it should become the Haryanan capital; for full measure, in Chandigarh itself the same party favoured giving the city the Union Territory status.

The organisational deficiencies of the opposition parties, combined with their lack of access to patronage, has made them very dependent upon the quality of their leadership. It has also made them exceptionally subject to the prevalent disease of factionalism and to the uncertainties associated with defection. The record of the Raja of Ramgarh and his personal supporters (numbering anything between seventeen and fifty) illustrates the tendency of opposition politicians to wander. Beginning his political life in the Janata Party, he first moved to the Swatantra, and then on to Congress. His last known centre of political loyalty was the Jan Kranti Dal. Just as opposition parties have provided a haven for disgruntled Congress party members, so Congress has provided one for members of the opposition parties, some of whom only joined the opposition to prove their worth to Congress. Sometimes Congress, at state level, has swallowed a whole opposition party, as with the PSP of Andhra Pradesh, which disbanded itself when Congress offered its leader the position of Chief Minister in a Congress government. For these reasons the opposition parties had to wait for their success until they became capable of creating united fronts. Once a united front was installed in office, the 'bandwagon' effect came into operation for their benefit, particularly as the new government could wield the patronage previously dispensed by Congress.

The Indian party system is now in the throes of massive change. Between 1967 and 1971, however, India appeared to be developing her own chaotic form of multi-party politics. A majority of states became governed by non-Congress ministries, while at the Centre the Congress government became dependent on opposition support. There were some who argued that this development was, in the long term, a healthy one, in so far as Congress's former dominance, together with its heterogeneity, had tended to inhibit the growth of a 'national' alignment of political forces. Some, indeed, foresaw that out of the multi-party chaos there might eventually emerge something that amounted to a two-party system, based on a confrontation between right-wing and left-wing coalitions. Such speculations have not been put to rest by Mrs Gandhi's overwhelming electoral victory in 1971, but it would nevertheless appear that, for the time being, the dominant party variety of politics has been restored, and indeed considerably reinforced, at least at the Centre. How far this is a flash in the pan, attributable to Mrs Gandhi's remarkable and unexpected capacity to appeal to the Indian masses over the heads of the machine politicians, cannot at present be reliably judged. Nor do the three state elections of 1971, in West Bengal, Tamil Nadu and Orissa, offer reliable evidence of the extent to which the sudden reversal of the 1967–71 trend has become operative at the state level. What seems certain, however, is that for the moment the 'new' Congress has established itself as the legitimate successor of the former undivided Congress, in so far as the Nijalingappa group is now reduced to an impotent rump. In view of the almost universal opinion among commentators on the Indian political scene that 'dominance' had gone for good, this is a quite extraordinary achievement.

(3) *Pressure Groups*

From parties we turn to pressure groups, the development of which is generally regarded as a vital element in the process of political modernisation, in so far as it represents a response to increasing functional differentiation and to the breakdown of traditional-type authority. In India's case, the ever-widening activities of government have stimulated the creation and consolidation of groups. The Congress Party was itself originally such a group, making a whole number of specific demands of the British raj, such as an increase in the number of Indians recruited to the administrative services. When it evolved into a national independence movement, it sought not only to accommodate as many political philosophies as possible but as many organised groups as could be persuaded to give it their support; moreover, as is the way with such movements, it fathered its own secondary organisations. Since Independence, the opposition parties have also formed such organisations, and the parties themselves, during the period when opportunities for the exercise of governmental responsibility were usually denied to them, were driven into the politics of pressure.

Today Indian pressure groups may be divided into two types: those that are based on traditional social structures associated with religion, caste, tribe or language, and those which spring from the modern centres of society, such as industry and the universities.

Hinduism, despite its diversity and lack of internal organisation, has produced one of the most powerful – and some would say sinister – pressure groups of all, the Rashtriya Swayamsevak Sangh (RSS), which boasts a membership of one million. On a very different level, although still at least partly traditionalist in origin, are the Gandhian Social Service Groups and the groups organised by the two great *gurus*, Vinoba Bhave and J. P. Narayan. Gandhi himself provided the elements of a pressure group theory when he said : 'Banish the idea of the capture of power and you will be able to guide power and keep it on the right path'; and it is obvious that the Community Development scheme and Panchayati Raj were inspired by notions of decentralisation most prevalent among the Gandhian groups.

Caste, however, has provided a far more fertile field for pressure group activities. Traditionally, the caste associations were primarily concerned with the behaviour of their own members and with the preservation of distinctive caste practices. They were predominantly local, non-political, and often hardly visible. But caste is a highly adaptive structure, and modern multi-functional and often state-wide caste associations have emerged in response to social, political and economic change. These are sometimes regarded as representing a half-way stage between traditionalism and modernity. Their membership is purely voluntary and their leadership sometimes elective. Many of today's powerful caste associations originated in the desire for upward social mobility on the part of economically-prospering castes with a low ritual status. Their activities were greatly stimulated, during the days of the British raj, by the registration of caste status in census documents. Today, although still very much concerned with ritual status, they tend to concentrate on achieving more material benefits for their members, e.g. places in the civil service and in educational institutions. They also provide a variety of service and welfare functions and some have even transformed themselves into joint stock companies, owning plantations, mills, banks, schools, hospitals, hotels, and newspapers. In *The Nadars of Tamilnad,* Robert L. Hargraves provides a picture of the Nadar Caste Association. In 1965 it had a membership of over twenty thousand and an annual conference attended by five thousand, which elected an Executive Committee meeting twenty times a year. The power of the caste association, however, is being frequently undermined by economic differentiation among its members, which inhibits it from adopting a consistent political line. The Nadar Caste Association, for instance, which advised its members to vote Congress in the early 1950s, made no attempt to influence their votes in subsequent general elections.

Tribal peoples, who number sixty million, have also become

susceptible to pressure group organisation; but they are far more likely to form separate political parties or, as in the case of the tribal peoples of Assam and Nagaland, secessionist groups. Linguistic groups, sometimes very well organised, have also played a very prominent part in Indian political life; but such groups are comparatively ephemeral, tending to subside into inactivity once their specific demands have been satisfied, whether through the creation of a linguistic state or otherwise.

For a land so overwhelmingly rural, there is pitifully little specific representation of peasant interests. As is well known, peasants are not great 'joiners'; nor do they command the educated leadership required for the articulation of their interests. Such peasant organisations as exist are almost invariably led by 'outsiders', who usually have purposes going considerably beyond the improvement of the peasants' conditions. The first major peasant association was created in 1936 by the Congress Party, as a means of mobilising the rural masses for the nationalist cause. Congress dared not use it for the out-and-out championing of peasant interests, since this would have brought the party into conflict with the landlords, which it also wished to include in the national front. The All-India Peasant Association (Kisan Sabha) consequently fell into the hands of the Communist Party, and although Congress and other parties have subsequently attempted to found new peasant associations, all attempts to unite the peasants organisationally have had to encounter the formidable obstacles of village factions, caste divisions, and economic inequalities. However, rural unrest, particularly among landless labourers and very poor cultivators, offers the possibility of creating militant group organisations, ephemeral as these usually are. Such unrest is strongest in the non-Hindi areas of India. In the late 1940s, the Communist Party organised an abortive peasant rising in Telengana. More recently, Communist dissidents have mounted a Maoist-type rising in Naxalbari in West Bengal, and at the time of writing 'Naxalite' activities are on the increase in Andhra Pradesh and Kerala. The Telengana and Naxalite episodes are, of course, examples of revolutionary rather than of pressure group activities; the rural pressure group itself is better represented by the Hill Cultivators' Union, organised by a Roman Catholic priest in Kerala.

Landowners as such have formed few formal organisations, but this does not mean that the farm lobby is any the less powerful. Its strength has been frequently experienced by state governments proposing to increase land taxation or introduce an agricultural income tax. Congress, in particular, is very well aware of its dependence on the votes and the influence of the more prosperous landowning peasants.

As might be expected, business interests show a much stronger tendency to form modern-type pressure groups. Business organisations are of many types: industrial associations, communal associations, regional organisations and all-India organisations. In Calcutta, community ties structure business representation, Muslims belonging to the Oriental Chamber of Commerce, native Hindu Bengalis to the Bengal National Chamber of Commerce, and Marwaris (a trading caste originating in Rajasthan) to the Bharat Chamber of Commerce. There is also an Indian Chamber of Commerce, which has a mixed but largely Marwari membership. The largest business organisation is the Federation of Indian Chambers of Commerce and Industry, which represents forty thousand firms and has a very effective central office in New Delhi. The kinds of pressures exerted by the business interests are extremely varied. The associations take part in joint consultative bodies and occasionally lobby MPs; but a greater effort is devoted to the bringing to bear of influence on the Planning Commission, the economic ministries and the various licensing bodies. From them the business men seek the maximum government aid and protection and the minimum government interference. In some respects they are in a strong position, since they can both withhold information essential to the public authorities and refuse to co-operate in the implementation of the plan. They also have considerable influence in the councils of the Congress Party, which has been heavily dependent on business contributions to its funds; but among some of the business communities, particularly in Bombay, disillusionment with the Congress record has lead to a switching of support to the Swatantra Party.

Important as are the business associations and the business connection with the Congress Party, it would be wrong to present these as the sole methods by which business brings its influence to bear. A big business such as the Birla or Tata group of companies is a highly effective pressure group in its own right. Moreover, individual businesses make extensive use of blood and caste relationships, as well as of bribery, to pressurise administrators who have favours to offer. Indeed, it has been suggested, by Myron Weiner among others, that only the 'baksheesh system' prevents the 'licence and permit raj' from grinding to a halt.

Industrial workers are a less well organised group, as might be expected, since many of them are still peasants in their mentality and behaviour and consequently heavily dependent upon outside leadership. The exploitation of factory workers at the beginning of the present century led progressive-minded middle-class professionals to take up their cause, and the first trade unions were formed before World War I. Under Congress influence, the all-India TUC was established in 1920, but by 1929 it had fallen under Communist control. In 1948, Congress formed a new organisation, the Indian National TUC, but its reluctance to take strike action – a consequence of the influence of business men in the councils of the Congress Party – tended to limit its attractiveness. When the Socialist Party defected from Congress in 1948, it established another Trade Union Centre. The non-Communist Marxist parties have also organised a federation. In all cases however the unions themselves are only patchily integrated in the federation to which they belong, the leadership of which is all too clearly a political arm of one party or another. The most effective unions are those based on local firms. Although poorly-financed and under outside leadership, they can be extremely vocal in their demands and militant in their methods. Lastly, but in these days certainly not least, there are the student organisations, of which the main examples are the Student Congress and the Communist-dominated Student Federation. They take up both university and wider issues, but have little control over the behaviour of their members and supporters, who have succeeded in utterly disorganising a considerable number of Indian universities.

Pressure groups, as distinct from political parties, have been very little studied in India. What is clear, however, is that the Indian political system has not yet developed to a point where groups are prepared to recognise any rules of the game.

Direct action, often involving a great deal of violence, is now assuming alarming proportions. To some extent this is a legacy from the nationalist movement, but the volatile behaviour of many sections of the Indian public is clearly the product of a situation in which there are too few goods to distribute among too many people. Moreover violence easily becomes a habit, particularly when the authorities seem unprepared to respond to any other kind of representation. Whereas in Britain an unpunctual train provokes the writing of a letter to the newspapers, in India it provokes a riot! From newspaper surveys, David Bayley estimates that between seventy to eighty serious riots take place each year. Riot leaders are predominantly members of the middle classes, who must be aware of the likely repercussions of their actions, particularly if they employ *goondas* (ruffians) – able-bodied, unemployed men who are prepared to hire out their services to any demagogue. But as long as violence brings returns and peaceful protest is ignored, direct action of this kind will continue to be the form of pressure to which Indians have frequent recourse.

5 Parliamentary Government

Despite the political conflicts described in the last chapter, there is a widespread belief in India that the ideal, and indeed the only sound, method of resolving differences is by discussion leading to consensus. This dislike of conflict is related to a suspicion of power. Traditionally, only those whose caste-status entitled them to exercise power but who did not deliberately seek it, could be entrusted with so dangerous a commodity. Familiar forms of thinking, therefore, have done little to legitimise parliamentary democracy, with its adversary and competitive norms, or to confer high status on parliamentary practitioners, who tend to be regarded as inherently self-seeking and even parasitic on their fellow citizens.

The British raj, however, significantly modified these traditional beliefs, at least among members of the upper echelons of Indian society. As we have seen, an elite absorbed the imported western attitudes which accompanied the imported western institutions. Among these institutions, one of the most novel to the Indian mind was the legislature, which made its first embryonic appearance in 1833, when the legislative were distinguished from the executive functions of Governor-General's Council. After the passing of the Indian Councils Act of 1861, so-called legislative councils, both at the Centre and in the provinces, gradually expanded their functions, in the performance of which carefully selected 'natives' were permitted to participate. Although the viceroys and governor generals still retained their power of veto, the influence of these bodies was permitted to increase, and by the Morley-Minto Reforms of 1909 the provincial legislative councils, as distinct from the Central Council, were endowed with unofficial, although still largely nominated, majorities, and the Legislative Council at the Centre, now strictly forbidden to transact any other business than legislation, was enlarged.

Until very late in the day, however, the British Government maintained that a full parliamentary regime was unsuited to India. Lord Morley, speaking in the House of Lords on the Morley-Minto scheme of 1909, proclaimed that 'if it could be said that this chapter of reforms led directly or necessarily to the establishment of a parliamentary system in India, I for one would have nothing to do with it'.

Nevertheless, by the end of the First World War, the British Government, in introducing the Montagu-Chelmsford reforms, was prepared to concede that 'the gradual development of self-governing institutions with a view to the progressive realisation of responsible government in India' was the order of the day. By these reforms, all the councils were enlarged and made more representative, and provincial legislatures were given their own 'nation building' powers and allocated their own sources of revenue. True, this transfer of powers was hedged about with safeguards, which caused Congress to condemn it as a fraud; nevertheless, one of its positive consequences was that several thousand Indians between 1919 and 1935 gained both legislative and executive experience in the provinces and the Centre.

Then came the Government of India Act of 1935, which abolished dyarchy in the provinces and transferred all provincial subjects, with a few crucial exceptions, to ministries responsible to enlarged legislatures elected on a greatly extended franchise. Although no responsible government existed at the Centre, and although for Congress even the provincial reforms seemed part of 'a new charter of bondage', British politicians could argue with some cogency that 'the centre of political gravity' was passing from British to Indian hands. Professor Morris-Jones rightly says that 'the "slave" Constitution gave legislative experience to a considerable number of politicians in the provinces; it installed what were in effect fully responsible popular governments; it began to accustom all concerned to a transfer of power', and 'gave experience precisely where it was needed.' Britain, therefore, may not unreasonably be given the credit for introducing Indians to the conception of representative parliamentary government.

Most of the delegates who met in the Constituent Assembly, therefore, had imbibed 'the spirit of the British Constitution'.

But was a parliamentary form of government suited to the Indian environment? Was it reconcilable with the lack of education, with the gap between the elite and the masses, and with the division of the country into a multitude of religious, communal and linguistic groups? The Congress majority in the Assembly was certain that, despite these difficulties, no other system of government was worth considering. What were the alternatives? Gandhi had called Parliament a 'prostitute' and Gandhians were advocating forms of government said to be more consonant with 'native' traditions. Their plans for a decentralised system based on 'village republics', however, were too vague to be seriously considered. Other members of the Assembly, by contrast, believed that only a powerful national executive, independent of the legislature, could muster sufficient strength to secure stability and promote development. Most delegates, however, shared the British prejudice against an American-type presidential system, with its rigid separation of powers, and most looked to Britain as a model. The strongest argument in favour of the British system was that India, to some degree, had already acquired familiarity with it. As K. M. Munshi said, 'After all this experience, why should we go back upon the tradition . . . and try a novel experiment?'

The Westminster model, therefore, found general favour. There was to be a Council of Ministers at the Centre, responsible to a bicameral legislature, consisting of an indirectly elected Council of States (Rajya Sabha), and a directly-elected Lower House (Lok Sabha). Both Houses were empowered to define their own 'powers, privileges and immunities'. Pending such definition, they were to adopt 'those of the House of Commons of the Parliament of the United Kingdom'. 'Ordinary' bills might be introduced into either House, and had to be passed by both before receiving presidential assent. As in the British Parliament, however, money bills might be introduced only in the Lower House, and the Upper House, although competent to consider them, was not competent to refuse them its assent. Provisions for state legislatures were similar, except that the bicameral principle was made optional.

The Lok Sabha is constitutionally required to convene twice a year. Its session is opened with a presidential address, equivalent to the Speech from the Throne in the British Parliament. Its rules are also modelled fairly closely on those of the House of Commons. The daily session opens with questions to ministers – a procedure so analogous to the British that Sir Anthony Eden was moved to declare that he felt more at home in the Lok Sabha than he had in the Australian Parliament. As in Britain, question time provides the back-bencher with his opportunity to turn the searchlight on government operations, and the minister with that of making or marring his reputation. All questions must be submitted to the parliamentary secretariat at least ten days in advance, and the Speaker determines their admissibility on the basis of the Rules of Procedure. The opportunities afforded by question time are used to the full. Between twenty and twenty-five questions are answered each day, and in the first elected Parliament there was a total of 87,972 submitted to the Table.

Most of Parliament's time is occupied with government business, as decided by the Cabinet and its Parliamentary Affairs Committee under the chairmanship of the Chief Whip; but to some extent the allocation of the Lok Sabha's time is controlled by a Business Advisory Committee under the chairmanship of the Speaker.

Legislation is dealt with in three stages, viz. (1) Introduction (2) Consideration and (3) Passing, which roughly correspond with (1) the First Reading in the House of Commons, (2) the Second Reading, Committee and Report Stages, and (3) the Third Reading. At the second stage, a motion that the bill be referred to a Select Committee may be made. One of the differences between the Lok Sabha and the House of Commons is the absence in the former of Standing Committees and Committees of the Whole House. Instead, the Indian Parliament uses *ad hoc* Select Committees, although few bills are actually referred to them. The size of these Select Committees varies from twenty to twenty-five; their membership is determined by the Government Chief Whip and the Speaker, having regard to the balance between the parties in the House, and no minister in charge of a bill may participate in them. Petitions are circulated with the bills to which they refer, and a financial memorandum must accompany any bill authorising expenditure. In practice, as a result of the fragmentation of the opposition, each bill attracts a vast number of

97

amendments, most of which are accepted by the Speaker. After the completion of its Third Stage, a bill is passed to the other House, which operates an identical procedure. In case of unresolved disagreement between the two Houses, the President, in consultation with the Speaker, must call a joint session.

Motions and resolutions are discussed mainly on government initiative; but motions of no-confidence may be introduced when fifty members have indicated their support. As in Great Britain, the adjournment may be used to discuss 'definite matters of urgent public importance'; but the Speaker shows a marked reluctance to accept such motions and treats the rules governing them very restrictively. More important, and without parallel in the British Parliament, are 'discussions on matters of urgent importance for a short duration', which require no notice but only the Speaker's permission. Each Friday, two and a half hours are reserved for 'non-official' business – private members' resolutions and bills; and additional time for private members may be allotted on any other day after consultations between the Speaker and the Leader of the House. The short-notice question, for which ministerial consent is required, and the half-hour discussion periods on Wednesdays and Fridays provide private members with further opportunities to exercise their initiative.

The basic financial functions of the Central Parliament were considered sufficiently important to be incorporated in the Constitution. Thus, no tax may be levied nor expenditure made from the consolidated fund without parliamentary authority. Taxation and expenditure proposals are the prerogative of the Executive, the legislature under no circumstances being able to take the initiative in these matters. Money bills are sent to the Rajya Sabha only to enable it to make recommendations; if not returned by the Rajya Sabha within fourteen days the bill is deemed to have passed into law. The Indian budget, introduced in mid-February, combines estimates of expenditure with proposals for taxation. Following its introduction, a few days are allowed for 'sober judgment' before the general discussion takes place. Following this, the Demands for Grants are presented. Each grant is taken separately and becomes subject to 'cut' motions (usually specifying a formal reduction of Rs 100), which enable the Lok Sabha, like the British House of Commons, to debate the policies behind the estimates. MPs belonging to the ruling party are discouraged from proposing 'cut' motions, but opposition members take full advantage of these opportunities, particularly to complain when they consider that the needs of their states or constituencies have been neglected. A vote-on-account procedure, of a kind also familiar to British MPs, permits the budget discussion to continue after the beginning of the new financial year; sometimes it stretches into the months of June and July. After all demands for grants have been debated, an Appropriation Bill is introduced and follows the normal legislative procedure. A corresponding Finance Bill, which sanctions the raising of taxes, is considered passed from the moment of its introduction, for reasons equally familiar to British parliamentarians. If amendments to it are subsequently passed, the proceeds of the taxes already collected under the original provisions are returned to their contributors.

Committees of the Lok Sabha exist for two purposes: to facilitate the conduct of the house's business and to scrutinise the activities of the government. Committees of the former type include a Rules Committee, a Business Advisory Committee, a Committee on Private Members' Bills and Resolutions, a Privileges Committee, a Committee on Petitions, a General Purposes Committee, a House Committee and a Library Committee. These perform essential 'housekeeping' jobs, but are of less interest to the student of government than the 'scrutiny' committees.

The most prestigious of these is the Public Accounts Committee, which is charged with the examination of 'all accounts showing the appropriation of sums granted by the House for the expenditure of the Government of India; the Annual Financial Accounts and any other accounts laid before the House as the Committee may think fit'. It is also empowered to examine the accounts of state corporations and other autonomous or semi-autonomous bodies whose audit is conducted by the Comptroller and Auditor General. The fifteen members of the Public Accounts Committee, all back-benchers, are elected annually by the Lok Sabha on a basis of proportional representation; another seven are nominated by the Rajya Sabha; the Chairman is selected by the Speaker. Very conscious of its role as guardian of the public purse, it has not been timorous in its investigations, although it often finds difficulty in separating technical from political considerations. Its influence is largely a product of the prestige attached to its published reports; but, conventionally if not legally, the Minister of Finance is obliged to implement its recommendations as far as possible and to report to the committee on any action he may have taken. Parliament rarely discusses the committee's reports except when important recommendations have gone unheeded by the executive, a situation which will be revealed in one of the Special Reports which the committee periodically submits. In appraising the committee's work, Professor Morris-Jones says that 'its mere existence . . . serves to remind officials that their actions are subject to scrutiny on behalf of Parliament'.

The Public Accounts Committee's *alter ego*, the Estimates Committee, was formerly, like its British counterpart, regarded with suspicion by the executive, as a body likely to be far too inquisitive for comfort. It examines such of the annual estimates as it thinks fit and suggests economies supposedly consistent with the policies embodied in them. Although it has no power to discuss policy matters as such, with the Speaker's approval it has placed a very liberal interpretation on its terms of reference, in this respect behaving very similarly to the British Estimates Committee. The Finance Minister is obliged to consider its suggestions on the form of the annual budget, and its reports are available to Parliament at the time of voting demands for grants. Its members are elected by the Lok Sabha, and their normal method of working is to select a number of departments and certain specific topics for examination. Together, the Public Accounts Committee and the Estimates Committee have tended to act, particularly during the period of Congress dominance, as a substitute for an opposition.

Although both committees were empowered to investigate public corporations and other commercial-type agencies, their enquiries in this field tended to be spasmodic and ineffective. To remedy this, a Committee on Public Undertakings has been constituted. Consisting of ten members of the Lok Sabha and five members of the Rajya Sabha, it examines the reports and accounts of selected public undertakings, together with the reports on them from the Comptroller and Auditor General, and enquires whether their affairs are being managed in accordance with sound business principles. Although the investigations of this committee are superficial and its reports scrappy in comparison with those of the British Select Committee on Nationalised Industries, it has done something to satisfy the demand that what an American critic has called the 'headless fourth branch of government' should not escape parliamentary scrutiny.

Among the more important of the other committees of the Lok Sabha is the Committee on Subordinate Legislation, which enquires whether the powers delegated by Parliament to the government have been properly used. This function is very similar to that performed by the British Select Committee on Delegated Legislation. Quite without any British parallel, however, is the Committee on Government Assurances, which scrutinises undertakings given by the government and reports back to the House on their implementation.

If this description of the Lok Sabha's proceedings looks familiar to students of British Government, the reasons are obvious. But although the husk is very similar, its content is often very different, since the Indian Parliament operates in a political environment which bears very few resemblances to the British, since its members have typically Indian presuppositions and backgrounds, and since the unique features of the Indian party situation are incompatible with that stately two-party confrontation which gives the House of Commons its peculiar and exasperating charm. Nevertheless, the attachment of Indian MPs to British-type parliamentary procedures remains very strong. Indeed, sometimes their imitativeness tends to be carried to quite unnecessary lengths.

The Upper House has never enjoyed the prestige of the Lower. The proposal to create a second chamber was very little discussed in the Constituent Assembly, which appeared to agree with the member who said 'after all no elaborate justification was needed'. What is its purpose? Although supposed to be a House of States, it is elected in a way that is hardly calculated to make it a vigorous champion of states' rights; since its socio-political composition differs very little from that of the Lok Sabha. In practice it tends to become a house for politicans whom the parties wish to 'kick upstairs'. As a 'second thoughts' chamber it may have some utility; but as its party composition is so similar to that of the Lower House, its thoughts rarely show any profound originality. For these reasons and for others it has encountered strong criticism. K. V. Rao denounces its power to clog legislation and to embarrass the Executive. He also criticises its co-equal right to approve the proclamation of an emergency, and its sole right to sanction the transfer of subjects from the states' list to the concurrent one. 'It is a Frankenstein', he says, 'and it should not have been let loose on the country; and the worst part of it is that its powers cannot be reduced without its own consent, given a two-thirds majority'. (Mrs Gandhi, who at the time of writing has just suffered defeat in the Rajya Sabha on a very important bill to abolish the princes' purses and privileges, would doubtless agree.) In a later passage, however, Rao tends to present it as a rather pathetic and ineffectual creature. 'This House', he writes, 'has remained a docile, neglected House, neglected by the public, neglected by its ministers, and neglected by its own members.' It is true that on several occasions not even one minister has attended its meetings, and that its sessions have often been curtailed and its meetings adjourned for want of work or a quorum. At best it has provided a few additional jobs in a country where the demand for such jobs greatly exceeds their supply. In view of its comparative lack of utility, one cannot be surprised that only half the states have chosen to adopt bicameral legislature, nor that one, the old state of Bombay, which possessed a second chamber, abolished it – with hardly a dog barking in protest.

During the period since Independence, the characteristics of Members of Parliament have changed in some ways and remained stable in others. Caste-wise, Brahmins still dominate the Lok Sabha, while Sudras, who form over 50 per cent of the total population, managed to occupy only 10 per cent of the seats. But educational backgrounds have changed considerably; the proportion of foreign-educated members has declined from 12 per cent in the Provisional Parliament to 9 per cent in the Third Parliament, and that of non-matriculants has increased from 4 to 9 per cent; but there are now very few illiterates. Graduates still occupy 60 per cent of the seats. An occupational classification shows a dramatic increase in agriculturalists (from

6 to 22 per cent), and a more modest increase in business men (from 8 to 12 per cent). The statistics for 'agriculturalists', however, are apt to be misleading, for although only 22 per cent of members state 'agriculture' as their occupation, it is known that half the MPs receive at least half their incomes from agriculture and that 70 per cent of them have some 'interest' in it. Representation of the professions has suffered a corresponding decrease. Lawyers are down from $33\frac{1}{3}$ to 20 per cent and teachers and journalists are also slightly fewer in number. Not unexpectedly, the House is ageing, and this means that fewer members are inexperienced, particularly as the percentage of members graduating to Parliament from state legislatures has increased from 26 to 34 per cent. All in all, the House is not very 'representative' of the Indian population, but the general trend, at least, is in the 'right' direction.

What of the attitudes of members towards their parliamentary duties? Observers frequently point to the alleged existence of a small group of active MPs (fifty or so), and classify the remainder as lightweights. The only formal study in this area of enquiry is that by Henry C. Hart. Using for interviewing purposes a random sample of 187 MPs, he concluded that 77 were 'influential' and that 88 had close contact with their constituents. About one in four of the sample, evenly spread amongst Congress and the opposition parties, were both 'influential' and constituency-oriented.

So long as Congress (or Mrs Gandhi's version of it) remains the ruling party, MPs who are members of it can exert an influence which does not depend on their activities on the floor of the House or in committee. They may raise their voices in the meeting of the Congress Legislative Party (CLP), where their complaints and suggestions may be brought to the attention of the leadership. These meetings take place at least once a month, and extraordinary meetings may be called at any time on the demand of fifty members. The size of the CLP, however, has made these meetings unsuitable for thorough investigation or lengthy discussion, and to remedy this a smaller General Council has been created, consisting of members elected by their fellow Congressmen. In addition, there is an Executive Committee of the parliamentary party, consisting of eleven office holders and twenty-one elected members, fifteen chosen by the

General Meeting and six by the council. The Constitution of the CLP prescribes that all important government motions, bills and resolutions shall be placed before the Executive Committee before being discussed in Parliament. There is also a network of Party Standing Committees, each responsible for a particular field of policy. Each MP normally sits on one or two of these. Their purpose is to minimise the gap between the government and the party, and to encourage members to develop specialised interests.

Opposition parties in Parliament have been in no position to build such complex parliamentary structures. Indeed, some of them are dominated by their organisational wings. Until recently no opposition parties held the vital 10 per cent of total membership of the House to qualify for recognition as the official opposition. This has been disadvantageous, as official recognition attracts certain privileges, such as the use of rooms in the Parliament building and the right to representation at official functions. Nevertheless, the forces of the opposition are not as weak and divided as they might appear to be, since the opposition parties tend to form groups for the purpose of demanding parliamentary time and of selecting common themes and speakers. The most successful of these groups was Mooker-jee's Democratic National Party, which consisted of the Jan Sangh, the Ganatantra Parishad, the Hindu Mahasabha, the Akali Dal, the Tamilnad Toilers' Party, and the Commonweal Party, reinforced by seven independents, and, surprisingly enough, by one member of the Forward Bloc, an extreme revolutionary party based on West Bengal. This group held discussions, planned common strategies, elected official representatives, and even attempted to 'whip' its members. However, it was never highly disciplined and petered out after Mookerjee's death. Recent attempts by the 'old' Congress, the Jan Sangh and the Swatantra to form a coalition in opposition to Mrs Gandhi's 'ruling' Congress Party have so far met with small success, owing to the mutual suspicions of the putative coalition partners.

The role of opposition parties in developing countries with democratic constitutions is never straightforward. Asoka Mehta, formerly leader of the Praja Socialist Party, maintained that 'the axiom that the opposition's job is to oppose would make economic development difficult' and suggested that 'a broad-based government holding power as a long-term tenure ... should replace the frequent changes in government that parliamentary democracy assumes'. Public liberties, he added, should be maintained, 'but opposition as distinct from criticism would be confined to those irreconcilables who are opposed to the fundamentals of the state.' Few of Mehta's party colleagues ever accepted this doctrine; but currently it would appear to be receiving some practical recognition, in so far as parties such as the CPI, CPI(M), PSP and DMK are adjusting their parliamentary tactics in order to save Mrs Gandhi's government from defeat.

Even in the heyday of Congress Party dominance, opposition parties were by no means without influence in the Lok Sabha. Krishna Menon has expressed his belief 'that Nehru was more sensitive to opposition parties than any other Prime Minister in the world that I have heard of'. It is also significant that, unlike some of his ministers, he hardly ever missed a meeting of Parliament when he was available to attend it. Every opposition party, moreover, has some *point d'appui* within Congress itself; for opposition members have usually been ex-congress-men and consequently have had long-standing connections with their rivals on the government benches. As Rajni Kothari writes, 'this role of the opposition parties in structuring the internal operation of the ruling party is a peculiar feature of the Indian system and enables the same party to be in power because the latter is constantly undergoing change and alteration in Parliament and government personnel'. It must also be noted that the opposition's lack of numbers has to some extent been compensated by the quality of some of its leaders. Brilliant parliamentarians, they have constantly harried the government on every possible issue. Consequently, Congress has never been able to ignore the opposition. However, in the days before the Congress split, the parliamentary eloquence of opposition members hardly compensated for their lack of numbers; and even when, as during the period of 1967–71, the government lacked the dominant position it had formerly enjoyed, both in the Lok Sabha and in the country, the tendency to equate opposition with disruption by no means disappeared.

The executive which Parliament is supposed both to support

and criticise is divided into four ranks – cabinet ministers, ministers of state, deputy ministers and parliamentary secretaries. Together, these compose the Council of Ministers referred to in the Constitution. In reality, this body never meets. A cabinet of senior ministers is the effective decision-taking body, though non-cabinet ministers may be called in when matters relevant to their departments are under discussion. In theory, non-cabinet posts are reserved for young and 'up-and-coming' politicians; in practice, their occupants tend to be established party stalwarts.

Since Independence, there have been frequent changes in the structure of departments and ministries. In 1947, the Council of Ministers numbered fourteen; by 1952 it had risen to forty; and Mrs Gandhi's present council includes no fewer than fifty-five. This increase is partly due to administrative proliferation, but it is also a consequence of the government's need to keep its leading supporters as happy as possible, by providing them with office.

The Cabinet system at the Centre dates from Independence. As in Britain, secrecy shrouds most of its activity. The principle of collective responsibility has been well maintained and is often used to keep in office certain individuals who, in its absence, might well have resigned. Permanent Cabinet Committees deal with such matters such as foreign affairs, home affairs, economic affairs, parliamentary affairs and defence, and *ad hoc* committees are frequently appointed, particularly in crisis situations. As in Britain, there is much controversy about the role of the Prime Minister. In the early years, Nehru's authority was tempered by the presence of powerful colleagues; but the office of Deputy Prime Minister was not retained after Patel's death and gradually the prestigious old men disappeared, leaving Nehru very much in command. 'Pandit Nehru was never *primus inter pares,* he always remained *unus inter pares*', was the verdict of V. M. Sirsikar. Dr Ambedkar resigned from the Cabinet in 1951 for this very reason, and in 1956 C.D. Deshmukh alleged that the Cabinet had not been consulted about states reorganisation. Under Shashtri's regime, leadership was more genuinely collective in character; nevertheless, we know that Nehru's successor took many decisions on his own responsibility, such as the decision to call a conference of chief ministers to discuss the language crisis. During her early days as Prime Minister, Mrs Gandhi behaved very 'democratically' but her subsequent actions, including the enforced resignation of Morarji Desai from the Finance Ministry in July 1969, and of Dinesh Singh from the Foreign Ministry in 1970, show that she is very much her father's daughter.

As we have seen, parliamentary government in India closely follows the British model. The system, however, contains an element for which there is no British counterpart, the presidency. The President is not equivalent to a constitutional monarch, nor is he – at least at present – an active politician. What is he then, and, more importantly, what is he capable of becoming? Nehru told the Constituent Assembly:

> We want to emphasise the ministerial character of the government – that power really resides in the ministry and legislature and not in the President as such. At the same time, we do not want the President just a mere figurehead like the French President. We do not want him to have any real power but we have made his position one of authority and dignity.

This was the essence of ambiguity, and the Constitution itself is no less ambiguous. In theory, the President is equipped with enormous powers. He appoints the Prime Minister and the Council of Ministers; he summons and dissolves the Lok Sabha; he gives his assent to all central legislation; he has a right of veto over state legislation; he can promulgate ordinances; and he can declare all types of emergency provided for in the Constitution. Yet his position is riddled with uncertainties. Does his right to appoint a Prime Minister also give him a right of dismissal? Can he, on his own initiative, refuse his assent to legislation? Must he always dismiss a ministry which has been defeated in the legislature? More importantly, is he invariably required to act on the advice of his Council of Ministers? The first President, Rajendra Prasad, although inclined to take an exalted view of his powers, in practice rarely went far beyond exercising the right to 'encourage, advise and warn', said to be characteristic of the British monarchy, and his rather frequent disputes with Nehru (as, for instance, over the Hindu Code Bill) were always resolved in the latter's favour. When, in 1960, Prasad asked for a legal review of his powers, opinion proved divided. Although the Supreme Court had already given its opinion that the Indian Executive was based on the British model, there were some legal experts who maintained that the President was endowed with powers of his own. The vital question, of course, is whether any President may attempt actually to assume and exercise such alleged powers. Mrs Gandhi's panic when the Syndicate nominated her political enemy, Sanjiva Reddi, to replace the deceased Dr Zahir Hussain, suggested that the issue might well become of immediate importance. Moreover, awkward problems could easily arise as a consequence of the method prescribed by the Constitution for electing the President. Parity between the votes cast by the MPs and those cast by the state assemblies, combined with the 'single transferable vote rule', makes it possible for a President to belong to a different party from that which commands a majority in the House, particularly if the five-year presidential term of office does not run coterminously with the life of Parliament. In the present multi-party situation, this method of election could acquire considerable political importance.

What of parliamentary government in the states? In essence, it differs little from parliamentary government in New Delhi. The social composition of the state assemblies, however, is very different from that of the Lok Sabha. 'Scratch a politician and you find a landlord', is an Orissa saying of very general applicability. In the assemblies there is a more rural, parochial and traditional atmosphere. Educational levels are lower and lapses into 'unparliamentary' behaviour much more frequent. Formerly all this was attributed to the inexperience of state legislators, and so was the comparatively high level of instability and corruptibility of the governments they created and toppled. Given time, it was suggested MLAs would become as sophisticated as MPs. Since 1967 there are far fewer grounds for such complacent optimism. Admittedly united fronts have not constituted an ideal environment for the development of political responsibility, but some observers have suggested that they could have been more stable and more successful if the average legislator had taken a more serious and public spirited view of his duties. As it is, any legislator, according to Professor Paul Brass, has become a 'potential blackmailer', with the result that 'the size of the state Cabinet has no relation to the amount of work to be done but bears an inverse ratio to the margin of the ruling party's majority'. Since the fourth general elections, 3,500 state legislators (14 per cent of the total) have defected from their parties. Haryana provides an almost classical example of this post-1967 situation. After the election, Congress held 48 seats out of a total of 81; yet after a week in office the Bhagwat Dayal ministry was defeated as a result of party members 'crossing the floor', on the grounds that a dissident leader had been denied office. The defectors, with the support of opposition elements, formed a new party, the Haryana Congress, whose leader, Birenda Singh, formed a government, only to resign from it, and from his party, when the Devi Lal Group threatened withdrawal of support. Having assumed the leadership of yet another new party, the Vishal Haryana, Birenda Singh was again appointed Chief Minister, and immediately embarked on a vote-buying spree by virtually putting ministerial offices up to auction. Eventually, after nine months of anarchy, Presidential Rule had to be imposed. Out of eighty-one MLAs, 64 had defected, twenty of them twice, three thrice, two four times, and one on no fewer than five occasions. A mid-term election brought another short-lived Congress majority, which was ended by the defection of a Congress leader with fifteen of his supporters. There followed 'a fierce battle of body snatching', during which one minister changed sides twice in a matter of hours. By offering ministerships to all and sundry, however, the Chief Minister managed to survive. To safeguard the ministry and its precarious majority, he decided to force through the budget within the narrow limits of the current session. This led to an opposition boycott of proceedings, with the result that twenty-one bills were passed in a hundred minutes. Appalled by this charade, members of the Lok Sabha voted, on a private member's motion, to set up an Investigating Committee. This discussed and rejected various suggestions made to curb migratory politics, such as a statutory ban on defections or a system of recall. It finally recommended a restriction on the size of cabinets and the barring of defectors from political office for a specified period. These proposals were not implemented.

Some commentators, even before the Congress split, were

forecasting that the kind of chaos illustrated by the Haryana example would inevitably spread to the Centre, and events in New Delhi seemed to confirm their views. In August 1969, Mrs Gandhi found it necessary to rebuke the Lok Sabha for its disorderly behaviour. 'The scene of disorder which prompted Mrs Gandhi to intervene', wrote Peter Hazelhurst in *The Times,* 'has become a daily one in the Lok Sabha. The House can hardly meet now without protracted bouts of angry shouting. Invariably ten members are talking at the same time, only one or two questions on the business agenda are answered and the Speaker is ignored almost completely.' Such behaviour seemed to bode ill for the coalition government that most observers expected to emerge at the Centre from the next round of elections, and despite the victory of Mrs Gandhi's Congress in 1971, it would be premature to foresee a restoration of parliamentary decorum. Much depends on how disciplined Mrs Gandhi's majority proves to be, and on the lengths to which the opposition parties are prepared to go in expressing their frustrations. Moreover, the new parliamentary situation at the Centre will not necessarily reproduce itself in the states. Nevertheless, one may hazard the guess that the strains that were threatening to make Indian parliamentary government unworkable will be significantly reduced, and one may even suggest the possibility that the country's twenty-one year old tradition of parliamentarism has been given a new lease of life.

6 Centre and States

Nowhere in the Indian Constitution does the word 'federalism' appear; yet the substance of federalism received considerable discussion at the Constituent Assembly. Moreover the question of how far, if at all, India's constitution and mode of government are 'federal' in character has remained important for those with a taste for definition and classification.

One of the outstanding features of the Constitution, casting doubt on its federal nature, is its flexibility. Although,

the Constitution is a federal Constitution in as much as it establishes what may be called a Dual Polity which will consist of the Union at the Centre and the States at the periphery, each endowed with sovereign powers to be exercised in the field assigned to them respectively by the Constitution [said Dr Ambedkar] yet the Constitution has avoided the tight mould of federalism . . . and could be both unitary and federal according to the requirements of time and circumstance.

This ambiguity both reflects a mixed political heritage and reveals the hopes and fears of the Founding Fathers. 'Federalism preceded the Constitution.' History and geography had always emphasised India's regional characteristics, with the result that the centralising policies initiated by the British in 1773 soon encountered difficulties. In 1861, legislative powers were given to the provinces, and by the India Act of 1919 the 'nation-building' subjects of education, health, agriculture, irrigation, and public works were devolved to the provincial legislatures, together with the appropriate financial ways and means. In 1930, the Simon Commission considered the efficacy of federalism as a means of mitigating the Hindu-Moslem conflict and of coping with the problem of the five hundred princely states, while the subsequent Round Table Conferences revealed widespread support for federal solutions. Finally, the Government of India

Act, 1935, prescribed a federal-type union of autonomous provinces whose governments were to derive their powers directly from the Crown. The division of powers between the Centre and the provinces was embodied in federal, provincial and concurrent lists. Moreover, although the Act never came fully into operation, it created a regime of responsible provincial government, and thereby brought into existence – or, more correctly, strengthened – a group of province-based politicians.

Although the provinces whose powers were thus enhanced had been essentially subordinate governmental agencies, they already possessed what Selig Harrison called 'the strength of age, of roots deep in the triumphs and humiliations of a venerable history'; and already there had been a considerable flowering of regional languages and literatures. All this experience suggested the possibility, and indeed the inevitability, of a federal-type solution to independent India's problem of unity-in-diversity.

Yet there was also need for a central authority powerful enough to counteract centrifugal forces. 'It is important for us not to take any step that might lead to the weakening of the fabric of India', said Nehru to the Constituent Assembly. The pertinence of this warning was underlined by a Communist uprising in Telengana, the activities of the Razakars* in Hyderabad, and the war in Kashmir. It was also considered, by Nehru in particular, that a strong Centre was essential for effective economic planning. The Constitution, therefore, sought the best of both worlds. Regional sentiments were to be satisfied, yet the Centre was to remain sufficiently powerful both to plan the economy as a whole and to deal with threats to national unity.

The federal-type provisions of the Constitution have already been summarised. Here we shall be concerned with the evolution of the actual relations between the Centre and the states, i.e. with what Carl Friedrich has called 'the federalising process'.

Such relations in all federations and quasi-federations are powerfully influenced by financial factors. As we have seen, the Constitution, while dividing powers of taxation, provides that periodically-determined proportions of certain centrally-

* An extremist Islamic para-military movement.

assessed and centrally-collected taxes shall be made over to the states for their exclusive use. In this way it was hoped to take care of the imbalance created by the restriction of the states' revenue to land taxes, sales taxes, certain excises, and various minor impositions. On the other hand, a once-for-all allocation to and division among states of centrally-raised revenues would have been totally unrealistic. The Constitution, therefore, reserves to the President the function of determining what proportion of the 'divisible' taxes are to be assigned to the states and the manner in which they are to be allocated. This power is to be exercised in accordance with the recommend-ations of a Finance Commission, an impartial, expert body, quinquennially-appointed. The specific functions of this Commission are to recommend (1) 'the distribution between the Union and the states of the net proceeds of taxes which are to be or may be divided between them ... and the allocation between the states of their respective shares of such proceeds' and (2) 'the principles which should govern the grants-in-aid' established by Article 275.

The First Finance Commission, which reported in 1952, advised that 55 per cent of the income tax should be allocated to the states and distributed mainly in accordance with size of population. It felt, however, that the 'source of collection' principle could not be entirely disregarded, and so recommended that 20 per cent of the total sum should be distributed according to its state of origin. Of the excise duties, the divisible portion (40 per cent) was to be allocated entirely on a population basis. In 1957, the Second Finance Commission raised the states' share of the income tax to 60 per cent and recommended that the 'source of collection' principle be abandoned, after a five year transitional period during which 10 per cent would be allocated on this basis. It also advised that the number of shared excise duties be enlarged to eight, although the states' share of their proceeds was to be reduced to 25 per cent. In 1962, the Finance Commission again felt it necessary to increase the states' share of the income tax – this time to 66⅔ per cent; but it abandoned the Second Commission's recommendation that the principle of collection be ignored, as it felt that recognition ought to be given to the special responsibilities of some of the richer states in respect of the preservation of law and order and maintenance of the social services. It therefore reverted to the principles of apportionment established by the First Commission. In addition, it recommended that *all* excises should be made divisible and 20 per cent of them distributed on the basis of population. At present, the allocation of inter-governmental finances follows the principles recommended by the Fourth Finance Commission, which increased the states' share of income tax to 75 per cent and approved the division of excise duties recommended by the Third Finance Commission. In the allocation of the latter, however, only 80 per cent was to be on a population basis, the remainder being subject to a complex formula designed to take different degrees of 'backwardness' into account.

In addition to dealing with the division of tax-raised resources, the Finance Commissions are also responsible for recommending the principles which should govern the making of grants-in-aid from the Centre to the states. Originally, six criteria were laid down for this purpose, *viz.* (1) the budgetary needs of the state; (2) the effort made by it to raise revenue through taxation; (3) the economy with which it managed its financial affairs; (4) the level of the social services which it had established or proposed to establish; (5) its specific obligations and special burdens; (6) the satisfaction of broad purposes of national importance. In practice these recommendations have proved difficult to apply, and budgetary deficits have therefore become the main determinant of the distribution of grants-in-aid.

When the First Finance Commission recommended grant-in-aid assistance to seven states, and also some special assistance for the expansion of primary education, this proved the beginning of persistent rivalry between successive Finance Commissions and the Planning Commission; for the latter has maintained that grant-aids for basic national purposes should be its own exclusive responsibility, so that planning priorities may be maintained. The Santhanam Commission, which investigated this dispute, recommended that grants-in-aid should be considered in the context of planning and that normal state expenditure should be assisted solely by way of tax sharing. Another recommendation, made by the Chanda Commission, was to the effect that the total grants in-aid should be sufficient to 'enable the states ... to cover 75 per cent of the revenue component of their plans'. In the nature of things, however, the dispute proved difficult to resolve, not only because the states were vociferous in their demands that they should receive the greater part of their centrally-provided assistance as of right, and not at the discretion of the Planning Commission, but because the distinction between 'plan' and 'revenue' expenditure was ambiguous. The Fourth Finance Commission of 1967, however, partially met the Planning Commission's point by recommending no special purpose grants – although it increased the size of the general grant-in-aid to meet an expected revenue deficiency in some of the states.

What is clear is that the operations of the Finance Commission have failed significantly to reduce the degree of financial imbalance as between the states and the Centre and between state and state. This failure is serious in a 'co-operative federal' context, and has produced considerable discontent in all states – not least in those governed by the ruling Congress Party itself. Minoo Masani, the Swatantra leader, has warned that the states 'will lose their rights' and 'become glorified municipalities and district boards if they do not look out'. In the present political context, this is an absurd exaggeration; but Masani is right to the extent that the centralising trend of Indian intra-governmental finances is not what the Constituent Assembly had intended. Yet there is little that the Finance Commission itself can do to remedy this gap between intention and achievement.

On the part of the states, the greatest discontent has been generated by the expansion of the so-called 'conditional' grants, authorised by Article 282 of the Constitution. Used to facilitate the planning process, these grants fall outside the purview of the Finance Commission, yet they now exceed in magnitude the states' portion of the shared taxes. Even by the end of the First Plan, the proportion of shared taxes and statutory grants to the total resources transferred from the Centre to the states had fallen from 43 to 20 per cent. During the Second Plan, the amount of 'conditional' assistance more than doubled, much of it being in the form of loans, which had already reached a total of Rs 900 crores by 1956. In 1961, the Third Finance Commission reported that the burden of state indebtedness to the Centre was so heavy that new loans were being raised to pay the interest on the old ones.

Some of the blame for this situation must rest on the states themselves, since they have generally shown a marked reluctance to engage in any vigorous use of the taxing powers conferred on them. The Union government has endeavoured to use the 'matching' grant as an incentive to financial effort, but without much success, since the *main* purpose of such grants is to finance projects which, having already been centrally approved, cannot be allowed to run into the sands simply because the State's promised support for them is not being fulfilled.

A device frequently used by the states, at least in former days, to evade their financial responsibilities has been to play off the Finance Commission against the Planning Commission. States will boast of their resource-raising capacities to the Planning Commission, in the hope of gaining sanction for expensive development projects, but to the Finance Commission they tell a very different story. As the latter is engaged in filling the revenue gap, the states, in their representations to it, are strongly tempted to underestimate their resources in the hope of receiving additional help.

Although one may criticise the states for their lack of effort to raise revenue, one should remember that they were never intended to be fully self-financing. The Constituent Assembly itself believed that the technique of shared taxes, the mainstay of which was to be the income tax, might be used to reduce the financial imbalance between the Union and the states that it had deliberately built into their respective revenue-raising powers. However, it did not foresee that grants and loans would be a more important method of transferring revenue and that 'tied' grants, in particular, would come to exceed the states' share of the income tax. There are several explanations of this outcome. One is that the income tax has ceased to be a rapidly-expanding tax. Its yield has been surpassed by that of the corporation tax, with the result that by 1963–4 only Rs 2,220 million of a yield from taxes on income, individual and corporative, amounting to Rs 4,006 million, entered the divisible pool; and, although excise duties, the other main 'divisibles', have become higher and more buoyant over the past twenty years, they cannot be expected to expand much further. However, the most important reason for the loading of the financial dice in the Union's favour lies in the central government's adoption of a planned economy. Planning and federalism make uneasy partners and the emphasis on the former has had a profound effect on Union-state financial relations.

Nevertheless, it would be an exaggeration to present the actual planning relations between Centre and states as totally one-sided. Partnership in fact, has tended to become more real in successive planning exercises. In the formulation of the First Five Year Plan, the states did little more than provide the Planning Commission with information. As the governments concerned were new, poorly equipped with statistical data, and without any planning machinery of their own, little more could have been expected of them. By the time the Second Five Year Plan was being formulated the states had acquired more experience and had even developed some rudimentary planning machinery; but it was still difficult for them to prepare their schemes in the absence of adequate indication about the total size of the Second Plan and the amount of central assistance they were likely to receive. In the drawing-up of the Third Plan, there was some improvement in this respect, and the states consequently played a more significant role. There were innumerable journeys between New Delhi and the state capitals, conferences were held in abundance, and some pretty hard bargaining took place. However, the close connections between the states' departments and the corresponding departments at the Centre meant that at least some of this bargaining was 'horizontal' rather than 'vertical' in character.

Both kinds, of course, spill over from implementation into execution. Responsibility for the implementation of a state's plan rests on the shoulders of its Council of Ministers, administrative departments and special agencies, working under the supervision and guidance of the Planning Commission and central ministries. How far this involves unwarranted intrusion by the Centre is a question very difficult to answer in general terms; but there is always a considerable volume of central direction on almost every conceivable subject. Moreover, up to 1958, agreement by the Planning Commission for the inclusion of a scheme in a state's Plan by no means ensured that work on it could proceed. Where central assistance was required (as in the majority of cases), specific sanction had to be issued by the appropriate central ministry or other agency. Each of these bodies operated its own system of detailed and meticulous checks and regulations. Subsequently these procedures were considerably streamlined, with the result that the states now enjoy greater freedom. In particular they have received the right, in most cases, to transfer funds from one project-group to another. The corresponding disadvantage of these new liberties, of course, is that the enforcement of national priorities becomes more difficult. Nevertheless, central control, in the form of driving from the back seat, still remains a marked feature of India's planning processes.

Planning conflicts between Centre and states have been at their fiercest on those subjects, e.g. education, health and agriculture, that are not only included in the states' lists of constitutional powers but are of greatest interest to state politicians, for rather obvious electoral reasons. In these, as indeed in other fields, the common complaint has been that the Planning Commission disregards regional differences and imposes on the states rigid and uniform programmes (see chapter 8 page 178). West Bengal, for instance, was asked to take measures to control filaria, a disease not widely prevalent in that area, but could get no central assistance for the implementation of a much-needed leprosy scheme. The actual impact of this centrally-imposed rigidity naturally depends on the degree to which a state is financially dependent upon the Centre for the implementation of a particular scheme. In respect of education, where this dependence is generally high, the views of the Central Ministry of Education and the Education Section of the Planning Commission naturally carry great weight. The same is true of health, which has been subject to central controls of an almost grotesque meticulousness. For instance, when the Central Ministry of Health received plans for a proposed Medical College at Kanpur, it suggested a reduction in the height of the rooms, and when the state government objected to this, replied that grants would be given for rooms only of the prescribed dimensions and that if higher rooms were insisted upon the extra expenditure would have to be met by the state. In community development, too, the imposition of centrally-determined patterns has been frequent and fierce. The Central Ministry of Community Development has even drawn up job descriptions for village level workers, extension officers and block development officers. In several cases, some of them conspicuous, the familiar 'matching grant' has been used to compel a state to modify its financial policies. For instance, the government of Uttar Pradesh, lacking resources to pay its share of the cost of a number of development schemes prescribed by the Third Plan, felt compelled to introduce a bill increasing the taxes on land. This highly unpopular measure caused a political crisis during the course of which the government of Mrs Sucheta Kripalani nearly fell from office.

On the other hand, it would be most unwise to generalise from these examples, since actual state-Centre relationships vary from time to time and from state to state, in dependence on a formidable complex of political factors. There is no doubt that 'states' rights' flourished as a result of the weakening of Congress but even in the comparatively early days of Independence, when the Party was both united and 'dominant', it was fully possible for a powerfully-placed state, itself under a Congress government, successfully to challenge the Centre. Case studies of the Damodar Scheme show the Union government unable to resist the demands of West Bengal even when these directly conflicted with centrally-determined policies of the highest importance. As the Damodar Valley Corporation was an autonomous body, centrally-financed, one might have expected that the two states in whose territories it lay, Bihar and West Bengal, would have had no more than minor influence on the policies it pursued. In fact, its original purposes became completely distorted as a result of pressures from the governments of these states (and particularly from that of West Bengal), and the Central government, feeling itself powerless to challenge the formidable party machine of Atulya Ghosh, simply accepted this situation. An even earlier conflict between West Bengal and the Centre, also resolved in favour of the former, was about land reform. Despite the fact that the Congress Party was fully committed to such reform, and despite the Planning Commission's persistent attempts to secure its implementation, West Bengal, in deference to the views of the property owners on whose financial support the State

Congress depended, refused to act, on the excuse that further 'research' was necessary. In the end, the state government came up with legislation so favourable to the landowners that its impact on the existing situation was minimal.

In the absence of many more case-studies (which might anyway present conflicting evidence), it is difficult to judge how far the planning process has tilted the federal balance towards the Centre. It has been suggested that 'a large part of each Five Year Plan in India has been drawn up in a fairly decentralised fashion'; but an officer in the service of the Uttar Pradesh Government has contradicted this in no uncertain way.

For practically every project, big or small, [he says] we are entirely dependent on the government of India. It is the government of India that releases foreign exchange, it is again the government of India that has to be approached for the sanction of schemes and the release of grants. So without the active participation of the central government it is well-nigh impossible to do anything substantial in this region despite the best intentions of the state government.

Wilfred Malenbaum confirms this view when he writes that 'the power of the Centre is so great that at the planning stage agreement will be reached fairly close to the Centre's position'. The discrepancies between these views may be partly explained by the fact that they are not contemporaneous. In respect of planning, as in other respects, Centre-state relations have not remained stable over the post Independence period. As a result of political factors we have examined (pp. 72–3), the states have acquired a greater *de facto* freedom. This fact has been implicitly recognised in the field of planning by the 'downgrading' of the Planning Commission and the attempted enhancement of the role of the National Development Council (see p. 128).

The planning process has been given some detailed discussion in this context because of its very important impact on Centre-state relations; but we must now deal in more general terms with the political factors that have been at work. 'Unitarism', of course, was promoted by the former dominance of the Congress Party. 'The existence of widespread state-Centre conflict', wrote Myron Weiner in *Party Politics in India,* 'has thus far been precluded by one-party control of the central government and most of the states'. Nevertheless, although one-party rule reduced public conflict, it was quite compatible with a great deal of in-fighting, behind only semi-closed doors. The victories of the non-Congress parties, in 1967 and subsequently, only intensified Centre-state disputes, which had been a major feature of the Indian political scene when Congress ruled both in New Delhi and in most of the state capitals. It is true, of course, that the Centre often won. The Kamaraj Plan, for instance, engineered the resignation of six chief ministers who still had the confidence of their various state assemblies. Moreover, the Congress Parliamentary Board on several occasions prevented chief ministers from freely choosing their colleagues, and on one famous occasion, known as the Katju episode, actually foisted a 'foreigner' on a state as Chief Minister. But one must also emphasise the degree of freedom enjoyed by B. C. Roy and Atulya Ghosh in West Bengal and the power exercised by the 'strong men' like C. B. Gupta in Uttar Pradesh and P. S. Kairon in the Punjab, both of them distrusted by the High Command. Indeed, it could be argued that during the period of Congress dominance, state politicans enjoyed an independence that derived from the High Command's anxiety not to be accused of undue interference.

Further important evidence about Centre-state relations is provided by the record of the Centre's use of its emergency powers. During the national emergency, consequent upon the Indo-Chinese conflict of 1962, the Union government, of course, freely invaded the states' reserved spheres. The states were directed to pay special attention to the expansion of scientific and technical education; to introduce double shifts in primary schools; to construct certain highways and bridges; and to establish co-operative consumer stores to prevent rises in prices. It is significant, however, that many of these 'invasions' were made with the states' own agreement. Of the other kind of emergency, resulting in Presidential Rule of a particular state, there have been seventeen examples by the time when this chapter was being written. Nine of these have occurred since 1967, and of the eight pre-1967 examples four applied to the chronically unstable Kerala. Despite the view of the Constituent Assembly that Presidential Rule should not be evoked simply to resolve a ministerial crisis, most of the proclamations have been used for this purpose, and it is not difficult to argue that the emergency provisions have thereby been abused. The Kerala case of 1959 and the Uttar Pradesh case of 1970 deserve examination in this context.

In 1957 a Communist majority was returned to the Kerala Assembly, and the policies of the government thus brought to power soon encountered widespread resistance, in which the Congress Party was prominent. By 1959 Kerala was in a state of chaos, mass agitation finding its main target in the new Education Bill, which sought to control private schools. This bill was reserved by the governor for presidential assent, with the result that some of its clauses were modified; but violent agitation and no less violent repression continued. Prime Minister Nehru, after touring the state, suggested the holding of a mid-term election, but this was refused by the Keralan Government. Finally, the governor reported a total breakdown of law and order and, despite the fact that the Keralan government retained its majority in the state legislature, Presidential Rule was proclaimed. Opinion about the legitimacy of this step was much divided. The Communists, of course, denied it vigorously; and K. M. Pannikar joined the protests. One criticism was that the President should have resorted to the use of Article 252 instead of Article 256; for the situation was one of internal disorder and, if an emergency had been declared under the latter article, the state government would not have been automatically dissolved. Supporters of the President's action justified the use of Article 256, on the grounds that in several instances the Communist ministry had violated the Constitution, e.g. by releasing political prisoners convicted of serious charges. But as the mainstay of anti-government agitation was the State Congress Party, suspicion that the pro-clamation was imposed for purely political motives has remained, particularly as a disorderly situation in Assam in 1960–61, the product of linguistic riots, did not provoke a similar presidential reaction.

The imposition of a brief period of Presidential Rule in Uttar Pradesh in 1970 raised, as we have seen, far more general controversy, as it appeared to be an openly partisan intervention, instigated by Mrs Gandhi. There was no ministerial crisis of a kind that could be measured by a vote in the legislature (since the State Assembly was not in session) nor was there clear evidence of widespread public disorder.

A word might be added here about the role of state governors. With one or two exceptions, all have been members of the Congress Party – often candidates defeated in elections or politicians due for 'pushing upstairs'. Have they always avoided pro-Congress bias? It would be difficult to argue that they have, particularly when confronted by the task of sending for a chief minister in a confused multi-party situation, or of granting or refusing a dissolution of the Assembly.

When all the contradictory features of the Union-state relationship have been duly noted, the fact remains that the substantive realities of Indian politics give a state ministry important sources of power. Whichever party is in office in New Delhi, its chief purpose is to remain popular with a predominantly unpoliticised Indian electorate. If anything rouses the citizens from their habitual torpor, it is a local issue which they can 'feel' if not understand. This means that, irrespective of the party which rules a particular state, the Centre simply cannot treat a state government as a passive agency. This has been true ever since Independence, but it has become an even more important fact of political life now that the Congress Old Guard has gone and central ministers have to look to their power basis in the states. Moreover, the state governments themselves, threatened by an opposition which exploits local issues, are strongly impelled to resist the Centre whenever it demands that they should imperil their electoral lives by taking unpopular actions.

Centrifugal forces have been seen most spectacularly at work in connection with the national language controversy and the agitation for linguistic states. The Constitution specified Hindi as the official language for all-India purposes but, as a consequence of robust opposition from non-Hindi-speaking areas, such as the Bengali-speaking West Bengal and the Tamil, Telugu, Malayalam and Kannada-speaking states of the south, it also provided that English could be used as an 'associate' language until 1965. In the intervening period the non-Hindi States made little effort to prepare for the change-over. Indeed, southerners vigorously raised the cry of 'Hindi imperialism'. In Madras, the controversy was exploited by the Dravida

Munnetra Kazhagam (DMK), the party of Tamil separatism, whose popularity caused growing alarm to the State Congress Party. Because of this deteriorating situation, Nehru opted for a 'go-slow' policy on the national language issue, announcing that he was opposed to a hurried switchover and that English must remain as an associate language for an indefinite period. This retreat was made official by a Presidential Order in 1960; but legislation on the subject was postponed and the south remained determined that it should not be forgotten. As 1965 approached, the situation in Madras became chaotic – the police fired on protesting crowds and thousands were arrested. As a result the official language policy was put in cold storage. But non-Hindi speakers demanded legal guarantees, and in 1968 the Official Language (Amendment) Act not only provided for the continued use of English, as an associate language for official purposes, but gave the non-Hindi states a veto over its discontinuance. This legislation illustrates the influence that disaffected states can exert, and also shows how tricky is the balancing act that the Centre has to perform from time to time; for in this case it had to attempt to buy off the opposition of the militantly pro-Hindi no less than that of the militantly anti-Hindi elements.

Since 1968, the controversy about Hindi has been rather less acute, which is perhaps a tribute to the wisdom of the policy embodied in the Official Language (Amendment) Act. Rather significantly, the Jan Sangh chose to soft-pedal the issue in its 1971 election campaign. Its manifesto spoke merely of 'developing Hindi as a link language' – a far cry from the aggressive 'Hindi imperialism' which had previously characterised its propaganda efforts. Moreover, the result of the election represented a set-back for those who had hoped to derive advantage from their championship of or opposition to Hindi as an exclusive national language. It may be, therefore, that much of the heat has now been taken out of this issue.

The Hindi controversy is inseparably connected with the more general phenomenon of linguistic regionalism. This, by the mid–1950s, had developed sufficient power to compel state reorganisation of a kind for which Nehru and his colleagues had little enthusiasm. Although India's heterogeneity had been responsible for the introduction of the federal element into her constitution, the state boundaries actually adopted bore little relationship to social, cultural and economic divisions – or to linguistic groupings. With such modifications as were necessary for the integration of the princely states, these boundaries remained essentially the same as those drawn by the British; and although the Constitution of India recognised fifteen 'associate' languages, the actual speakers of these tongues were frequently divided by political lines which looked increasingly arbitrary. Congress itself had long been committed to linguistic reorganisation, and this demand, as might have been expected, was vigorously raised in the Constituent Assembly itself; but the Congress High Command, which feared the effect that the creation of 'linguistic' states might have on the unity of India, remained cool towards it. However, a commission under Mr Justice Dar was set up to look into the question. Dar's verdict was that a reorganisation according to linguistic criteria would damage the unity of India, and that any redrawing of boundaries should be based on the principle of administrative convenience alone. Continuing agitation among the peoples of the states, however, was sufficient to worry Congress and late in 1948 the party appointed a three-man commission, consisting of Nehru, Patel and Sitaramayya, to have another look at the question. In their report they followed Dar in advising against any wholesale linguistic reorganisation, but expressed sympathy for the claims of the Telugu speakers, suggesting the creation for their benefit of a predominantly Telugu-speaking state of Andhra to be cut out of what was then Madras. The Communists, already committed to the principle of linguistic organisation, took up the Andhra cause specifically and the 'linguistic' cause generally. In Madras, with the State Congress Party divided, the continuation of coherent government became virtually impossible. Finally, the fast to death of Potti Sriramulu, together with the wave of unrest which followed it, forced the Union government to agree to the creation of the new state. The floodgates were now open and, partly to head off increasing pressures from other 'linguistic' claimants, a third investigation into state reorganisation was confided to a States Reorganisation Commission in 1956. Its report accepted the basic principle and recommended substantial changes, with the result that the Union government decided to act. India was divided into fourteen states, their boundaries largely drawn on linguistic criteria.

There were, however, two outstanding areas to which the new principle was not applied: Bombay and Punjab, which were left as 'bilingual' states. In these areas, therefore, the agitation continued and intensified. In Bombay the demand was for the separation of the Gujerati-speaking from the Marathi-speaking areas. The opposition parties joined together to form linguistic front organisations, the Samyukta Maharashtra Samiti and the Maha Gujerat Janata Parishad. This agitation was so violent and so effective that in the 1957 elections the Bombay Congress Party found its former massive majority reduced to a highly precarious one. After further campaigns, in which the two front organisations managed to secure support from almost all sections of the population, the Union government, in 1960, agreed to the division of Bombay into two separate States, Gujerat and Maharashtra.

In the Punjab, the situation was more complex. Whether the demands of the Sikh Party, the Akali Dal, were based on language or religion is disputable; but after innumerable investigations a Punjabi-speaking state was created in 1965, by the division of the Punjab into a truncated state of that name and a predominantly Hindi-speaking Haryana.

At the time of writing, these pressures are less intense than they used to be, and the question raised in the late 1950s by Selig Harrison (in his *India, the Most Dangerous Decades*) whether the Union would be able to survive them is consequently less acute. Indeed, in Tamil Nadu, the DMK Government now appears to be faced with student revolt *against* the 'Tamilisation' of the educational system. 'English', reports the *Hindustan Times*, 'had become the status symbol, with English medium private schools being the Mecca of every middle-class family with any aspirations. Some DMK Ministers sent their own sons to these schools while deciding to impose Tamil alone on others. This opened them to the charge of hypocrisy.' But even if these signs of reaction against linguistic particularism were absent, it could still be argued that the survival of the Union, if ever in real jeopardy, was threatened by the central government's *delay* in satisfying linguistic demands rather than by its eventual acceptance of them. For, while undoubtedly reinforcing regionalism, linguistic reorganisation has at least tended to reconcile the dissident elements to the Union's *existence*. From the point of view of successfully operating federal institutions, this would seem to be sheer gain.

On the other hand, it must be admitted that the snowball effect of the agitation for linguistic states has induced the central government to concede to demands for further subdivision which have have little justification politically and none at all economically. Statehood has now been conferred on Nagaland, Manipur and Himachal Pradesh, and even a 'substate', named Meghalaya, has been carved out of Assam. These concessions, moreover, have had the effect of stimulating further demands, of which currently the most powerful is the demand for the establishment of a 'Telengana' at the expense of Andhra Pradesh. In the elections of 1971, the Telengana Praja Samiti, which heads the agitation, captured ten out of the fourteen regional seats in the Lok Sabha, thereby indicating to Mrs Gandhi's Congress, which almost swept the board in the rest of the state, the strength of the local feeling.

It is also clear that the establishment of linguistic states has dangerously reinforced sentiments of regional patriotism, and facilitated the rise to power of politicians whose outlooks differ radically from those of the New Delhi elite. As a consequence, the Centre's power and influence have been diminished. Such changes in mentality and in personnel were not without responsibility for Congress's poor showing in the elections of 1967. Whether its brilliant performance in the Lok Sabha elections of 1971 means that the balance is now shifting back to the Centre remains to be seen. It may mean merely that Mrs Gandhi is the sole remaining politician of national standing.

Even before these results were known, however, there were few serious students who held that India was about to become a confederation rather than a federation; still less that it was on the edge of disintegration. Those that did were perhaps misled by false analogies. Because our own political culture leads us to stress the competitiveness of federal relationships, we tend to underestimate the viability of federalism, particularly for developing countries. We fail to realise, for instance, that an Indian may be proud of his regional inheritance yet possess a genuine all-India patriotism. After all, the spirit that drove men to seek Indian independence was not extinguished the moment Independence was won. But this combination of loyalties, as everyone admits, is difficult to achieve.

To the extent that it can be promoted by appropriate institutions and practices, the Indian system of government has already done its best to make the combination possible. The Founding Fathers were undoubtedly wise in providing a 'concurrent' list of powers, an Independent Finance Commission and, in general, an institutional framework designed to facilitate voluntary co-operation. Within this framework, much has been subsequently done to make the states realise that they possess common interests and to persuade them that the Centre is not a hostile power.

Potentially important organisations, devised for this very purpose, are the Zonal Councils, which were brought into existence by the States Reorganisation Act of 1956. There are five such councils, based on geographical groupings of states and Union territories. Each consists of a Union minister as chairman, the chief ministers and two other ministers from the participating states, and not more than two representatives from each centrally-administered territory, where such territories are included in the zone. Its functions, as laid down by the States Reorganisation Act, are to 'discuss any matter in which some or all of the states represented in that council or the Union and one or more of the states represented in that council have a common interest, and to advise the central government and the government of each state concerned as to the action to be taken on any such matter'. In particular it is concerned with matters of common interest in the field of economic and social planning, and questions relating to border disputes, linguistic minorities and inter-states transport. Purely advisory in character, the councils have not yet fulfilled many of the hopes of their originators. Nevertheless, if the political situation should prove favourable, they could become important growing points for inter-state collaboration. But at the present moment relations between states – particularly adjoining states, such as Bengal and Assam – are much more competitive than collaborative, and have been so for many years.

Another institution which attempts to serve a similar purpose is the National Development Council, created in 1952 as a means of promoting inter-state and Centre-state cooperation in economic planning. The Cabinet resolution which established it defined its functions as follows: (1) to review the working of the National Plan from time to time; (2) to consider important questions of social and economic policy affecting national development; and (3) to recommend measures for the achievement of the aims and target set out in the National Plan, including measures to secure the active participation and cooperation of the people, improve the efficiency of the administrative services, ensure the fullest development of the less advanced regions and sections of the community and through sacrifices borne equally by all citizens, build up resources for national development. So far, it has done little more than provide the Planning Commission with a sounding board of moderate utility; but, with the recent reorganisation of the planning machinery, there is at least a possibility that its role will become very much more important.

One must also not disregard the less formal types of inter-state and Centre-state collaboration. There are, for instance, very frequent meetings in New Delhi of state ministers concerned with particular subjects, such as education, agriculture, housing and finance. Many of these are infructuous, but some have taken decisions of major importance. In 1962, for instance, state housing ministers agreed on the freezing of land values and the imposition of a levy on industry to finance housing programmes for workers. In 1963, a meeting of state finance ministers decided to introduce uniform rates of sales tax on certain commodities. In 1964, a meeting of education ministers agreed to take steps to achieve uniformity in standards of secondary education. Centrally-promoted meetings and conferences of this type have, in fact, become one of the regular features of Indian political and administrative life. Even Benjamin Schoenfeld, no great admirer of Indian federalism, admits that such get-togethers 'provide a forum for discussion of mutual problems and set the stages for a cooperative solution to these problems'.

But it would be unwise to imagine that these swallows make a summer, and we must necessarily end this chapter on Centre-state relations with a series of unanswered and possibly unanswerable questions. Will the centrifugal forces eventually split the Indian Union wide open, with the result that it dissolves into what Selig Harrison once described as a motley of 'feuding principalities'? If so, would this really matter very much, provided that the 'feuding' did not reach damaging proportions? It can be argued with some cogency that 'India' is too varied and too heterogeneous to provide the long-term basis for an even partially unified political community – and, indeed, that her unification has never actually been achieved except as a result of the efforts of a foreign conqueror, whether Moghul or British. It can also be argued that, despite all that Nehru said on the subject, the retention of unity is not a *sine qua non* for effective economic development, since a community of far fewer than five hundred million people can provide a perfectly viable economic unit, even in our modern technological age. On the other hand, in these days when everyone is preaching regional economic cooperation, it would seem a retrograde step if an area already large enough to constitute a region in itself should split up into a series of separate states, each pursuing its own autarchic economic policies. On the cultural plane, moreover, one has to admit that there does exist a sense of 'Indianness', however vague and amorphous, and that this is not solely the result of the predominance of the Hindu religion and of the caste institutions that characteristically go with it. Moreover, political disintegration would spell the end of what Indians themselves admit to have been a valuable British achievement – an achievement that was damaged, but not destroyed, by the partition that created Pakistan.

India's unity-in-diversity, as underlined and underpinned by her Constitution, has so far been maintained, and her federal-type institutions have successfully withstood tensions of a strength which, in many other developing countries, have reduced federalism to dust and ashes. Whether Indian federalism can avoid this fate, and whether it deserves to do so, are questions on which neither of the authors of this book would care to hazard a clear answer. All we can say is that the 1971 elections have considerably restored confidence that an effective unity can be preserved.

7 Administration

(1) *The Civilians*

It has become the merest commonplace to say that the acquisition of independence brings with it new administrative tasks. The contrast between the predominantly 'law and order' function of colonial administration and the 'nation-building' function of administration in the successor regime is almost equally familiar. This dichotomy is often presented in an exaggerated form, since no colonial government has ever confined its activities to the maintenance of law and order, and since independence usually increases rather than diminishes the difficulties of maintaining it. Nevertheless, the withdrawal of the colonisers does involve the adoption of a new approach to administration, particularly for a government such as the Indian, which is serious about economic and social planning and anxious to combine it with those new forms of popular participation which go under the name of *panchayati raj* or Democratic Decentralisation.

The ambiguities of the British administrative legacy have already been stressed (see Chapter 1 pp 23-4). Its strength, which was considerable, lay in the high quality and remarkable adaptability of the small administrative aristocracy. Its major weakness was to be found in the routine-bound nature of the administrative processes below that level. A tiny body of senior men, highly educated and trained to think in problem-solving terms, was attempting to run the affairs of a vast country through a mass of not-very-highly-motivated minor bureaucrats, educated in the arts of absorption and regurgitation rather than in those of thinking, and trained mainly in the literal application of a formidable collection of detailed regulations, hopefully providing for every possible contingency. Correctness rather than initiative was its watchword: find the right regulation, apply it and, for the rest, carry out orders, treat superiors with deference, and do nothing that might prejudice job-security.

This administrative ethos has suffered very little change during the twenty years of independence. In some respects it has become reinforced as a result of the decline in the quality of secondary and further education and the increase in the severity of competition among the growing mass of the half-educated for a limited number of government jobs. Hence, despite the development-mindedness of many of the newly-recruited top-level administrators and the capacity shown by some of the older ones to take on new and unfamiliar tasks, together with some rather half-hearted attempts to implement the impeccable recommendations of innumerable administrative reforms commissions, both central and state, Indian administration remains, to a remarkable extent, stuck in its pre-Independence posture. This is the despair of the social and economic planners, who are always proclaiming, although with decreasing hopefulness, the urgent need to 'ginger up' the administrative machine, so as to make it a more efficient instrument for the attainment of their goals.

Another source of tension is the difficulty experienced by politicians and administrators in coming to terms with each other. At Independence there was a reversal of roles. Despite the introduction of limited self-government, the administrator, at least up to 1946, regarded himself as master. Nationalist politicians, from Nehru downwards, presented him with a 'law-and-order' problem. Whatever his private opinions may have been, his professional loyalties were to the British raj. When the British went and the Congress took over, he found himself having to make a sizeable effort of psychological adjustment. The rebels, having become the masters, necessarily looked at him with a certain suspicion. He had to win their trust by proving the genuineness of his change of allegiance. If he leant over backwards to carry out their orders, he was liable to be regarded as a stooge; if, on the other hand, he attempted to pit his experience against their inexperience, he might well find himself shunted into some position where he could do no harm. Victorious rebels are always impatient of criticism, which they find difficulty in distinguishing from sabotage, and when that criticism comes from bureaucrats who were enjoying well-paid jobs while their more nationalistically-minded contemporaries were, as often as not, languishing in prison, it is particularly resented. Hence during the years immediately after Independence, the relationship between politicians and civil servants was a very delicate one. More importantly, the attitudes characteristic of these years have proved remarkably persistent. The give-and-take partnership between V. P. Menon and Sardar Patel, one of the few Congress leaders who really understood administrative problems, has been the exception rather than the rule.

Indeed, there were many Congress politicians who would have liked to disband the ICS, not only because they doubted its loyalty, but because they considered its inbred, elitist and caste-like characteristics to be incompatible with India's new democratic institutions. This demand, however, was strongly resisted by the more experienced leaders, who saw the virtues of an Indian equivalent to the British Administrative Class, both as a source of much-needed administrative competence and as a means of cementing national unity. They won their point, but only at the cost of building tensions into the system. The situation became worse as the older generation of Congress leaders disappeared, to be replaced, particularly at the state level, by new men who were often socially and educationally the inferiors of their own administrative top brass. Hence, as the colonial period receded into the background there has been no lack of fresh fuel to keep the old antagonisms smouldering. One of the less endearing characteristics of the politician is his tendency to pass the buck, by openly criticising his civil servants and making them take the blame when things go wrong. Nehru himself was by no means guiltless of this bad habit, but the outstanding example was Krishnamachari's largely successful attempt to place responsibility for a financial scandal on the shoulders of his extremely distinguished Permanent Secretary, H. M. Patel. This had a very deleterious effect indeed on civil service morale.

All this was happening, it should be remembered, at a time when the government's wide-ranging social and economic programmes were placing an enormous strain on the top-level administrators. This strain was further increased by the introduction in the late 1950s of democratic decentralisation (panchayati raj), which involved giving responsibility for the implementation of many of the government's socio-economic projects to a pyramid of locally-elected authorities. Previously, although civil servants at the secretarial and departmental levels had had to adapt themselves to new political masters, those operating in the districts enjoyed considerable discretion, within the ambit of policies formulated by the Central and state governments. Panchayati raj, however, means that the District Officer has to work in cooperation with an elected Zilla Parishad, the Block Development Officer with an elected Panchayat Samiti, and the humble Village Level Worker with an elected panchayat. With the consequent politicisation of administration in the district and below, the tensions inherent in the relations between administrators and politicians begin to affect the *whole* of the administrative machine, and not merely its top echelons. Indeed, the field administrators find themselves in an even more difficult position than their Secretariat-based bosses, since they become simultaneously responsible to the relevant elected body and to their own hierarchical superiors. Moreover, in the so-callad *mofussil* areas, where elected representatives tended to be a pretty rough-and-ready lot, the difficulties of political-administrative communication are even more severe than in the capitals. The administrator, say Kothari and Roy, 'responds to the challenge in two ways. In the first place, he seeks the support of powerful local leaders for protecting his own position. In the second place, he treats administrative rules, regulations and procedures as protective devices and tries to protect himself by greater adherence to them'. The result, as the two authors point out, is a 'displacement of goals'.

Coping with these many-sided problems has been primarily the responsibility of the ICS and of its successor, the IAS. Those in the older service, proud of its traditions, did their best, with considerable success, to pass them on to the IAS recruits. Changes in organisation and in spirit, therefore, have been gradual, although some observers see them as significant. Whereas Morris-Jones, for instance, stresses the continuity between the ICS and the IAS, Bottomore, among others, considers that the gap between the old hands and the new recruits is widening, as a result of the attractions for the latter of 'regional as opposed to western culture' and of their greater awareness of the need to adapt their behaviour to politicians in whose presence 'public school manners are not always likely to be very helpful'.

At the 'business' end of the administrative machine, the District Officer has retained his predominance, and to some extent his prestige. Occupying a position comparable in many respects with that of the French *préfet,* this generalist administrator is the government's maid-of-all-work, exercising jurisdiction over an area which, depending on local circumstances, may be as large as 27,000 square miles and contain as many as three million people.

It is in the field, however, that the change in the administrator's role has been most obvious. In British days the DO regarded himself – and indeed was sometimes regarded – as the 'father of his people'. This self-image, however, lost a great deal of its lustre as Indians replaced Britons on the captain's bridge, as the complexity of the post's duties, with the accompanying flood of paper-work, increased, and as district administration, particularly after the introduction of panchayati raj, became more and more politicised. The DO now has less direct contact with 'his' people and more with their political representatives, who have to be conciliated, cajoled and 'squared'. Moreover, work in rural areas (which, in a country where some seventy per cent of the people are dependent on farming, is necessarily the lot of most DOs) does not possess the charm for the upper-class, high-caste and highly educated Indian that it often possessed for the British expatriate, particularly as the opportunities for developing a personal style have become greatly diminished. Secretariat service at New Delhi or in one of the state capitals seems much preferable. There lie the power and the opportunities for advancement, as well as the amenities of civilised living. Few DOs, therefore, now regard their translation to the secretariat in the manner of David Symington, who, in his pseudonymous memoirs, wrote:

With the passing weeks I grew more and more certain that I did not like the secretariat. Both the nature of my work and the surroundings in which it was done were repellent. To read a score or two of files, to write something on them, to drop them on the floor of my gloomy cell – what a contrast to the teeming life of my offices in the districts! I had grown used to having the world flow around me, clerks, police officers, lawyers, applicants, witnesses . . . and prisoners.

Nevertheless, it is in the district – although initially in a subordinate capacity, not as DO – that the IAS recruit normally starts his career. As Indian government is federally organised, and as the district is an administrative unit of the state government, the new officer, although centrally recruited to an all-India service by competitive examination organised by the Union Public Service Commission, is assigned to a state 'cadre', just as in British days he would have been assigned to a provincial cadre. To this cadre he remains attached, at least in theory, for the rest of his official life, even though the greater or at least more significant part of it may be spent in one of the coveted secretariat posts in New Delhi. For when serving the Union government he is 'on assignment to the Centre', with the agreement, willingly or unwillingly given, of the state government concerned.

This use of members of the all-India civil service 'aristocracy' as occupants of some of the key positions in the service of the state governments is a very important feature of Indian administration. It makes for a degree of uniformity which would otherwise be unattainable, and it is generally and rightly regarded as one of the main unifying forces that mitigate the fissiparous tendencies which have grown so strong in the political arena. The provision that no more than fifty per cent of the IAS personnel recruited in a given state shall serve in that state's administrative cadre shows that the IAS is being consciously used as a nation-building instrument. But how long this provision can survive the upsurge of linguistic exclusiveness and regional patriotism is open to doubt; for a situation in which many of the state's senior administrative officers have imperfect command over the local language (such as Taub discovered in Orissa) becomes increasingly intolerable. Already, the rule that twenty per cent of the IAS officers in a state shall have been promoted from the state's own administrative service is making for greater 'localisation'.

The IAS is not the only all-India service. There are other services which, although centrally recruited, are available to the state governments as well as to the central government. In British days, a variety of specialised all-India services was created. The most vital of these was the Police Service, but there were also services for agriculture, forestry, engineering and education. These, as Asok Chanda says, were intended 'to provide manpower at the higher levels for the technical departments, both at the centre and in the provinces, and were supported by corresponding services organised on a provincial basis'. With the advent of provincial autonomy, in the 1930s, however, all except the Police Service were abolished. In Chanda's view, this was 'unquestionably a retrograde step', the impact of which 'was visible in a deterioration of the development of forestry, agriculture and irrigation in the provinces and a fall in their educational and engineering standards'. Owing to the suspicion felt by state politicians towards all-India services, a product of their dislike of undue dependence on the centre for the supply of top-level personnel, independent India had to wait many years before it became politically possible to restore some of the disbanded corps, by means of constitutional amendment. In the 1960s, partly as a result of the states' realisation that their development programmes were suffering, the necessary support was enlisted for the reconstitution of the Engineering and Forestry Services and for the creation of a Medical and Health Service. This fresh departure was facilitated by the fact that the same party ruled both in New Delhi and in most of the state capitals. However, with the loss of Congress dominance and the growth of centrifugal tendencies, one cannot feel confident about the future of these recreated and newly-created all-India services.

Although members of the ICS and IAS occupy the key administrative posts in New Delhi, the centre obviously cannot do without services of its own, not to be shared on an all-India basis with the states. In British days the most important of these 'superior' services were Imperial Customs, Indian Audit, Indian Political, and Income Tax. Today, there are more than twenty of them, ranging from Audit and Accounts to Archeological. Personnel for the more technical ones are separately recruited from among applicants possessing relevant qualifications; the others, although operating independently, rely on a common competitive examination. One of the characteristics of these services (which is paralleled by the corresponding services at the state level) is a strong tendency to develop a caste-like exclusiveness, which is inevitably accompanied by considerable and sometimes bitter inter-service jealousy. As each service has evolved its own grades, salary-structure, promotion rules and disciplinary regulations, transfer from one to another becomes difficult and usually impossible. Normally, a man's only way out of the narrow confines of the superior service which he has joined is deputation to the secretariat – a privilege that cannot be enjoyed by more than a small minority.

In addition to the all-India services and the central services, there are separate public services, both generalist and specialist, in each of the states. These are recruited by the states' own Public Service Commissions. Structurally and organisationally, the states' services are very similar to the all-India and central services; but in quality they are generally, and in some cases markedly, inferior. The all-India and central services tend to cream off the best administrative talent, leaving the states' services with the second-best. Differences in level of competence of locally recruited administrators are, however, very wide as between one state and another. An advanced state, such as Maharashtra or Tamil Nadu, has a sufficient reserve of administrative talent both to provide a disproportionate number of recruits to the all-India and central services and to equip itself with a comparatively reputable service of its own. A backward one, such as Orissa, Assam or Rajasthan, has to scrape the bottom of the barrel. This, undoubtedly, is the main reason for the decision to reconstitute or create certain all-India specialist services, the existence of which enables the backward state to obtain the help of administrators educated in and recruited from its more advanced neighbours.

Structurally, Indian public administration follows the 'Whitehall' model as faithfully as is possible in conditions so different from those prevailing in the United Kingdom. There are departments with ministers, advised by the equivalent of an administrative class, at their head, and a bewildering collection of *ad hoc* agencies, under varying degrees of departmental supervision. Also, as in Whitehall, there is an enormous and persisting problem of demarcation and co-ordination, which in India is greatly exacerbated by federalism. Neither at the Centre nor in the states are departmental jurisdictions made to conform with any clear principle. The familiar process of creation, fission and fusion has been in continuous operation, propelled by political rather than by administrative needs. Overlapping and poor coordination of related functions are perennial problems, giving rise to periodical *cris de coeur* from ministers themselves. For instance, S. K. Patil, then Minister of Irrigation and Power, in a speech to the Lok Sabha in 1958, complained that 'there was little coordination even in such a vital matter as food production.'

He said that if he had his way, he would like a thorough stream-lining of the entire administrative structure. There was, at present, the Planning Commission which went far beyond mere planning. There was his ministry responsible for the construction of irrigation projects to increase food production. Then came the Food and Agriculture Ministry and a host of departments in different states dealing with the same subject. On top of all this, there was the Community Projects Department, also concerned with food pro-duction. He was aghast to find how many departments were dealing with the same subject. But when it came to a question of fixing responsibility, everyone wanted to get out of it.

Since Independence, two attempts have been made to con-sider the administrative structure as a whole and to produce realistic proposals for its reform. The first, undertaken for the Cabinet by Gopalaswami Ayyangar in 1948, gave rise to plenty of discussion but little action. The second, undertaken by the Administrative Reforms Commission in 1968, is too recent for one to be able to assess its influence.

The task of administrative rationalisation is more difficult in India than in England, since the obstacles in its way are more frustrating. The heavy weight of administrative tradition is reinforced by the self-interest of civil servants, anxious to protect themselves against redundancy in a country where governments have totally failed to reduce the high proportion of unemployed among persons with secondary and higher education. Except at the very highest level, administrative personnel are in-adequately educated and trained, and consequently obstinately devoted to the routines with which they are familiar. There is a very strong sense of hierarchy, and an almost automatic promotion system which discourages initiative and encourages inertia. Inter-service jealousies and inter-departmental rivalries increase the sensitivity of civil servants to reforms which affect the relativities of status and the distribution of career-opportunities. Lastly, as we have seen, there are built-in resistances arising from the sheer size and variety of the country and from the federal features of its political constitution.

Of these, the dead weight of tradition is probably the most important single cause as in a sense it embraces all the others. It is felt from the top to the bottom of the administrative hierarchy. For instance, the organisation of the secretariat, where, both at the centre and in the states, the most vital of administrative decisions are taken, is not substantially different from what it was in British days, except to the extent that, with the expansion of governmental functions, particularly in the field of social and economic development, it has become more cumbersome and complicated. To understand why this organisation is now outdated, one must contrast the functions it performed under the British raj with those that it is being called upon to perform today. Comparatively little concerned with the promotion and organisation of development, its main duties then lay in the disposition of individual cases in accordance with the law and the regulations. Most of its business was not self-generated, but came to it from outside, to be dealt with in the light of well-established and only slowly-changing policies. In the words of Asok Chanda, it acted as a 'tribunal of reference and general supervision'.

As long as this situation persisted, there could be little objection to the senior officials being birds of passage and holding their posts on a 'deputation' basis. The 'office', consisting of members of the central or provincial secretariat service, provided the experience and embodied the traditions. Nor was there very strong objection to a long line of command, stretching from the humble Assistant (who made the first note on the file) to the Secretary, who made the final decision in all important matters not sufficiently important to be referred to the appropriate member of the Viceroy's Executive Council. Yet, even before Independence, the sheer length of the line (Assistant – Section Officer – Assistant Secretary – Under Secre-

tary – Deputy Secretary – Joint Secretary – Secretary) was causing some concern. Today, it causes serious delay, without, by
way of compensation, reducing the burden of detailed decision-
making on the men at the top. Over-centralisation, of course,
tends to be typical of administration in developing countries,
and is not merely a product of organisational inertia; pushing
the final decision-taking responsibility up the administrative
hierarchy is a reflection of lack of self-confidence among subordinate personnel and of an often well-justified fear of being
'bawled out' by superiors. Nevertheless, organisational reform,
particularly if accompanied by better job-description and more
adequate training, could offer a useful counter-weight to these
tendencies.

Procrastination and congestion are the enemies, which draw
additional sustenance from a number of other features of
Secretariat organisation and procedure. The decision-making
process, for instance, is made more complex and time-consuming as a result of the multiple inter-departmental and inter-
agency clearances that are now required, particularly in respect
of proposals that involve the use of scarce resources. This has
been illustrated, by one of the present authors, in . a previous
book, by means of the following little case-study:

The agency concerned is the Andhra Pradesh Mining Corporation,
a state-owned public enterprise. . . . The subject-matter is foreign
exchange. When the Managing Director requires further supplies
of this scarce commodity to purchase equipment, he first has to
apply to the Bureau of Mines for an 'essentiality certificate'. Before
rendering it, the bureau may have to consult with the Export
Promotion Department (Ministry of Commerce and Industry), which
is naturally anxious that imported equipment should be used, as
far as possible, in industries with good export potentialities. Clearance is also needed from the Development Wing of the ministry,
which is concerned with plan priorities, and which will certainly
inquire whether there is any possibility of obtaining the equipment
from an indigenous source. Another application goes to the 'sponsoring' ministry, the Ministry of Mines and Fuel, which will refer
the matter to the Department of Economic Affairs (Ministry of
Finance) for foreign exchange clearance. If problems arise at this
stage, there will be correspondence with the Bureau of Mines and
the Development Wing. When these have been settled, the Ministry

of Mines and Fuel issues a clearance letter, of which one copy goes to the Chief Comptroller of Imports and another to the Andhra government. The Corporation then prepares its application for an import licence and sends it to the Chief Comptroller, who will require another copy, for confirmation, from the Ministry of Mines and Fuel. When the comptroller has issued the licence, together with a letter of authority, the corporation is at last free to place its order with the overseas supplier.

Since that was written, the names of some of the ministries and other agencies have changed, but the problem which it illustrates remains. Procedures, originally devised in British days to ensure that everyone is consulted and that no-one makes a 'mistake', have been extended to new fields of policy where speed rather than 'correctness' is the first requirement. It is hardly surprising that an International Bank Mission should have demanded that some way should be found 'of eliminating at least the major of these detailed checks and controls and of decentralising the process of economic decision'. Since 1963, when the mission reported, a considerable effort has been made to simplify and rationalise procedures of the kind illustrated by our case-study. Indeed, if this had not been so it is possible that the mission's ominous prediction to the effect that the government of India would break down under the strain might have been fulfilled. But few students of Indian public administration would claim that as yet reform has gone far enough.

Nowhere is the traditional 'checks-and-balances' approach to the problem of coordination better illustrated than in the operations of the Ministry of Finance. Its efforts to ensure that every item of expenditure is properly authorised and correctly accounted for have had the effect that no-one is prepared to take responsibility for an expenditure decision who can pass it on to someone else. In a vigorous criticism of the system whereby all items of expenditure were subject to multiple sanctions by the ministry, the Estimates Committee of the Lok Sabha pointed out that fear of disallowance was so deep-seated that 'even where there are delegations of powers and the administrative ministry could normally take the decision itself, it has often resorted to consultation with the Ministry of Finance in order to escape any criticism later on'. The committee also showed how the frequent failure of spending departments to plan their project outlays compels the Ministry of Finance to engage in the *ad hoc* sanctioning of individual items, with the result that by the time the spending department 'prepares to start a scheme or to go ahead with it, a good part of the year is already over and it is suddenly found at the end of the year that the non-utilised funds may lapse' or that the department 'may have to approach again the Ministry of Finance for including the amounts in the budget and according fresh expenditure sanction'. Both the pre-eminence of the Ministry of Finance and the complex of regulations through which it endeavours to ensure the correctness of expenditure decisions and disbursements of funds date from the period of the British raj. Their total effect, oddly enough, is to reduce rather than to enhance the sense of financial responsibility in the operational agencies and hence to 'prove' the necessity of subjecting them to a whole battery of time-consuming checks. Admittedly, there have been significant improvements in financial procedures since the Estimates Committee produced its critical report, quoted above. Nevertheless, right up to the present day the planners have found it necessary to engage in persistent criticism of the system itself, which is undoubtedly responsible for much infructuous expenditure and many delays in the realisation of objectives.

The most encouraging thing is that informed Indians are fully aware of these organisational and procedural defects. They have been the subject of many reports, both at the centre and in the states, particularly since the adoption of economic planning raised the strain on and the tensions within the administration to new levels. Right at the beginning of the period of planning, the government had the benefit of two highly critical, if over-generalised, reports from A. D. Gorwala, a distinguished civil servant, and Paul Appleby, the well-known American consultant. Moreover, something has been done to reduce the length of the line of command, to speed up the decision-taking process, to expedite clearances and to improve coordination; and much attention has been paid at all levels to 'O and M' and to the diffusion, through in-service training, of knowledge of up-to-date administrative methods.

Some of the more important modifications of the traditional administrative system actually pre-date Independence. One of the most important of these was the creation of a Finance and Commerce 'pool', consisting of persons, recruited from the ICS-IAS and the central services, who specialise in and receive training for economic administration. This represented the first overt recognition that there were certain top posts that could not be suitably filled by 'birds of passage' and for which experience of district administration was not the most relevant qualification. The pool underwent reorganisation as the 'Central Administrative Pool' in 1957, when it was also supplemented by an Industrial Management Pool, consisting of public servants available for employment in the increasing number of public enterprises. Neither of the pools, however, has worked very successfully; indeed, the Industrial Management Pool has virtually been written off as a failure.

One of the difficulties experienced by the student of Indian administration is that of arriving at a just assessment of its achievements. Failures are so obvious that they tend to obscure successes, which receive far less publicity among a hyper-critical Indian public. One persistently receives the impression that administrative collapse is just around the corner, particularly if one accepts, *au pied de la lettre,* the alarmist statements of certain distinguished retired civil servants. Some of this alarmism has rubbed off on to the International Bank which, in its enthusiasm for free enterprise, has presented a horrifying picture of bureaucratic procrastination and mismanagement. A more balanced and realistic assessment was produced by the framers of the Third Five Year Plan. As this remains as relevant today as when it was written, it is still worth quoting:

The past decade has been a period of considerable change and adaptation in the field of administration. Innovations have been introduced and new institutions established, although perhaps many of them have yet to be integrated with one another and with the structure as a whole. With the increase in the range of government's responsibilities and in the tempo of development, the volume and complexity of administrative work has also grown. The administrative machinery has been strained and, at many points in the structure, the available personnel are not adequate in quality and numbers. The administrative burden of carrying out plans of development, large as it is at present, will increase manifold ..., and doubtless new problems of public relations will also come up.

In the recent past, certain aspects of administration have attracted pointed attention. These include the slow pace of execution in many fields, problems involved in the planning, construction and operation of large projects, especially increase in costs and non-adherence to time-schedules, difficulties in training men on a large enough scale and securing personnel with the requisite calibre and experience, achieving co-ordination in detail in related sectors of the economy and – above all, enlisting widespread support and co-operation from the community as a whole.

Perhaps the most useful feature of this very generalised assessment is its emphasis on personnel problems. So far, our concern has been mainly with questions of organisation and procedure; but it would be grotesquely inadequate to look at these in isolation, if only because no administrative system can be better than the people who man it. Indeed, the most vital questions confronting Indian administration are how to improve the quality of personnel at all levels, how to provide them with more adequate motivations, and – most important of all – how to enlist a sufficient number of properly qualified persons to staff the ever-expanding government departments and the proliferating specialised agencies (such as those concerned with the stimulation of agricultural and industrial development) that the process of planning has spawned. These problems have now received full recognition, but in the early years of Independence they were comparatively neglected, with results that are writ large in the records of the second and third planning exercises. In particular, the work-capacity and adaptability of the 'generalist' ICS-IAS were strained to the breaking point, and too little attention was paid to improving the quality and capacity of lower and middle-level personnel.

Even today, although training courses, both in-service and pre-service, abound, training of the highest quality tends to be reserved for those recruited to the IAS and the other 'superior' services. The most important part of this training is that provided by the yearly induction course at Mussoorie, where the main subjects of study are administration, social and political history, economics, criminal law, the Constitution and the Five Year Plans, and where theoretical instruction is combined with some three months' practical experience, comparable with the more prolonged 'stage' that is one of the features of the French *Ecole Nationale d'Administration,* which has provided the Mussoorie school with some of its inspiration.

Mussoorie must be counted as one of the successes of Indian administrative reform, not only because it provides the administrative recruit with the basic knowledge he needs, but because it has made an important contribution towards the preservation of the top administrators' *esprit de corps.* 'No-one who has met a class of probationers', writes W. H. Morris-Jones, 'can fail to be impressed by their keenness and awareness. The valuable part of the ICS 'ethos' has been astonishingly preserved.' One may legitimately ask, however, whether the preservation of the ICS ethos, valuable as it has been in so many respects, can now be regarded as a priority task – and, indeed, whether the old type of *esprit de corps,* quasi-aristocratic in implication and expression, can be sustained in a country that not only claims to be democratic but almost daily becomes increasingly politicised.

Aloofness from ordinary people is generally said to be characteristic, not only of the ICS-IAS, but of administrators generally, but how far that is so and, more importantly, how far it is resented by the administrators' 'clients' is not easy to determine. Popular attitudes towards administrators in India have been comparatively little studied, and the difficulties in the way of obtaining hard information on such a topic are formidable. Eldersveld, Jagannadham and Barnabas, in a survey confined to the New Delhi area, found a higher incidence of 'supportive' attitudes and a lower incidence of 'complete alienation' among rural than among urban people. On the other hand, it was also revealed that one third of the farmers had no contact whatever with the officials responsible for administering the agricultural programmes and that over half did not know their community development officer. The ambiguity of such findings precludes the drawing even of tentative conclusions from them.

General observation, however, tends strongly to support the view that, although there has been much discussion about the development of a more democratic administrative style, there has been little change in the actual style, except to the extent that administrators at all levels have, of necessity, acquired the habit of treating elected politicians with at least outward respect. Moreover, there are several reasons why changes in style are unlikely to be more than very gradual. An obvious one is the fact that what is loosely termed casteism in the administration is constantly stimulated and sustained by the casteism that is still the predominant feature of the whole social order. Another is to be found in recruitment of the IAS (and, to a considerable extent, of the other superior services, both at the Centre and in the states) from a very narrow social stratum. Typically, the top administrator comes from an urban family which enjoys something that approaches a western standard of living and has at least some of the elements of a western outlook. Morris-Jones has indicated that of 350 appointees to the IAS over a few years, 200 were sons of government officials and a further 100 came from professional families. Nearly 100 had received a 'public school' education in India or abroad, and only 15 per cent came from the rural areas. When to all this is added a need for proficiency in English, as the main all-India language for mutual communication among the educated, it is clear that one has a public service which, at least in its higher echelons, is hardly more representative than it was in British days. Given the actual distribution of both opportunities and expectations, it is inevitable that this should be so.

There is some evidence, however, that it is becoming rather less homogeneous, both caste-wise and class-wise. Posts reserved for the 'backward' castes have of recent years been filled, and there seems to have been some increase in the number of recruits from families earning less than Rs 300 a month. 'Agriculturalists' also provide a higher proportion of recruits – although it must be remembered that this term covers a very wide range of socio-economic status. The greatest diversification has been the product of the provisions for promotion from the state services, and of the 'emergency' and 'special' recruitments of the post-war years, intended to fill up gaps left by the departure of the British and to increase the total size of the cadre. Recruitment by promotion from the state services continues, but the 'emergency' and 'special' recruitments, being apparently once-for-all, are not likely to have a long term effect on the services' composition. By and large, therefore, Taub's generalisation holds good, that 'the IAS officers ... come from that section of society which would be most likely to produce offspring who could pass (the) competitive examination: that, is the wealthy, urban and educated classes.' Moreover, as wealth, town-dwelling and education are concentrated in particular regions, it is not surprising that, as in British days, a very high proportion of them come from New Delhi, Maharashtra and Madras.

This social distance of the IAS and State services from the mass of the population has been, to some extent, reinforced since Independence by greater physical distance, despite the advent of panchayati raj; for much of the top-level talent has become desk-bound in the Secretariats, while the administrators in the districts, being overwhelmed with paperwork, also spend a higher and higher proportion of their time seated in offices. Yet the very nature of the Indian government's policies would seem to demand a more intimate and continuous contact than ever before between the administrator and his clients, particularly in the rural areas; since the administrator is supposed to be inspiring and leading a great, popularly-based development effort. This is perhaps the most important of the situation's built-in contradictions.

As we have already seen, it is intensified by the administrator's persistent quest for the greater job-satisfaction that he thinks he will obtain from service in the secretariat. Even if he succeeds in this quest, he finds himself confronted by much the same kind of contradictions at a higher level. The politicians and pressure groups at New Delhi and in the state capitals, although somewhat more sophisticated than the local politicians and pressure groups, are no less importunate. Relations with the business community, in particular, tend to be unsatisfactory, not merely because the civil servant is the operator of numerous controls (e.g. over prices, industrial licenses, foreign exchange, distribution of commodities, etc.) but because he belongs to a professional group (and sometimes a caste-group) that regards the businessman with deep suspicion and 'business' as an inferior occupation.

The latter point is well illustrated by the answers given by Mr Taub's Orissa respondents, most of them civil servants and all belonging to the professional classes. Eighty-four per cent 'thought that businessmen needed to be controlled in every sphere by rules that limit their behaviour'. One response, presented by the author as reasonably representative, ran:

What is the businessman's motive? Maximum profit. What is the government's motive? That everybody gets a fair share. The two motives or first principles are in basic conflict. . . . Our businessmen have no self-restraint. . . . Government must simply curb these fellows.

This rather naive view of the relationship between government and business, although not typical, is common enough.

Fruitful contact between civil servants and other members of the community, therefore, tends to be limited. It is also not greatly desired by the administrators themselves. The service has tended to become inward-looking, obsessed with questions of status, pay and promotion. Status, with its concomitant exclusiveness, is more highly valued precisely because it has been eroded. This erosion is partly a consequence of relative economic deprivation. Civil service pay has notoriously lagged behind increases in the cost of living, and for senior civil servants has even declined in money terms. The top IAS scale is now Rs 3,500 a month, in comparison with a top ICS scale of Rs 4,000, despite a 200 per cent inflation since 1947. (One should note, however, that to some extent this is offset by the enjoyment of considerable privileges and perquisites, particularly in respect of transport and housing.) Although having a standard of living far exceeding that of the majority of his countrymen, the civil servant compares his rewards with those that accrue to the private businessman, the professional business manager and even, particularly since the 'green revolution', the more prosperous, kulak-type agriculturalist. Status increasingly coincides with income, even in a country such as India, where traditionally this coincidence has been weak and even negative. Relative economic deprivation, however, is not the whole story. There has also been a certain decline, of which the Indian public is well aware, in the quality of the service, which is partly due to the undermining of university standards, and partly to the increased attractiveness of other occupations, such as business management, for some of the best of the young men who would previously have regarded membership of the

ICS-IAS as the summit of their ambitions. Business now seems to offer not only higher rewards but greater freedom. For the man with initiative, opportunities for promotion are superior and, despite government controls (which the man with initiative can often evade) there is far less red tape. One should hardly be surprised, therefore, that there is something of a crisis in civil service morale, and that the Planning Commission's frequent exhortations about 'toning up the administration' have not been very effective.

Together with declining morale has gone increasing corruption. This, in the nature of things, is difficult to document, but it is certainly a persistent worry to Indian administrative reformers. How much corruption there was in British days is uncertain, but it seems to have been largely confined to the lower echelons of the administration, and to have been extremely rare in the ICS and the other superior services. That most of the members of those services remain relatively immune to improper pressures seems probable, but that at least some of them have fallen from grace is universally admitted. When politicians are corrupt and clerks are corrupt, it is difficult for the administrative 'aristocrats' to remain immune, particularly when their opportunities for malpractice have been so greatly increased by the advent of the 'licence and permit raj' and their temptations to engage in it by the fall in their standards of living. Efforts to stamp out corruption by the establishment of Vigilance Committees and the like, both at the Centre and in the states, have not been very effective. For reasons now very well known, administrative corruption is almost unavoidable in developing societies, where western-type bureaucratic norms have not become fully internalised, and when the social system is such that the distinction between corruption and the loyalties associated with caste, community and the extended family cannot easily be made. Nevertheless, if it goes beyond a certain point, and particularly if it is seen to be on the increase, it cannot but undermine both the efficiency of the adminstrator and the trust that members of the public are prepared to place in him.

Again, one should beware of exaggeration. Administrative collapse has been as frequently staved off as it has been predicted. Indian critics of administration tend to think in apocalyptic terms, and to predict disaster unless the service immediately undertakes the exercise of self-purification. These Cassandra-like pronouncements are sometimes taken too seriously by foreign observers. Mr Taub, for instance, recognising that self-purification is highly unlikely, foresees nothing but woe if present trends continue. In his view, salvation depends on the restriction of administrative tasks to what he regards as manageable ones.

Unless the bureaucratic organisation can contract, emphasising those tasks it can do well, while creating independent sources of initiative to manage those it cannot, the administrative apparatus will one day collapse, prey to the rage of its hungry and frustrated people, who will turn to demagogues to accomplish what their present national leaders have so far failed to do.

This, in our opinion, leads nowhere. It would be very difficult to specify precisely what tasks the administration could abandon, and equally difficult to envisage just how a bureaucracy could 'create independent sources of initiative'. Nevertheless, it must be admitted that a situation not very dissimilar from the one Mr Taub predicts has actually arisen in certain areas, and particularly in West Bengal. Although bureaucratic resources are by no means exhausted, India will certainly have a tight corner to turn, administratively as well as politically. If she is to get round it, she will need to strengthen and diversify her public service rather than attempt to restrict it to the tasks that it has traditionally performed well.

(2) *The Military*

Whereas there is an abundance of information about Indian civil administration, comparatively little is known about her military institutions. Publications on the subject are rare and not always very informative, while the student of military matters receives even less encouragement than students of other politically sensitive subjects. As might be expected, there are a number of useful commentaries on India's defence *policies*, but for information on defence *organisation* we have to rely mainly on the formal information contained in handbooks.

Command of the armed forces is vested in the President of

the Republic. Policy is the responsibility of a number of Cabinet committees, of which the most important are the Defence Committee and the Defence Minister's Committee. The Ministry of Defence coordinates the work of the three services, and also has direct administrative responsibility for research and development, production, inter-service training and the National Cadet Corps.

Army headquarters, under a Chief of Army Staff, is divided into the familiar branches: General Staff, Adjutant General's, Quartermaster General's, Master General of Ordnance's, Engineer in Chief's and Military Secretary's. Territorial organisation is based on four commands, Eastern, Central, Western and Southern, each under a General Officer Commanding-in-Chief, with the rank of Lieutenant General. In addition to the regular army, there is a Territorial Army, which dates from 1949. Recruited from Indian nationals between the ages of eighteen and thirty-five, its main duties are to relieve the regular army of some of its more static responsibilities, to man coastal defence and anti-aircraft units, and, in case of need, to strengthen it with additional units. Members of the Territorial Army cannot be required to serve outside India.

The Naval Headquarters, under a Chief of the Naval Staff, has four branches, Staff, Personnel, Material and Naval Aviation, each under a Principal Staff Officer. It operates through four commands, one (under the Flag Officer Commanding, Indian Fleet) afloat and the other three (at Bombay, Cochin and Vishakhapatnam) ashore.

Air Headquarters, under a Chief of Air Staff, is divided into Air Staff, Administration, Policy and Plans, and Maintenance. The five commands are Eastern, Western, Central, Training and Maintenance.

Each service has its own training establishments, and a series of Defence Colleges, under the Ministry of Defence, is provided for inter-service training. Of these the most important are the National Defence College, modelled on the Imperial Defence College in Britain, to conduct training for senior officers, and the National Defence Academy, which gives a combined basic training for officer-cadets of all three services. Admission to the National Defence Academy is through written examination, conducted by the Union Public Service Commission.

Defence production is organised by the Department of Defence Supplies (established in 1965), the Department of Defence Production (established in 1962) and the Research and Development Organisation (established in 1958). One of the main purposes of these three bodies is to reduce India's dependence on foreign equipment for the three services by developing indigenous production, in both public and private sectors. The first serious effort in this direction was made during the period of Krishna Menon's occupancy of the Defence Ministry (1957–62), and the tempo was greatly stepped up, with more consideration for the real operational needs of the services, after the major border conflict with China in 1962. Public sector production is divided between the Ordnance Factories and a number of state-owned companies, such as Hindustan Aeronautics Ltd, Bharat Electronics Ltd, and Praga Tools Ltd.

In recruitment to the regular services and to the Territorial Army, the voluntary principle has been firmly maintained, both for officers and for other ranks. Compulsory membership of the National Cadet Force was introduced for male students in 1964, but has subsequently been abolished.

As with civilian administration, independent India took over from the British a going concern – a sizeable army, together with a much smaller navy and air force, trained by the British, subject to British-type organisation and discipline, and firmly indoctrinated in the British tradition of subordination to the civil authorities. The main immediate change was the replacement of British officers by Indian officers in the most senior posts. This, although it involved some pretty rapid promotion all the way up the line of command, was achieved with very little disruption, since a handful of Indian officers had already attained the rank of Brigadier. There was no question, as in the Congo at a later date, of giving staff rank to sergeants.

Opposition to the policy of continuity, however, made itself felt, and rather more strongly than in the case of the civil service. The more intense Indian nationalists, and particularly those on the Left, were not slow to point out that the armed forces had been the loyal servants of the British and had fought in a British war at a time when the Congress Party was sacrificing its leading cadres to the 'Quit India' campaign. But the Congress leadership, when in power, stood firm on the issue. It was as determined to retain the British-created armed forces as it was to retain the British-created ICS. The demand for the politicisation of the services, through the general absorption into the officer corps of members of the so-called Indian National Army, which, under Subhas Chandra Bose, had fought with the Japanese for a 'Free India', was resisted. Although the INA was honoured and fêted, there was no attempt to convert it into the nucleus of independent India's new army. Here the Congress leaders took a wise decision, from the point of view of maintaining civilian control over the armed forces. So far, the political subordination of the army has never been open to serious doubt. Not even a would-be coup d'état as feeble and ill-organised as that of 1962 in Ceylon has been attempted. One may guess that it might have been otherwise if the men on horseback had been graduates of the INA.

The nature of the armed forces, therefore, was predetermined by a clear political decision. Their mode of employment was dictated by an inescapable political fact – that of partition. At first, the army was heavily engaged in the holding of Kashmir against Pakistan-supported tribesmen; it then had the job of patrolling a long and sensitive frontier, including the cease-fire line in Kashmir itself. As, however, Partition had left India with the lion's share of both men and materials, this was a manageable task. It certainly made heavy demands on the national revenue budget, which saw an increase in the sums allotted for defence expenditure from Rs 1,451 million in 1948–49 to Rs 2,567 million in 1957–58. But over the same period items under 'development services' increased much faster, from Rs 292 million to Rs 1,541 million, while the share of defence in total revenue expenditure declined from 45.4 per cent to 40.7 per cent.

During the first decade of Independence, therefore, India's finances were by no means dominated, to the extent of those of many other new states, by defence expenditure. Nor did the military enjoy the social prestige or the political influence that it often enjoyed elsewhere. Politically, it played no role at all; socially, military service was just one honoured occupation among many. On the whole, this is still so. As

Lloyd and Susanne Rudolph write, 'the marriage market, a reasonably faithful barometer of career status in a society where marriages are still arranged, rates young men in the 'foreign firms' highest, in the Indian foreign and administrative services next, and then perhaps those in the defence forces'. In some parts of India, however, military service has such low prestige that practically no-one volunteers for it. Orissa, Gujerat and Andhra Pradesh, for instance, are virtual deserts for the recruiting-sergeant. The traditional 'martial races' of northern India, and particularly the Punjabis, still provide some 40 per cent of the recruits and a further 40 per cent (with a predominance of Tamils) come from the far south.

The prestige of the armed forces, however, increased significantly during the 1960s, when India felt her security to be seriously threatened and became involved in undeclared wars with both China and Pakistan. From the late fifties, moreover, the army once more became the subject of active political dispute and even, to a limited extent, found itself drawn into the political arena. Krishna Menon provided the provocation. Incapable of behaving other than as a stormy petrel, he was a curious choice as Defence Minister. In some respects he was a success – for instance, he gave a considerable fillip to defence production; but his blatant disregard for the sacred principle of seniority and his alleged regard for political conformity in matters of promotion to the senior posts created a crisis of morale, which culminated in an offer of resignation by the Chief of Staff, General Thimayya, in protest, among other things, against the rapid rise of General B. M. Kaul. Strategy as well as promotion was an issue in this dispute; for Menon firmly insisted, in the face of growing military doubts, that Pakistan was the only serious enemy, that China was friendly, and that the defences of the North-East Frontier Area were (to quote *Link,* a periodical active in the Menon cause) 'as safe as houses'. Both issues were raised again on the eve of the Indo-Chinese conflict, when Kaul's appointment as Chief of the General Staff provoked a parliamentary debate. Neither Kaul nor Menon, of course, professionally or politically survived the actual fighting of 1962, which revealed that the North-East Frontier Area defences were virtually non-existent.

This conflict proved the turning-point in the history of the

Indian armed forces since Independence. The necessary re-organisation of the army was undertaken by a new, dynamic and highly professional Chief of Staff, General Chaudhury. The aim was to raise the army's strength to over 800,000 effectives, disposed and equipped to meet the worst possible contingency: a simultaneous attack by Pakistan and China. Under a new programme for the indigenous production and foreign purchase of arms, care was taken to ensure that equipment supplies were closely related to the military training which the soldiers were required to undergo – a somewhat obvious requirement which had been rather badly neglected in former days. The Indo-Pakistan conflict of 1965, together with the apparent inability of the Indian army to put down the rebellion of Naga tribesmen, gave a new urgency to India's rearmament. Considerable funds were diverted from civilian to military expenditure, much to the detriment of the Third Five Year Plan, which in any case was not looking very healthy. Allocations for defence were stepped up from Rs 2,820 million in 1960–61 to Rs 9,430 million in 1966–67. (The projected figure for 1971–2 is Rs 11,110 million). The total strength of the armed forces reached 1,250,000 in 1968, of which the army accounted for 800,000. Assistance for this programme was obtained from the United States, Commonwealth countries, the Soviet Union, France and Germany. How much of this constituted 'aid' is not known, since the details of the arrangements made by India with each of the supporting countries have never been disclosed. We do know, however, that since 1965 the USSR has become the dominant supplier of India's military hardware.

The success of the new policy is hardly open to doubt. India is now the dominant military power in South Asia – so much so, in fact, that her soldiers are of the opinion that adequate defence capability has now been provided, with something to spare. Today, the army is more than ever available to the civilian authorities for internal security duties, and the increase in political and communal violence has considerably enhanced its law and order role. During the elections of 1971, for instance, an entire army division was deployed in West Bengal. This change of emphasis certainly gives no pleasure to the soldiers, as it tends to get them involved in political controversies and could result in the imposition of new strains on the army's hitherto exemplary unity. That the use of the army as a security force brings with it dangers to the army itself as well as to democratic institutions is too well known to need emphasis.

Fear of increasing this strain beyond the breaking point must give pause to those officers – if there are any – who may be thinking in terms of supplanting rather than supporting the civilian authorities. Another obstacle to an all-India *coup d'état* is the structure of the four territorial commands, each of which is more or less independently organised under its General Officer Commanding-in-Chief. Simultaneous action in the eighteen states, which are, to say the least, highly unlikely to adopt a common attitude towards a soldiers' rebellion, would be difficult. In the event of the military playing a direct political role, this is more likely, as we have seen, to take the form of a 'loyal' response to a call from a President who has decided actively to exercise his prerogatives as Commander in Chief – but this is hardly conceivable so long as the presidency remains in the hands of N. V. Giri or some other nominee of the 'new' Congress Party. So although a military take-over obviously cannot be ruled out, the obstacles to it, both objective and subjective, are far more serious in India than in many other new states. There is certainly no possibility of exact comparison, in this respect, between India and Pakistan, where democratic institutions had no opportunity to take firm root.

India, therefore, has not only a civil service which, by the standards of developing countries, is unusually competent, but armed forces which, so far, have proved entirely amenable to control by the civilian authorities. So long as the administration is able to ensure that the normal processes of government are carried on, and so long as the democratic politicians do not disgrace themselves irrevocably, there is a reasonable chance that constitutional forms of government can be preserved. Obvious countervailing forces are political confusion, political and communal violence, and corruption – all three of which are at present increasing dangerously. These, however, will have to reach a level far higher than that which has proved intolerable in countries whose political systems are less well-founded than the Indian and whose people are far more volatile than India's hitherto patient masses, before a Pakistan-type situation is likely to occur.

(3) *The Police*

As yet, the maintenance of law-and-order is mainly a matter for the police, whose duties are becoming increasingly onerous and, indeed, dangerous as the various forms of political and communal violence require the employment of forces which would normally be used mainly for the detection and prevention of 'ordinary' crime. Since the police play a pivotal role in India's administrative system, it is important to know something about their organisation and their relations with the public.

Again, the British legacy is obvious; in fact the basic structure of the police services is still that which was originally prescribed by the Police Act of 1861. Admittedly, the forces are now mainly under the control of the states; but each state force has an almost identical structure and operates under almost identical rules.

As we have seen, the Indian Police Service was the only all-India service, other than the ICS, that the Founding Fathers of the Constitution chose to retain; this, in itself, made for continuity and uniformity. Today, the superior positions in the state police forces (Inspector-General, Deputy Inspector, Superintendent and Assistant Superintendent) are normally occupied by members of the IPS, while the subordinate positions (Deputy Superintendent, Inspector, Sub-Inspector, Head Constable and Constable) are the prerogatives of the state police services.

In addition to this hierarchical division, there is a vertical one between the armed and unarmed branches. The latter run the police stations, investigate crime and perform a variety of duties most of which would be familiar to the British policeman. The armed police, on the other hand, live in cantonments and are comparatively remote from the public. They can be used – and nowadays are used with increasing frequency – to put down riots; they guard buildings and escort prisoners; and they attempt to exercise control over crowds.

In addition, the Union government has two police forces of its own. The Central Reserve is mainly used – nowadays with increasing frequency – to assist the state police forces in situations of emergency. The Central Bureau of Investigation is mainly concerned with the detection of corruption. It can operate in the states only with their approval, which up to now has been freely given. Both the Central Reserve and the CBI are responsible to the Union's Home Ministry.

Recruited by the Public Service Commission through competitive examination, the 'top brass' of the Indian police is highly educated. Among the rank-and-file, however, educational standards are abysmally low. For the ordinary police constable, the conditions of service are unattractive; the pay is very poor and the prospects of promotion are negligible. Recruitment at this level of the able and enterprising is therefore almost unknown. Consequently those members of the police force with whom the public has most frequent contact are not highly regarded, and their notorious propensity for petty corruption means that they receive very little cooperation. Whenever possible, Indians avoid the police.

Our principal concern here is with the police as maintainers of law and order, which is currently becoming a major problem, as political violence escalates. Broadly, there are four types of 'law and order' situations with which the police are expected to cope.

The first is organised protest in the urban areas, which may take the form of the demonstration, the *satyagraha*, the strike, the *hartal* or the fast, and can very readily become violent. Partly a legacy of pre-Independence politics, these types of action have also reflected the frustration felt by the opposition parties in a 'dominant party' situation. Today they are a habit, most firmly established in Calcutta, but hardly less common in the other major cities. Having so frequently conceded to agitation, as over the linguistic states issue, Indian governments have made a rod for their own backs, the full force of which is felt by their policemen. Organisers of demonstrations and comparable forms of public protest, however, have objects additional to, and sometimes more important than, the bringing to bear of influence on the political decision-making process; for a 'good' demonstration is a surer, as well as a more spectacular, way of recruiting members for an organisation than the canvass or the ordinary meeting. Moreover, if its leaders are lucky enough to be apprehended, they can wear that crown of martyr-dom which in India is so frequently the passport to a political reputation. If the police could simply concentrate on controlling demonstrations and on breaking them up as soon as they begin to get violent, their task would be reasonably manageable. In fact, it is much less simple, since they cannot nowadays rely on the support of the political authorities. Minority governments and disorderly coalitions in the states have stimulated ministers themselves to use the demonstration as a means of strengthening their own uncertain positions, and even those who have an occupational interest in the maintenance of law and order, such as Home Ministers, are reluctant to give the police too free a hand. Not surprisingly, the morale of the police has been thoroughly undermined in many urban areas.

The second category of 'law and order' situations is that which now arises with increasing frequency in the rural areas, as a result of violence organised by the Naxalites and other leftists. For this, the 'green revolution' is at least partly to blame, to the extent that it has widened the gap that separates the more substantial landowning peasantry from the sharecroppers, tenants and labourers, and in some cases has increased the incidence of unemployment. Forcible occupation of the land, sometimes accompanied by the murder of landlords, has spread from West Bengal, Andhra Pradesh and Kerala, where there is a long tradition of rural protest, to Assam, Rajasthan, Madras, Madhya Pradesh, Gujerat, Mysore and Orissa. In coping with it, the police are at a severe disadvantage, even when adequately supported at the ministerial level; they are very thinly spread on the ground, hampered by defective communications and unable to obtain the cooperation of members of the public, who, even when hostile to Naxalite activities, fear the consequences of providing information about them.

The third category is the 'confrontation' between groups of citizens stirred by mutual hatred. The standard example, with which India has long and sad familiarity, is the Hindu-Muslim riot, but caste hostilities within the Hindu community also pro-vide the police with a sizeable problem, as when Untouchables attempt to take advantage of their formal legal equality to infringe traditional taboos. Currently, it is the antagonism between Hindus and Muslims that provides the police with its major headache. Since 1960 communal riots have shown a marked if irregular increase, reaching a horrifying climax in the Gujerat 'killing' of September 1969, when over a thousand Muslims were murdered and a great deal of property was destroyed. As the police inevitably have their own sympathies in these situations, they can hardly avoid charges of partisanship, particularly if they stand by and do virtually nothing, as is frequently the case. Similar to communal riots, but without the additional animus provided by religious differences, are the fights between rival political groups. Of recent years these have become very frequent in West Bengal, where they are often associated with the kidnapping of politicians. During the period when the Communist Party (Marxist) was the dominant coalition partner in West Bengal's government and occupied the Home Ministry, the police found itself almost totally inhibited from doing anything effective about these affrays, which became so common as to cease to be particularly newsworthy.

Finally, the police have to contend with the more or less spontaneous outbursts occasioned by the frustrations of urban life. Calcutta, with small wonder, is notorious for such outbursts, which are often difficult enough to distinguish from political demonstrations, since the same *dramatis personae* are to be seen in the leading ranks. Calcutta's trams are the worst sufferers on such occasions, since the burning of trams – which started in the days when they were foreign-owned – has acquired an almost ritual significance.

The cliché about the unhappiness of the policeman's lot, therefore, is rather more than a cliché in India. His situation, moreover, becomes increasingly difficult. New forms of violent demonstration, such as the *gherao,* in which the management of a business or administration of a government agency is subjected to siege tactics, present him with unfamiliar problems, while political demonstration becomes less and less distinguishable from ordinary crime. The distinction, for instance, between a Naxalite, who is a politico of a new type, and a *dacoit,* who is familiar enough to the police as a member of a band of organised robbers, is a fine one, since Naxalite activities provide dacoits with convenient 'ideological' cover. In the same way, urban demonstrations of an overtly political kind provide profitable opportunities for *goondas*, those professional strong-arm men who are prepared to hire their services to any demagogue in search of trouble. Inadequately supported, occasionally suborned, and always criticised by the political authorities, the police often do not know which way to turn, in the most literal sense. If they hold their fire, they may be held responsible for a massacre; if they fire, they may be condemned as fascist pigs.

One must not, however, exaggerate. The law and order problem that confronts the police is difficult enough in the big cities and in certain areas of the countryside; but over the greater part of India the situation is not, as yet, substantially different from what it was in the days of the British raj. For most of the time, the police are concerned with ordinary crime, which they deal with by the time-honoured methods of investigation and apprehension according to the best of their limited abilities. The Indian man in the street, while showing little disposition to cooperate with them, is glad enough of their presence. According to Professor David Bayley's findings, even demonstrators, in their calmer moments, are prepared to justify the repressive police actions of which they have been the victims. Nevertheless, with the growth of violent behaviour, political and otherwise, the task of the police is increasing in difficulty, and so is their exposure to improper pressures. Numerically, with one policeman to eight or nine hundred Indians, they are strong enough to cope, neither better nor worse than their counterparts in many other countries, with the more normal forms of lawbreaking; but now that, in so many areas, the abnormal has become the normal, they are subjected to strains that can quickly become intolerable.

Oddly enough, there are few general works on Indian government and politics in which the police receive more than a peripheral mention. The comparatively extended treatment which they have here been given is intended to redress the balance. As we said at the beginning of this chapter, independence usually increases rather than diminishes the problem of maintaining law and order. The police, therefore, are as essential to the preservation of India's democratic system as are the 'development' administrators; and their task is certainly no less difficult.

8 Planning the Economy

Logically, if not chronologically, the first task of the government of any newly independent country is to consolidate its own authority and to establish the legitimacy of the political system under which it operates. Only then can the tasks of the rehabilitation and development of the economy be undertaken with hope of success. For the achievement of the first task, the government formed by Nehru in 1947 was comparatively well placed. Congress, being an 'aggregative' party and continuing to enjoy the great reputation it had acquired during the course of the national independence struggle, was popular among the politically-vocal classes and at least accepted by the remainder of the community. The process of integrating the former princely states was skilfully acomplished with remarkable speed. Moreover, Nehru, and to a lesser extent the other members of the top Congress leadership, had acquired considerable charismatic powers. It is not surprising, therefore, that the government was able to proceed without very much delay to the formulation and implementation of national economic policies aimed at the elimination of India's 'backwardness'.

The urgency of this task needed no underlining, and Nehru in particular was extremely conscious of it, with his deep hatred of poverty and profound belief in the necessity of economic growth. Indeed, all well-informed Indians were aware not only that India was miserably poor, even by the standards of the less developed parts of the world, but that during the later years of British rule she had suffered from economic stagnation and even, in some respect, retrogression.

Admittedly the 1930s and 1940s had seen significant progress in manufacturing industry, as may be illustrated by the rise in the average number or workers employed in manufacturing concerns from 1.6 million in 1935 to 2.5 million in 1944. Moreover, the country had become a major exporter of textiles, and had achieved self-sufficiency in certain commodities, such as cement, sugar and soap. Power for industry, however, was perpetually in short supply, and many primary products, such as oilseeds, were being exported raw for lack of local processing plants; while industry as a whole provided employment for little ·more than 10 per cent of the productively-employed population, well over 60 per cent of which remained engaged in agriculture. It was here that the situation was truly alarming. The average annual production of rice, which formed the staple food of a substantial part of the rapidly increasing population, had undergone no increase between the quinquennium 1925–29 and the quinquennium 1935–39, while during the 1930s there was an actual decrease in the net area sown with crops. Furthermore the Second World War, while accelerating the development of India's industries, had inevitably introduced grave distortions into her economy as a whole. The only major advantage it had brought with it was the accumulation of considerable sterling balances on which India, with Britain's permission, could draw. The need for a coherent economic policy, if India was to overcome her disadvantages and realise her opportunities, was fully evident. Indeed, the Congress leadership had long been committed to the development of the economy through planning, and even before Independence had been engaged in drawing up plans of its own.

The question of the general shape that rehabilitation and development were to take had, therefore, already partly been answered. There was general agreement that it should be as rapid as the mobilisation of resources would permit and that its benefits should be widely diffused rather than concentrated in a few hands. As we have seen, the Constitution's Directive Principles of State Policy registered this agreement in proclaiming the right of all citizens to 'an adequate means of livelihood', in asserting that 'the ownership and control of the material resources of the community' should be 'so distributed as best to subserve the common good', and in enjoining that 'the operation of the economic system' should not 'result in the concentration of wealth and means of production to the common detriment'. It was also generally agreed that major attention would have to be given to the improvement of infrastructural services (e.g. transport, electricity, water, sewage, irrigation, education, etc.), that industrial expansion and diversification would have to be actively promoted, and that a programme of land reform would have to be combined with one of community development. All this obviously seemed to demand economic planning, and already the new government had a considerable number of alternative plans (including Congress's own) available to it – for instance a plan drawn up by a group of Bombay industrialists, a so-called Gandhian plan (drafted by one of the Mahatma's disciples, Shriman Narayan), a plan produced by the ex-Communist, M. N. Roy, on behalf of the Indian Federation of Labour, as well as a series of detailed sectoral plans formulated during the later years of the war by the British bureaucracy, with the assistance of officially acceptable Indians. All of these, however, required further consideration, considerable elaboration, and adaptation to the new circumstances of independence.

Behind this wide consensus on the general principles of economic policy and planning, there was, of course, considerable disagreement among the members of the Congress political elite. Nehru, for instance, was a socialist of Marxian sympathies, while Patel, the other member of the initial duumvirate, had strong business connections and adopted a far more sympathetic attitude towards private enterprise. There were also the Gandhians, who lacked Nehru's and Patel's enthusiasm for industrialisation, and thought in terms of a predominantly agricultural and handicraft economy, with the more or less self-sufficient village as its base. These disagreements, which necessarily imposed certain constraints on the government's economic policy-makers, reflected the diversity of Congress's support. Socialism, of one sort or another, had captured the imaginations of most of the intellectuals, but private business men and the more prosperous peasants were naturally suspicious of it – a suspicion which became clearly more evident when, during the 1950s, the government's economic policies gradually took shape and were given a 'socialist' label. These constraints, however, were as nothing in comparison with those imposed by what Marxists would call the 'objective situation'. Predominantly, India was an agrarian, peasant economy, much of it non-monetised, in which the centres of economic decision-taking were dispersed, attachment to traditional ways of doing things was extremely strong and the kinds of motivation said to be characteristic of 'economic man' were correspondingly weak. There was, indeed, nothing that could be justly described as an 'economic system', and the only public force which might conceivably help to bring one into existence, the administration, was thinly spread and ill-adapted to the task. Clearly there were severe limitations on what any government could achieve in fulfilment of Congress's promise of a better life for all.

Nevertheless it was inevitable that heavy emphasis should be placed on the pioneering, stimulatory, and regulatory role of the state. The former British bureaucracy, impelled by the needs of war, had itself come to recognise the need for public initiative, and Nehru, as a socialist, was determined that the state should pioneer on a scale far exceeding anything that had been hitherto attempted. By 1954 he had persuaded Congress, without too much difficulty, to adopt the objective of 'a socialistic pattern of society'. His personal influence may also be seen in the important role which was given to the Planning Commission, in the statements of objectives contained in the Five Year Plans and in the emphasis placed by the plans on increasing the role of public enterprise in the economy and on extending cooperative forms of organisation (e.g. for credit, marketing, and even production) in the countryside. In all this, India was attempting to follow, in her own democratic way, the example of the USSR, a country greatly admired by Nehru for its economic if not for its political achievements. This influence became considerably strengthened when P. C. Mahalanobis became Nehru's top economic adviser. In the later 1950s even the Chinese cooperatives evoked a sympathetic and would-be imitative response among a section of the Congress leaders. But as the political systems of both Russia and China were rejected, and democracy continued to be strongly emphasised, it seemed that India was embarking on an experiment in democratic socialism – an experiment unique among the countries of the Third World, which was regarded by foreign observers with a mixture of hope and apprehension, according to their political predilections.

In the immediate aftermath of Independence, these interesting developments were still some distance ahead. The solution of urgent political problems necessarily took precedence over the planning of the economy, and indeed for several years the economic policies of the new government displayed very little coherence. Despite an attempt to define the respective roles of the public and private sectors by an Industrial Policy Resolution of 1948, uncertainty about the future among business men tended to inhibit new investment. Agriculturalists, too, tended to wait for the government to make up its mind about the pattern of land reform, while the decontrol of food-grains, intended to provide them with incentives, did little to reassure the masses of the people about the government's proclaimed solicitude for their welfare. There was, in fact, little that could be described as an economic policy, apart from a series of *ad hoc* efforts to keep the economy going by any means that lay readily to hand. Nehru himself admitted as much.

I am afraid [he said in 1950] that in spite of a good deal of talk about planning we have not done much . . . we have tried to make good in many directions but there has not been that amount of coordination even within the government or between state governments and the central government. I am frank to confess that in the central government there has not been a careful attempt to see the overall picture.

Nevertheless, even during this period there were a number of developments which proved of long-term importance. For instance, a series of important economic development agencies, such as the Industrial Finance Corporation and the Cottage Industries Board, were established; and the central government entered into negotiations with foreign firms for the creation of important new industries, such as machine tools, heavy chemicals, steel, penicillin, fertilisers, telephones, and loco-motives. Many irrigation projects were also being considered, investigated, or executed. There were even attempts at sectoral planning, such as the Ministry of Agriculture's Five Year Plan for food production and the Central Cotton Committee's Five Year Plan for cotton. The most important steps, however, were those taken to equip the government with an *apparatus* for the formulation and implementation of economic development policies. These came to fruition in 1950, with the establishment of the Planning Commission.

Created by Cabinet resolution in March 1950, the Commission was given the following seven duties:

1 Make an assessment of the material, capital and human resources of the country, including technical personnel, and investigate the possibilities of augmenting such of these resources as are found to be deficient in relation to the nation's requirements;

2 Formulate a Plan for the most effective and balanced utilisation of the country's resources;

3 On a determination of priorities, define the stages in which the Plan should be carried out and propose the allocation of resources for the new completion of each stage;

4 Indicate the factors which are tending to retard economic development, and determine the conditions which, in view of the current social and political situation, should be established for the successful execution of the Plan;

5 Determine the nature of the machinery which will be necessary for securing the successful implementation of each stage of the Plan in all its aspects;

6 Appraise from time to time the progress achieved in the execution of each stage of the Plan and recommend the adjustments of policy and measures that such appraisal may show to be necessary;

7 Make such interim or ancillary recommendations as appear to be appropriate either for facilitating the discharge of the duties assigned to it, or on the consideration of the prevailing economic conditions, current policies, measures and development programmes; or on an examination of such specific problems as may be referred to it for advice by the central or state governments.

In addition, the Cabinet resolution attempted to define the position to be occupied by the commission in the total governmental system.

The Planning Commission [it said] will make recommendations to the Cabinet. In framing its recommendations, the commission will act in close understanding and consultation with the ministries of the central government and the governments of the states. The responsibility of taking and implementing decisions will rest with the central and the states' governments.

The original Planning Commission consisted of six members under the chairmanship of the Prime Minister, Jawaharlal Nehru. The Deputy Chairman, Gulzarilal Nanda, was a prominent Congress politician, and three of the 'ordinary' members were men of long and varied administrative experience. The fourth was a business man. From the beginning, the commission was equipped with an 'expert' apparatus, largely staffed by administrators and economists. As time went on, this tended to proliferate in a manner which caused considerable alarm among those who feared that the commission was developing into a 'second Cabinet', with executive as well as advisory powers. Another development, during the 1950s and early 1960s, was an increase in the number of politician members of the commission, of whom the most important – and indeed, in the opinion of the commission's defenders, the most necessary – was the Finance Minister, who came to hold a virtually *ex officio* position.

Whatever may be thought of the manner in which the Planning Commission evolved, there is no doubt that its constitutional position was, and remains, an anomalous one. Although a body wielding very considerable power – just how much has always been open to dispute – it owes its existence not to any law (still less to any constitutional provision) but to a mere Cabinet resolution; and in theory it is no more than an advisory committee of the Cabinet. This anomaly has attracted a great deal of criticism, among the advocates as well as among the opponents of a planned economy.

The first duty given to the commission was to formulate a Five Year Plan and to oversee its execution. This First Plan, which was little more than a collection of projects, covered the years 1952 to 1956. It was followed by a much more ambitious Second Plan (1956 to 1961), and an even more ambitious Third (1961 to 1966). Both the Second and the Third Plans ran into difficulties, one of the consequences of which was that the commencement of the Fourth Plan, currently in operation, was delayed. For three years between the end of the Third Plan and the beginning of the Fourth, India had to make do with annual plans. Of recent years, many have questioned the value of the quinquennial exercises, and *a fortiori* of the long-term perspective plans which are supposed to provide their framework; the Indian Government nevertheless persists with both.

The main characteristics of India's plans, being well known, require no more than brief summary in the present context. Each Plan aims at raising a given quantum of resources for the purpose of increasing the national income by a specified percentage. Each attempts to be systematic and comprehensive, establishing certain developmental priorities as between the different sectors of the economy, e.g. heavy industry, light industry, agriculture, infrastructural services etc. Each endeavours to enlist the participation of the 'people', by combining planning from above with planning from below, right down to the village level. Each displays a combination of the imperative and the indicative principles.

The Plan is imperative in that it raises a high proportion of the required resources by imposing taxation, in that it involves the positive regulation of private trade and industry (through licensing, the issue of foreign exchange permits, the control of capital issues etc.), and in that it makes extensive use of public enterprise, particularly for the development of heavy industries and infrastructural services. Public enterprise has been particularly emphasised since the adoption of the 'socialistic pattern' in 1954, and the fields of economic activity which it is supposed to occupy, either totally or partially, are specified in a general way by the (Second) Industrial Policy Resolution of 1956. This scheduled as the state's 'exclusive responsibility' the further development of most heavy and extractive industries, together with aircraft, air transport, railway transport, ship building, telephone, telegraph, and wireless apparatus, and the generation and distribution of electricity. However, even in this 'reserved' field, it did not preclude 'the expansion of the existing privately owned units, or the possibility of the state securing the co-operation of the private enterprise in the establishment of new units when the national interests so require.' Nor was private enterprise to be denied its opportunities in a second category of industry, where it was said the state would 'increasingly establish new undertakings'; and there was a third category where development would be undertaken 'ordinarily through the initiative and enterprise of the private sector'. It will be seen, therefore, that even in industry a 'mixed economy' was envisaged, in which the efforts of the private sector would be vital to the achievement of the planned targets. In agriculture, of course, the private sector would remain overwhelmingly preponderant for as long as could be foreseen. Soviet-type reliance on 'command' planning, therefore, was never seriously contemplated, and consequently the judicious use of 'indicative' methods was vital to success. This involved, among other things, the selective stimulation of the various branches of the private sector by credit and fiscal policies.

Another feature of the Plans, at least until recently, has been their high degree of centralisation. Although the states have been encouraged to plan – and indeed are required to draw up their own five-yearly and annual Plans – the Planning Commission and the central government have used their grant-awarding powers to exercise a tight control – some would say far too tight. The reluctance of the state governments to raise resources for plan purposes, together with the concentration of planning expertise at the Centre, have made planning at the state level a rather sketchy affair. Both Centre and states are nevertheless agreed about certain broad objectives. One of these, which everybody treats seriously, is that the object of the planning exercise is to create a situation in which the country as a whole will become capable of rapid self-sustaining growth. Another, now more honoured in the breach than in the observance, is that India should become increasingly socialist and egalitarian. Many have regarded, and some still regard, the Indian Plans as inspired by the Soviet model. This is true only to the extent that there has been considerable emphasis, particularly in the Second and Third Plans, on the creation of a heavy industrial base. This came first among Nehru's economic objectives and was given pride of place by Professor Mahalanobis in his famous 'Plan Frame' of March 1955 which stated that the development of heavy industries was essential 'to strengthen the foundations of economic independence'. Subsequently, as a result of bitter experience, higher priority has been given to agriculture.

It is all too easy to emphasise the deficiencies of Indian

planning. Only the First Five Year Plan reached its main quantitative targets; the other two completed ones showed serious shortfalls. In the Second and Third Plans there was a particularly serious failure to realise objectives in agricultural production, and the development of heavy industry itself was subject to considerable time-lags. Furthermore, the social objectives of the Plans – objectives far too often expressed in terms of vague aspirations rather than of specific policy proposals – have certainly not been realised. Far from being a more egalitarian society than in 1950, India may even be a *less* egalitarian one, and unemployment (particularly among educated persons where it is *politically* most significant) has increased, not diminished.

These gaps between aspiration and achievement may be attributed to several causes. One is the setting of Plan targets that in the event have proved to be mutually incompatible. Another is the isolation of the planners in New Delhi, and their lack of sufficiently continuous contact with the grass roots. This is one of the reasons for their frequent use of inappropriate methods, a product of miscalculation of the response to certain stimuli. One might instance the planners' excessive reliance on the Community Development Projects as a means of raising the level of agricultural production. Even more evident, from even a superficial comparison of the plans and their results, is the over-optimism that has informed the planners' calculations. They have tended consistently to assume the 'best possible case', relying on a series of optimistic assumptions and predictions which could not possibly be realised *in toto*, even if *some* of them were realised. As one of us has written elsewhere:

Too many of their aims are contingent upon the adoption, by various sections of the Indian community, of attitudes they are exceedingly unlikely to adopt, at least to the desired and requisite extent. If people work harder and are less selfish, if they make the plan their own and contribute unitedly and enthusiastically towards its achievement, if the administration is less corrupt and more efficient, if the peasants make full use of the irrigation waters, if the Community Projects evoke the planned responses, if the business community becomes public spirited, if the prejudice and antagonisms associated with region, caste, and community are significantly diminished, if there is more whole hearted co-operation between the states and the Centre, then we shall achieve our aims : so runs the argument.

Such are presuppositions that tend to get written into the Plans. A further and allied inhibiting factor is the worship by the planners of certain 'idols', whose veneration has been required of them by Congress politicians, and particularly by Nehru. Objectives such as the socialistic pattern and economic equality, techniques such as planning from below, institutions such as panchayati raj and cooperative societies have been virtually above criticism. As a result, certain policies have been doggedly pursued long after their impracticability, or their irrelevance to the task of promoting economic growth, has been conclusively proved.

Yet when all this has been said, it must also be said that the development achieved has borne a recognizable relationship to the development planned – although how far this can be attributed to the planning process itself is wide open to dispute. *Per capita* incomes have been significantly raised. Although the annual average rate of increase of 1.8 per cent is obviously insufficient, it represents a trebling of the pre-Independence figure, to the extent that this may be reliably calculated. More importantly, there has been a great strengthening of the infrastructure of the economy. For instance, over the fifteen-year period, 1950–1 to 1965–6, installed electric power capacity has increased four-fold, the freight-carrying capacity of the railways more than two-fold, and the length of surfaced roads nearly two-fold. Moreover, the industrial achievements of the Second and Third Five Year Plans have been particularly impressive. Over the whole period of the three Plans the index of industrial production (using 1956 as a base line) has increased from 74 to 182. In particular, certain key industries (upon which the planners, rightly or wrongly, placed very great emphasis) have developed spectacularly. One might instance aluminium ingots, machine tools, iron ore, petroleum products, and sulphuric acid and nitrogenous fertilisers, the last two being of particular importance for agriculture. Such achievements give some substance to the planners' claim that India 'is poised for faster growth during the years to come'.

As we have suggested, the extent to which these achievements are due to planning itself is a very open question. It can hardly be doubted, however, that they are connected with certain *political* advantages which India possessed during the period under review. Among these, we would stress the political continuity provided by Congress's maintenance of its dominant position, and the high priority placed on the tasks of economic development by Congress's unchallenged leader, Jawaharlal Nehru. But now that Nehru has gone and Congress dominance is less well assured, the question is whether the admittedly inadequate developmental momentum already attained can be maintained, let alone increased. In the absence of these two vital advantages, it must be admitted that India's political system is hardly the planners' dream.

Federalism, for instance, presents the Planning Commission and its associated organs with problems of a peculiarly intractable kind. According to the constitution 'economic and social planning' is a concurrent subject. This means, in practice, that the Centre and the state formulate their quinquennial and annual plans more or less simultaneously, and that the central planners have the task of coordination. The performance of this task involves an annual autumnal pilgrimage of states' representatives to New Delhi, where some very hard bargaining takes place. It is also assisted – in theory if not always in practice – by the meetings of the National Development Council, where, under the chairmanship of the Prime Minister, the chief ministers of the states confer with the representatives of the Central Government and Planning Commission to take major policy decisions and to arrive at compromises about the share-out of resources (or, perhaps more correctly, to register compromises already made).

In this bargaining process the Centre possesses an important source of strength – it has gifts to offer. By granting or withholding assistance, it can make or mar a state plan. Yet this sanction is much less effective than it might appear to be. Centre-state political relations are such that a cutting off or serious reduction of 'plan money' is inconceivable, and even moderately effective control over its utilisation by the states has proved impracticable.

Moreover, the states are increasingly critical of a planning process which seems to relegate them to a client status. One of them, Kerala, has gone to the extent of drawing up the outline of a national plan alternative to that presented by the Planning Commission – an unheard-of thing in former days. Organisationally, this situation is reflected in the recent downgrading of the Planning Commission. Once regarded, as we have seen, as a 'second Cabinet', and formerly possessing very great authority in the process of day-to-day decision-making, it is now a body whose purely advisory status is consistently emphasised. The decision-taking status of the National Development Council has been correspondingly enhanced – although whether such a 'round-table' body can ever succeed in giving coherent leadership to the planning process is very much open to doubt. As a result of all these developments, planning has become considerably more difficult. It is also less subject than in former days to considerations of economic rationality, and more affected by the hard political bargaining that increasingly characterises the relationship between Centre and states.

All this imposes severe limitations on what the planners can attempt to do. Equally severe limitations, of course, are imposed by the fact that India's political culture is democratic as well as federal. Admittedly, democracy offers the advantages of 'planning by consent', and these should not be underestimated; but such consent is not easy to obtain in an underdeveloped country where resources are few and claimants many, insistent and vociferous. Moreover, its enlistment is hampered by several communicational difficulties. Consent requires a knowledge and understanding which is extremely deficient, if not completely absent, at the grass-roots level. This deficiency is partly due to the low level of literacy, but even more to the fact that Indian politics displays a sharp dichotomy of style, as Professor Morris-Jones has emphasised. Among the political and administrative elite, particularly in New Delhi and to a lesser extent in the other large towns, the 'western' style predominates. Elsewhere the traditional style is overwhelmingly prevalent. In the so-called mofussil areas politics, as we have seen, is largely a matter of caste, community and faction. This does not mean that there is no link between the two styles, for, again as we have noted, the local political bosses play the role of 'brokers', as Professor Bailey has so vividly illustrated in his studies of Orissa. But communication of *planning* objectives and techniques from the upper levels to the lower ones is virtually impossible, although it has taken a very long time for the Planning Commission to realise this fact. Hence, even if such objectives and techniques enlisted the unanimous support of the political parties (which they do not), there would still be a strong element of utopianism about attempts to mobilise popular democratic support for plan fulfilment. What the planners have to do is to develop, by a process of trial and error, the appropriate individual and group incentives. This they now realise in practice, but even in the original Outline of the Fourth Five Year Plan they were still talking in 'mass mobilisation' terms. In fact the model of the Soviet Union, which Nehru so greatly admired and so seriously misunderstood, has continued to influence the prevailing planning ideology, to the detriment of realism.

These political difficulties constitute some of the more important reasons for the critical situation which Indian planning now faces. There are, however, more immediate and obvious reasons for the virtual collapse of the Third Five Year Plan and the abandonment of the original version of the Fourth Plan. The most obvious of these was an enormous – although fortunately temporary – set-back in agricultural production, due to the successive failure of the monsoons in 1966 and 1967. Except under circumstances of complete political and administrative breakdown, this is unlikely to be repeated, for the new technological break-through has been accompanied by the adoption of more realistic agricultural development policies, while the new Foodgrains Corporation has now accumulated sufficient buffer stocks to meet any foreseeable crisis situation. A second reason, which continues to operate, is India's serious balance of payments situation, a consequence of the insufficiency of foreign aid and the sluggishness of exports. This is unlikely to be quickly rectified, because, although exports have taken a favourable turn, foreign aid prospects remain poor. A further component of the crisis is the strain imposed on the Indian economy by the conflicts with China and Pakistan, which as noted above (p. 156) have resulted in a considerable stepping up of defence production. Whether this strain will increase or diminish cannot be reliably predicted, although the outcome depends to some extent on the kind of foreign policy that India decides to pursue. Over and above these external factors is the inadequate mobilisation of internal resources, where short-falls from planned targets have been particularly conspicuous. Whether such mobilisation will be significantly improved is hard to say, although it is not difficult to predict that the tax-resistance by the more prosperous peasantry and tax-avoidance by business men will remain prominent features of the Indian economic scene.

These, in brief, are the difficulties that have stimulated a great deal of talk about the 'failure' of planning, for which the Congress Party in general and the Planning Commission in particular have been blamed. The very prevalence of such talk is symptomatic of the deterioration in the political environment to which the planners have had to adjust themselves. More seriously, the centrifugal and divisive tendencies already noted have had the effect of shifting the attention of governments, both at the Centre and in the states, away from growth-promotion and toward sheer preservation. The advent to power of the Communists in West Bengal and Kerala and of the DMK in Madras; the rise and fall of unstable governments, based on shifting and unprincipled coalitions, in many of the states; the consequent frequent imposition of Presidential Rule; the deepening of divisions, particularly over the national language issue, between north and south; the agitation against cow slaughter; student unrest; the rise of violent, fascist-type movements such as the Shiv Sena in Maharashtra; 'Naxalitism' and 'landgrabbing'; and Congress's successive loss of dominance and loss of unity – all of these things have not merely distracted attention from planning but have made the planning process itself very much more difficult. Now that Congress once again reigns supreme at the Centre, the situation could improve; but whether it actually does so depends in part on the uses to which Mrs Gandhi is able to turn her overwhelming majority.

So far, the main reaction of the central government to these difficulties has been to make certain institutional adjustments, the nature of which have already been briefly mentioned. Some of these were inspired by the recommendations of an Administrative Reforms Commission, which placed at least some of the blame for planning failures on the organisation and modus operandi of the Planning Commission itself.

According to the ARC, the Planning Commission has fallen

into grievous procedural and organisational sin. It had immersed itself excessively in executive (as distinct from advisory) activities, such as vetting important economic decisions, watching over the progress of land reforms, and participating in the work of a large number of regulatory committees, to the detriment of its more central duties of formulating plans and reporting on their implementation. It had created an over-centralised planning system, in which insufficient initiative was left to the states and centrally-formulated schemes were in-appropriately and unimaginatively imposed upon them. By a process of administrative proliferation, it had equipped itself with an unnecessarily swollen bureaucracy. Lastly, it was over-dominated by its ministerial members, who tended to treat its non-ministerial members and officials as mere servants, with the result that it was inhibited from giving the government unbiased advice, based on objective economic analysis. To rectify these alleged faults the ARC recommended that the commission should become a purely 'expert' body, entirely advisory in character. The government, while generally sympa-thetic to the ARC criticisms and recommendations, did not go so far as entirely to deprive the commission of ministerial membership. The Prime Minister remains its chairman and the Minister of Finance is still a member. Significantly, however, it appointed to the key post of deputy-chairman the man who for many years had been making criticisms of the Planning Commission similar to those made by the ARC, Professor D. R. Gadgil.

Although changes which tend to deprive the Planning Commission of much of its former power and influence are necessarily regretted by most enthusiasts for economic planning, a case can be made out that they are both necessary and inevitable in the new political situation. One must nevertheless point out that they seem to have been accompanied by what appears to be a marked deterioration in the coherence of the planning process. In one of its periodical planning reviews, the National Council of Applied Economic Research points to economic dislocation as well as stagnation as a feature of Indian production in 1971, and suggests that the Fourth Plan should be revamped to promote price stability and improve employment prospects. This causes Mr Balasubramaniam, writing in the

Hindustan Times, to ask with some justice 'But what and where is the Fourth Plan?'. Perhaps the implications of the question are over-pessimistic and it may be that the new government, emergent from the elections of 1971, will succeed in restoring credibility to the planning exercise. The last information available to us is that President Giri, in addressing the joint session of the new Parliament on 23 March 1971, announced that the government intended to reappraise the Fourth Plan and make major changes in it, with the objects of 'increasing the pace and effective use of investment in the economy', reducing unemployment, promoting 'an egalitarian social order' and 'maximising agricultural production'. This sounds like an old refrain; nevertheless, one can hardly doubt that the fate of Mrs Gandhi's government depends very considerably on the substance it succeeds in giving to this song.

A further reconstruction of the Planning Commission also seems to be in the offing. Any such reconstruction, however, could hardly be expected to restore to the commission the prestige and prerogatives it had in Nehru's day. For planning everywhere takes place in a political context and this has changed radically since Nehru's death. Therefore, whatever further reforms Mrs Gandhi's government makes in the planning machinery, the process of planning is bound to be different from what it used to be. Its future depends not primarily on the technical expertise that Indians can bring to it, which is now considerable, but on the as yet unanswered question whether the country can maintain that degree of unity of purpose without which even the most sophisticated of Plans will become inoperable.

9 Local Government

Readers of texts on government and administration usually greet the above heading with a sigh of relief. It provides evidence not only that the book is drawing to a close but that all the more important things have already been dealt with. Such a reaction would be quite inappropriate here, for local government in a developing country – and particularly in one of the size and diversity of India – has a significance quite different from that which it possesses in a developed one. In the latter it signifies a collection of subordinate instrumentalities, restricted in both jurisdiction and geographical coverage and concerned with the provision of more or less routine services which, for one reason or another, are considered suitable subjects for administration by locally-elected bodies. In a developing country it signifies – or *can* signify – something of far deeper importance. Through local government institutions the new political elite, emerging from the process of independence, makes an attempt to mobilise the masses, hitherto no more than peripherally involved in public affairs, for the nation-building tasks of economic and social development, and to commit them more actively to the maintenance of the political system of which they are now supposed to constitute an integral part. Particularly in developing countries endeavouring to operate a democratic system of government, local self-governing institutions can play a vital role in the process of political legitimisation and offer a means of developing a sense of participation in people who, except during brief periods of crisis, were previously uninvolved in the making and implementation of political decisions.

For this purpose, institutions have to be *created* where none of much significance previously existed. Their creation is necessarily a task of great difficulty, since nation-building demands for its accomplishment both firm and central control and independent local initiative: a sophisticated combination which, as is well known, presents problems even to the most politically mature of countries. Local initiative, once stimulated, may find expression in ways irrelevant or even contradictory to the purposes of the central political elite, as expressed in Five-Year Plans and ministerial decisions. Yet, if the hand of the centre bears too heavily on the nascent councils, their growth may be prematurely stifled and with it the political involvement they are supposed to foster. The alternative then becomes one between stark centralisation and decentralised chaos. These problems have been acutely experienced in India, as we propose to illustrate in the following account of the development in that country of the unique system of local institutions known as panchayati raj.

Independent India, as we have seen, inherited from the British a well-articulated system of central administration; but it inherited very little in the shape of effective and firmly-based local government. The districts, together with the sub-districts, *tehsils* (or *talukas*) and revenue circles into which they were divided, were administered by provincially-appointed officials, from the Collector downwards. Not until the Ripon Resolutions of 1882 was any attempt made to associate local people in the rural areas with the administrative process, through the creation of nominated District Boards, endowed with meagre financial resources for the building of roads and schools and the promotion of public health. Later, some rather half-hearted efforts to extend representation 'downwards' resulted in an uneven patchwork of sub-district boards and village councils. Further progress, of a sort, came with the India Act of 1919, when responsibility for local government passed into the hands of ministers responsible to the newly-created provincial Legislative Assemblies and the district and sub-district boards became more genuinely representative, at least in the sense that their members were elected on a restricted franchise. But limitations on their resources, together with the absence of a local government service, prevented them from achieving very much, and membership of them held few attractions for politically active Indians, except to the extent that it could offer them vantage points for harassing the British administration and advancing the nationalist cause. Similar considerations applied to most of the urban centres which were equipped with representative institutions; although it is worthy of note that certain prominent Congress leaders, such as Sardar Patel, first made their political reputations as presidents of Municipal Boards, and that the actual or proposed reform of a major corporation, such as Calcutta or Bombay or Madras, could create a very considerable political storm.

The local government situation that confronted the new rulers of independent India was certainly confused, and in some respects it remains so even to-day. Little attention has been paid, for instance, to municipal organisation, which varies widely from state to state and, in general, achieves a level of efficiency no higher, and often considerably lower, than it achieved in British times. As for local authorities in the rural areas, with which we are here principally concerned, the British heritage is thus summarised by Professor Henry Maddick:

In the state of Uttar Pradesh the District Boards were strong. In Madras and in Bengal the groupings of villages, in which sub-district or sub-subdistrict unions had some achievements to record, provided a significant framework for future operations. Bombay state, the home of modern local government in India, had quite a developed system of District Local Boards, District School Boards (both largely elected), Taluka Committees, District Building Committees and District Rural Development Boards. In parts of Madhya Pradesh there were local boards and District Councils, whose members were mostly elected. No District Boards existed in Assam or Kerala, while in the former princely states the pattern varied even more widely but, in most, local institutions had not been favoured.

The constitution-makers, rather than making any effort to clean up this mess, handed over responsibility for it to the states. This did not mean, however, that the Congress leaders had failed to envisage a nation-building role for local government, but simply that those interested in it were looking to indigenous rather than to British-created institutions to provide a foundation for the popular democratic participation they wished to enlist. For them, it was the ancient village panchayat, refurbished, modernised and equipped with a wider range of powers, that seemed to offer the best possibility of progress at the local level. This somewhat shadowy self-governing institution, partly a figment of the historical imagination, was alleged to have been disrupted and almost destroyed by bureaucratic forms of government; its revival as a popular substitute for bureaucratic rule had been envisaged by resolutions of the Indian National Congress passed as early as 1909 and 1910, and its popularisation had subsequently been vigorously undertaken by Mahatma Gandhi, who considered that 'the nearest approach to civilisation based on non-violence' had been 'the erstwhile village republic of India'.

Even so, the tough-minded westernisers among Congress's top level leadership had little use for what they tended to regard as Gandhi's 'political mysticism', however deeply they may have revered the Mahatma as the father of the nation. As a result, there was no mention of panchayats in the draft originally circulated to the Constituent Assembly. Only protest from the Gandhians themselves and from those who regarded the omission as an insult to India's most distinguished political leader produced the concession contained in Article 40, the Directive Principle that instructed the states to 'take steps to organise village panchayats and endow them with such powers and authority as might be necessary to enable them to function as units of self-government'.

During the early years of Independence no great efforts were made to give effect to this directive, despite periodical exhortations, mostly couched in general terms, from the central government and the planning commission. Although some existing panchayats continued to function and a few new ones were created, the states were more interested in protecting their own powers from encroachment by the Union government than in divesting themselves of any portion of such powers for the benefit of untried, and probably highly inefficient, subordinate authorities. 'Available evidence', wrote the Mehta commissioners in 1957, 'indicates that possibly no more than 10 per cent of the panchayats are functioning efficiently'. In the following year, the Programme Evaluation Organisation's survey of sixty panchayats revealed that only twenty made any provision at all for lighting and sweeping and that none could make more than a 'negligible' claim to have promoted rural economic development.

By this time, however, events had compelled the central government to consider more seriously the potentialities of the panchayat as a developmental agency, if not as a general-purpose local authority. To understand why this happened and to follow the course of events which led to the establishment of the system known as panchayati raj, which represents India's distinctive contribution to the theory and practice of local government, we must look at the problems which, by the middle 1950s, were facing the Community Development Projects.

When Independence was achieved, community development was already a familiar concept. Basically, the idea was to take a village or group of villages as a point of concentration, and to send into it an organised group of social workers and technicians, who were to proceed by way of eliciting expressions of the villagers' own 'felt needs' and showing them how, by appropriate forms, organisation and mutual aid, they could provide for the satisfaction of these needs through their own efforts, suitably guided and assisted by the imported personnel. The projects based on this conception were few, but several of them, such as Albert Mayer's Etawah Project, Rabindranath Tagore's and Leonard Elmhirst's Sriniketan Project, Spencer Hatch's Martandam Project, the 'Firka' Development Scheme in Madras, the Rural Reconstruction Centres in Baroda, and F. L. Brayne's 'Gurgaon' experiment, had become famous. With the exception of Brayne's scheme, which was the favourite child of a British District Officer generally regarded by his fellow administrators as an inspired eccentric, all these were organised and financed privately or by princely governments. Soon after Independence, a further fifteen, regarded as pilot projects, were organised by the Ford Foundation with the approval of the Indian government. Results seemed to live up to expectations and, with further aid from the United States, the government decided to bring into existence a Community Development Programme, with 'service through guidance and assistance and inspiration to self-help' as its slogan. The chosen unit of operation was the 'block', covering an area of some 50,000 acres of cultivated land and embracing about a hundred villages with a total population of between 70,000 and 100,000. Originally fifty-five 'block development areas' were scheduled, but by 1956 the number had risen to 1,200, covering about a quarter of the Indian people, and a target of complete nation-wide coverage by the end of the Second Five Year Plan had been announced. This proved rather too ambitious; nevertheless, it was attained, at least on paper, by 1963. At the centre a Projects Administration was created, later to become a fully-fledged Ministry of Community Development. This arranged for the recruitment, training and deployment of the new type of official required for community development work. At the block level, the key man, supposed to coordinate and give direction to the work of specialists, was the Block Development Officer (BDO), while for each group of five or so villages there was another multi-purpose man known as the Village Level Worker (VLW) – the so-called 'friend of the people'.

The Community Development Programme was integrally linked with the National Extension Service, in such a way that each block was expected to pass through three distinct stages. The first, known as the pre-intensive or NES stage, was of one year's duration. Characterised by concentration on preliminary surveys and agricultural demonstrations, it prepared the way for the second, known as the intensive or CD Programme stage, lasting five years, during which the full team of block-based officers was to be on site. The third or post-intensive stage, also of five years' duration, was to be one in which the local people would progressively assume greater responsibility for the assets created and practices developed during the second stage, and in which most of the government-appointed personnel were to be phased out. Later, these three phases were reduced to two, but the implied 'catalytic' principle remained unchanged. Financially, the main responsibility was with the state and the Ministry of Community Development, each block being equipped with a so-called schematic budget; but the raising of resources locally, by taxation, voluntary contribution or provision of labour services, was obviously to be encouraged.

In retrospect, it is easy to see that the CD scheme was based on several fallacious assumptions. The first, and probably the most damaging, was that the success of the pilot projects could be generalised and that government-appointed officials could provide a leadership not conspicuously inferior to that provided by dedicated volunteers. The second, closely linked with the first, was that the new CD personnel could be persuaded, by precept and example, to develop an administrative style radically different from that characterising the old forms of district and sub-district administration. The third and most unrealistic of all was that the village people could be readily induced to forget caste distinctions and factional conflicts and develop a collective enthusiasm for the improvement of village amenities and of agricultural practices. This last assumption was obviously based upon the 'little republic' fallacy.

The progenitors and top-level administrators of the CD programme proved extremely reluctant to discard these beliefs, which had rapidly become articles of faith among them; but by the mid-fifties it was obvious to every impartial observer that the programme was not working as intended. Administratively, it was causing considerable confusion by complicating the lines of command and placing new and unwelcome burdens on the shoulders of the district officers. 'Frankly', said one of these, 'I do not like to spend a night in a village. I have nothing to say to the villagers nor have they to me.' BDOs, underpaid and over-worked, tended to behave just as arbitrarily as any other officers posted to rural areas, while the Block Advisory Committees (later Block Development Committees) with which they were associated, were made up, for the most part, of local notables whose main object was to use the inputs and amenities provided by the CD programme for their own advantage. Corruption and extravagance abounded, and the essential component of self-help was difficult to discover. For, although CD was often popular, particularly with the village rich, it was almost universally regarded as a *government* programme, brought *to* the people *by* the officials. Hence, when the officials began to depart, at the end of Stage II, the newly created assets, such as wells, tanks, schools and *pukka* roads, tended to fall into neglect, sometimes scandalously so. Furthermore, the rigidities of the schematic budget, together with the orientation of officials towards obedience to superiors rather than towards responsive-ness to local need, ensured that, even when there was no corruption, expensive resources were conspicuously wasted. The Report Teams on Plan Projects, during the course of their visitations, had frequent occasion to note that equipment was lying around unused, simply because it was ill-adapted to local conditions. In short, this great programme, launched amid such high hopes, appeared to be running into the sands as a result of a combination of administrative inefficiency and popular apathy.

Clearly, something had to be done. Either CD could be abolished, as totally misconceived, or provided with an entirely new basis. The first alternative was unthinkable; hence a process of rethinking was inaugurated. Public initiative was taken by the Planning Commission which, in its Second Five Year Plan document, expressed the opinion that lack of genuine popular participation was the root cause of the failure and suggested that the whole problem should be remitted to a 'special investigation under the auspices of the National Development Council.' Accordingly, the NDC decided to set up, as an arm of the scrutinising body known as the Committee on Plan Projects, a special team 'for the study of Community Projects and National Extension Service'. This team, led by Balvantray Mehta, an ex-Chief Minister of Gujerat and a member of the Lok Sabha, worked very fast to produce a massive report within a few months. Accepting, more or less without question, the basic 'philosophy' of Community Development, it confirmed the now-prevalent opinion that the deficiencies of the movement were due to its failure to arouse local interest and to develop popular enthusiasm.

We have found that few of the local bodies at a higher level than the village panchayat have shown any enthusiasm or interest in this work; and even the panchayats have not come into the field to any appreciable extent. An attempt has been made to harness local initiative through the formation of *ad hoc* bodies mostly with nominated personnel and mainly advisory in character. These bodies have so far given no indication of durable strength nor the leadership necessary to provide the motive force for continuing the improvement of economic and social conditions in rural areas.

Almost inevitably, and without much research or serious consideration of alternatives, it came to the conclusion that the only way to rescue and revive the projects was to throw the ball to the people, by establishing local institutions, based on the panchayat, which would exercise real control over the operations of the development administrators. Thus,

so long as we do not discover or create a representative and democratic institution which will supply the 'local interest, supervision and care necessary to ensure that expenditure of money upon local projects conforms with the needs and wishes of the locality', invest it with adequate power and assign to it appropriate finances, we will never be able to evoke local interest and excite local initiative in the field of development.

Accordingly, it recommended the creation of a new representative institution at the block level, which it christened the *panchayat samiti.* This, linked with the village panchayat by a system of indirect elections, was to be entrusted with

the development of agriculture in all its aspects . . . , the promotion of local industries, the supply of drinking water, public health and sanitation, medical relief, relief of distress caused by floods, earthquakes, scarcity, etc., arrangements in connection with local pilgrimages and festivals, construction and repair of roads . . . , management and administrative control of primary schools, the fixation of wages under the Minimum Wages Acts for non-industrial labour, the welfare of backward classes and the maintenance of statistics.

Some of the money for these purposes it was to raise through taxes under its own control; more importantly, it was to be given control of 'all central and state funds spent in the block area'. Its various officers, although not appointed by it but 'lent' to it by the state government, were to act under its direction, at least in 'administrative and operational' matters.

The village panchayat, which provided the electoral base for the samiti, was itself to be elected by universal franchise, with due provision for the representation of various 'disadvantaged' groups. Its basic duties were to be

(i) provision of water supply for domestic use; (ii) sanitation; (iii) maintenance of public streets, drains, tanks, etc., (iv) lighting of village streets; (v) land management; (vi) maintenance of records relating to cattle; (vii) relief of distress; (viii) maintenance of panchayat roads, culverts, bridges, drains, etc.; (ix) supervision of primary schools; (x) welfare of backward classes; and (xi) collection and maintenance of statistics.

It was to be provided with its own sources of revenue, but also to receive 'grants from the panchayat samiti on lines similar to those suggested for grants from government to panchayat samitis'. Its budget was to be supervised by the superior body, which could also use it as an agent for the execution of development schemes.

The committee's rather optimistic view was that as soon as this new democratic structure had been created there would be 'very little left for any higher ... executive body other than the government'. District Boards and the like would, therefore, become superfluous. Coordination at the district level of the activities of the samitis would, however, remain necessary, and to provide for this the committee suggested the creation of a *zilla parishad,*

of which the members will be the presidents of the panchayat samitis, all members of the state legislature and of the parliament representing a part or whole of a district whose constituencies lie within the district, and district level officers of the medical, public health, agriculture, veterinary, public health engineering, education, backward classes welfare, public works and other development departments.

This body, meeting under the chairmanship of the Collector, was to examine and approve panchayat samiti budgets, recruit and post officials, coordinate and consolidate block plans, distribute government funds, and exercise general supervision over the working of the whole new representative apparatus.

Two things must be said at once about these recommendations. Firstly, they were brought into effect with extraordinary promptness – more or less in their original form, although with significant variations as between state and state. Secondly, although they were not successful in achieving the purposes for which they were designed, i.e. the rehabilitation of the CD Programme, they did have profound effect (often of an unanticipated kind) on the nature of India's political culture. The panchayat, that afterthought of the Indian constitution-makers, was back in the centre of the picture.

Indian intellectuals, when not experiencing complete disillusion with politics, are somewhat addicted to panaceas – and here was a panacea of a quite spectacular kind. Its welcome, therefore, was highly satisfying to its inventors. The Minister of Community Development and Cooperation, always distinguished for his delight in hyperbole, went to the extent of proclaiming that 'the panchayati raj institutions could offer patterns before which Plato's Republic would pale into insignificance'. Gandhians felt that an important step forward had been taken. Even that rigid custodian of Gandhian doctrine, Jayaprakash Narayan, expressed his welcome for the Balvantray Mehta Report, with which he said he had 'much in common'. Machine politicians were hardly less enthusiastic, although it soon became evident that they had rather more earthy reasons for their welcome, since panchayati raj could provide them with a much-needed additional source of local patronage. Dissenting voices were few. There was some muted opposition among the bureaucracy, however, and one of the most famous of India's retired civil servants, A. D. Gorwala, gave heavily ironical expression to the scepticism which many officers of the central and state governments must have felt.

A village panchayat does not work well. It performs its simple duties most inadequately. But a committee of representatives of village panchayats must do splendidly. Let us call it a 'Taluka Samiti', give it ample powers, repeat the sacred charm of democratic decentralisation and all will be well.

Perhaps some of them recalled the savage attack on village 'democracy' made by the leader of the Harijans, Dr Ambedkar, at the Constituent Assembly: 'I hold that these village republics have been the ruination of India. . . . What is the village but a sink of localism, a den of ignorance, narrow-mindedness and communalism?' Indian villages, after all, had not changed fundamentally since these words were spoken. It could be argued, indeed, that whatever sense of community had once bound the villagers together had suffered further erosion, largely as a result of the rise among the richer peasants, of a spirit of individualism, partly fostered, ironically enough, by the Community Development Projects themselves. There was some justification, therefore, for the opposition to panchayati raj expressed by another minority group, the Marxists, who held that the new institutions would merely provide a convenient cover for the activities of the 'exploiters'. Such 'Doubting Thomases', however, hardly disturbed the chorus of approval, and one state after another passed the necessary panchayati raj legislation, until by 1962 the coverage was virtually complete.

As local government is a subject on the states' list, the

structure and powers of panchayati raj institutions necessarily differ from state to state. In most states, for instance, the chairmen of the village panchayats (*sarpanches*) are ex-officio members of the panchayat samiti, but in some (e.g. Assam and West Bengal) the panchayat members themselves elect their representatives, while in one (Mysore) elections to the panchayat samiti are conducted in the village assembly (*gram sabha*). Cooption of panchayat samiti members also follows variable rules. Maharashtra, for instance, is unique in its failure to coopt MLAs and MPs; but certain states that do coopt them do not give them voting rights. Perhaps the most radical departure from the recommendations of the Balvantray Mehta Committee has taken place in Maharashtra, which has made a directly-elected zilla parishad, and not the panchayat samiti, the key body in the panchayati raj set-up, on the grounds that 'the district body is the best operative unit of local administration as it alone will be capable of providing the requisite resources, necessary administrative and technical personnel and equipment for the properly coordinated development of the district'. In choosing this pattern, Maharashtra has decided to disregard the Mehta Committee's warning to the effect that 'people cannot be expected to make personal sacrifices for common institutions at local government level unless these are small enough for their comprehension and are near enough for their influence to be demonstrably apparent'. West Bengal is another odd man out in having a four-tier instead of a three-tier structure of panchayat institutions. There an anchal panchayat (replacing the old Union Board) is interposed between the panchayat and the panchayat samiti.

The financing of panchayati raj insititutions shows even greater state-to-state divergencies. Houses, vehicles, professions, businesses and land provide the main tax bases, but there is no general rule about whether a particular tax should be monopolised by a particular panchayati raj institution or shared with others or with the state itself. In some states a cess (or surcharge) on the state land tax is an important source of revenue. Grants, which – owing to the extreme reluctance of local bodies to wield the fiscal weapon – are generally much more important than taxes, may come from the Union government, the state government, or particular agencies of either.

Only Madras (Tamil Nadu) has made any effort to coordinate them. National data on expenditure is not yet available. All one can say with confidence is that whereas the panchayat samitis (and, in Maharashtra, the zilla parishads) often dispose of considerable sums, expenditure at the panchayat level is rarely more than derisory. Of eighteen panchayats sampled by Professor Maddick in 1961–2, one third failed to spend more than one rupee per capita, five spent between 1.06 and 1.75 rupees, and the remainder between 2.12 and 7.35.

The financial weakness of the panchayati raj institutions, together with the fact that they are dependent for the performance of their duties on state-appointed officials, necessarily means that they enjoy far less autonomy than that which the Balvantray Mehta Report envisaged for them. Formal controls are also not lacking. They are essentially *subordinate* bodies, created by state legislation and subject to state supervision. They can be suspended or dissolved, and in most states they can be ordered to execute works considered by the state government to be in the public interest or prohibited from undertaking works regarded as contrary to it. As with Centre-state relations, however, political factors can sometimes ensure that they receive rather more liberty than, on strictly administrative grounds, they would be willingly conceded.

From the long-term point of view, one of their most serious structural weaknesses may be that which arises from their purely rural character. In India there are some 2,700 urban units which are organisationally separate from the panchayati raj structure. Admittedly, some states have provided for the representation of urban authorities on panchayat samitis or zilla parishads, but this kind of *ad hoc* device does not solve the problems created by the structural divorce of the provincial town, great or small, from its rural hinterland. For the peasant, the town is important as a market, a centre of social amenities, and a source of part-time employment; and pressure of population on resources in the rural areas causes increasingly country-to-town migration, particularly among the younger and more active countrymen. Yet the creation of town-cum-country local government areas, which would appear to be indicated by the development of economic interdependence, is inhibited by the pattern of rural government prescribed by panchayati raj. Perhaps, for the moment, this has the balance of advantages on its side, since there is an obvious danger that in any 'combined' institution the simple country-dweller would be swamped by the more sophisticated townsman. Nevertheless, it must not be forgotten that the village rich, who so often succeed in dominating the panchayati raj institutions, are sometimes town-based.

How far has the introduction of panchayati raj succeeded in giving the rural areas of India a 'new' political leadership, less traditional and more progressive in outlook than the old? On this subject it is very difficult to generalise, as the impact of the new local government system has varied widely from one part of the country to another. When it was being intro-duced, many observers found evidence to suggest that its effect would be to confirm and, so to speak, legalise the dominance of those who were already dominant; and this, indeed, has often happened. More recent studies, however, indicate that in many areas – and not invariably in the more advanced ones – it has assisted the rise of new elites, usually described as neo-tradi-tionalist rather than modernising, composed of the younger and better-educated members of those middle castes who benefited both from the land reforms of the 1950s and from the Community Development Schemes themselves. Even in backward Rajasthan, the former 'natural' leaders of the rural community, the *jagirdars,* have fared badly in the panchayati raj elections. In some areas, election to one of the higher panchayati raj bodies appears to have widened the political horizons and stimulated the political ambitions of the 'new men'. A Maharashtrian survey, for instance, revealed that most of 306 interviewed members of zilla parishads were aware of at least some of the problems confronting India and professed a belief in 'democratic socialism'. Eighty per cent of them had enjoyed the support of a political party when waging their election campaigns; all but twenty-three were members of Congress and no fewer than 120 occupied positions in the party's organisation. Most significant of all, over half had political ambitions which went beyond zilla parishad member-ship, which they regarded as a step up the ladder towards the State Assembly or even Union Parliament. It would be absurd to regard this situation as typical, but it would also be unsafe to treat it as entirely exceptional.

The manner in which leadership changes can be brought about at the village level is amusingly illustrated by Paul Brass's 'incident of the fish'. In the district of Faizabad, Uttar Pradesh, the village panchayat, at the instigation of the Pradhan (President) and the VLW, sold stocking and fishing rights in the village pond to an outside interest. Apparently there was little objection to the sale, but trouble arose when the beneficiaries arrived to catch fish on a day when the village was engaged in a religious ritual necessitated by the presence of a case of smallpox. The interruption was strongly resented, and from then onwards the Pradhan's position came under attack. Previously, as a Rajput who had inherited a leadership role, he had been elected without contest, by show of hands. At the next election, however, he found himself confronted by no fewer than five rival candidates, including one of the leaders of the 'fish incident' protest. He finished at the bottom of the poll and had to yield his pradhanship to a prosperous middle-caste man who had previously played no more than a minor role in village politics. Clearly the coming of panchayati raj had made the villagers aware that the Pradhan was born responsible and replaceable, thereby undermining the traditional conception of leadership that had hitherto held sway among them.

When the neo-traditional elite is a united body, the villagers may well have no more than a choice between King Log and King Stork, so powerful are the socio-economic sanctions that normally prevail. But when, as may be more usual, the elite is divided by faction, there can be a more genuine 'appeal to the people', affording an opportunity for the poorer and less articulate members of the village community to make independent demands. In such circumstances, panchayati raj makes possible, for the first time, some small advance towards the democratic sharing of power at the local level. This, to be sure, should not be over-emphasised, since it could well be that poor villagers will come to the conclusion that direct action is much more effective than the exercise of the vote as a means of scaring their 'betters'.

Panchayati raj has also had the effect of expanding the range and increasing the depth of a more modern type, or at least a less traditional type of political activity. Here again the actual introduction of the system has had effects very different from those intended by its originators. The Balvantray Mehta Committee conceived that the panchayat institutions, being mainly occupied with matters of village uplift, would take their decisions in the time-honoured Indian manner – by discussion leading to consensus. Political conflict was to play no part in their proceedings, and the idea that parties might carry their inherently disruptive activities down to the village level was regarded with extreme distaste. Initially, the Congress Party accepted this view and renounced the idea of sponsoring candidates in panchayati raj elections. In some states, the governments actually offered financial bonuses to areas which elected their panchayati raj representatives by unanimous acclaim. This self-denying ordinance, however, could not be maintained for long, since rival factional groupings in the village, block and district inevitably tended to seek the organisational support which rival political parties could provide, and the political parties, in their turn, sought out village factions as potential sources of electoral strength. In most areas, therefore, panchayati raj became thoroughly politicised. This was naturally deplored by the idealists of the Community Development movement, including, of course, the Gandhians, as a serious fall from grace. Many other observers, however, saw it as an inevitable stage in the political modernisation of rural India. Factions at the local level, like caste associations at the state level, provided, they thought, an essential brokerage function whereby the traditional and the modern political styles might be brought together. Other interpretations, less optimistic in their implications, may be offered of this increased localisation of party politics that the adoption of panchayati raj stimulated. What is certain is that the political consciousness, if not the political understanding, of the ordinary villager received a certain stimulus, that the areas of activity covered by the practices of democratic competition were considerably widened, and that a new dimension was added to the Indian political culture.

For the political parties, panchayati raj offered new opportunities; for the administration, it presented new problems. The main difficulty, as we have already suggested (see pp. 186 and 188) was one of divided loyalties and fractured chains of command. To see why, a brief explanation of the staffing pattern of the new institutions will be necessary.

In most states, the village panchayat is serviced by the Village Level Worker, whose duties have remained virtually unchanged. Although politically responsible to the panchayats within the area of his jurisdiction, however, he remains administratively responsible to his immediate hierarchical chief, the Block Development Officer. At a still lower administrative level, there is the panchayat secretary, who is supposed to keep the records of the panchayat and to ensure that its decisions are implemented. In some states, he is a full-time government servant; in others, he is appointed by the panchayat itself. Often the local schoolteacher performs the purely record-keeping function on a part-time basis, in which case responsibility for implementation falls to the lot of the panchayat president, usually known as the sarpanch. Maharashtra, unorthodox in this respect as in others, has appointed a new type of official who combines the functions of secretary, VLW and revenue collector.

The samiti is equipped with a 'general purposes' man, still generally known as the Block Development Officer, who combines the functions of secretary with that of chief executive. In most states, he is also responsible for financial transactions and for the safety of the block's funds. Almost everywhere, he is required to fulfil simultaneously the tasks of carrying out the orders of the samiti, under the supervision of the samiti's chairman, of complying with central directives conveyed to him by his hierarchical superior at the district level, of coordinating the work of the block's team of specialists (e.g. for agricultural services, medical services, public works, etc.) each of whom has a 'technical' responsibility towards a higher official in the service of which he is a member, and, through the VLWs, of galvanising the panchayats into at least some appearance of constructive activity. Well may he envy the comparative simplicity of the functions performed by a French *préfet*! The manner in which this putative paragon is recruited varies widely from state to state. Where, as is usual, he is a state officer, he may be selected from the administrative service or from one of the technical services – or even recruited directly to a separate 'service' of BDOs. His opportunities for advancement are usually very limited.

Local Government

The parishad also has a chief executive officer cum secretary, with responsibility for coordinating whatever parts of the work of the departmental officers at the district level have been brought under the parishad's supervision. In some states the Collector himself performs this function; in others the Collector does his traditional jobs, while attempting to liaise constructively with his 'developmental' *alter ego,* who may or may not be his subordinate. In Maharashtra, where the key responsibilities in the panchayati raj set-up have been given to the parishad, the Chief Executive Officer, although distinct from the Collector, is his equal, and sometimes his superior, in rank and experience.

Even in the best-regulated states, panchayati raj administration presents a rather untidy appearance, and confronts certain officers – usually the BDOs – with problems of a kind that only a hero or a fool would willingly take on. Why has this happened, and why is the normal relationship between the elected members and 'their' officials one of tension, sometimes rising to the level of acute mutual frustration? Obviously, what we have already said (p. 132) about the general nature of political-administrative contacts is applicable to the districts, blocks and villages, as well as to New Delhi and the state capitals. Within the panchayati raj structure, however, there is an ambiguity, not to be found elsewhere in the Indian polity, that arises from the fact that the scheme's inventors, while expressing almost unbounded enthusiasm for local democracy, were really rather afraid of it. Had they possessed the full courage of their democratic convictions, they would have made the administrator fully responsible to the politician at every level. As it was, they felt that the new authorities would require a long period of tutelage before they could be given complete control over the apparatus through which they were required to perform their duties, and that during this period, at least, there had to be someone on the spot who could ensure that they acted in conformity with national and state priorities, that they faithfully followed the regulations (including their own), and that they assumed responsibilities only of a size and complexity with which they could reasonably be expected to cope. It was the attempt to reconcile these requirements with local democracy that gave rise to the ambiguity. Technical and executive officers were 'lent' to the system rather than made an integral part of it. Most of them are, to use the familiar phrase, on deputation to panchayati raj, while remaining members of their state or union cadres. They are paid by the state and their recruitment, promotion, transfer and discipline are provided for by the service to which they belong. Moreover, to varying degrees they are subject to 'technical' instruction by their hierarchical superiors, and in no way can they claim exemption, on the grounds that they have been deputed to work with a democratically-elected local agency, from responsibility for giving effect to national and state policies. Yet they are also required to implement, as faithfully as possible, the decisions of the panchayats, panchayat samitis and zilla parishads. This indeed is a matter of national and state policy. The dilemma, of course, appears when this *general* instruction to follow the expressed wishes of the panchayati raj institutions comes into conflict, as it frequently does, with *specific* instructions to carry out departmental programmes and to follow the priorities laid down in the quinquennial and annual Plans. For any assumption which may once have been made about the 'essential' identity of local, regional and national interests has by now been fully revealed as unrealistic.

Although this device of dual responsibility has sometimes worked successfully, its general effect has been to undermine the morale of the administrator. For him, responsibility to a local politician spells loss of power, authority and prestige. His commitment to panchayati raj is, therefore, rather low, and his interests tend to become concentrated on job-security and promotion rather than on constructive achievement. It is true, of course, that he is unlikely to win the approval of his superiors if his relationship with the chairman of his panchayat samiti or zilla parishad is bad, but unless he is rather stupid he can usually fix up some publicly-presentable *modus vivendi* with this potential tormentor. Once this has been done, the important thing for him is to 'keep in' with his state government; for he knows that his attachment to a panchayati raj institution is likely to be a temporary one (indeed, in most cases he profoundly hopes that it will be so) and that personal advancement depends on his capacity to make himself agreeable to the higher-ups in his service and to the state politicians rather than on the quality of his work as a local official. Like all such generalisations, this one needs to be qualified in many different ways; nevertheless, its basic truth is clear enough to anyone who has seen a number of panchayati raj officials in action. 'The District Collector is my boss and the slogan of considering the people as his ... real master is political bunkum', said one executive officer of a zilla parishad, during the course of being interviewed. Few, perhaps, would find the courage to express themselves with equal vigour, but many – perhaps most – would give their silent approval to the sentiment.

The position of the Collector himself in the panchayati raj set-up also presents problems. How far is he still 'boss' of the district? In matters of law and order and of revenue administration he continues to remain supreme, but the precise degree of his responsibility for economic and social development is often rather obscure. Much of this, at least in theory, is now within the jurisdiction of the panchayati raj institutions, with which his relations vary considerably from state to state. In Madras, for instance, where the zilla parishad is purely advisory, he functions as its president. In both Madras and Mysore, he is chairman of a district development council on which members of the parishad and nominated members sit side by side. In Andhra Pradesh, he is a member of the parishad and chairman of all its standing committees. In most other states, he has membership of the parishad, but sometimes without voting rights. In Maharashtra, Gujarat and West Bengal, however, he is entirely excluded from it. These variations provide evidence of the difficulty that states have experienced in fitting this prestigious and powerful official into the new system. If he is incorporated in it, whether as chairman or as member of the district body, he is liable to dominate it. If he is kept out, district administration is liable to suffer from a lack of co-ordination. If a parallel official, of equal power and prestige, is appointed, there are likely to be damaging top-level conflicts unless the two men are able to develop happy personal relations. Whatever arrangements are made, there will inevitably be a suspicion in the minds of the suspicious that the Collector, as the state government's 'general purpose' agent in the district, is exercising *de facto* authority either by by-passing the panchayat institutions or by 'fixing' their decisions with the help of a small group of local political bosses. These are some of the difficulties which arise from the attempt to graft a new system of democratic local government on to the old system of bureaucratic administration. They are not, of course new problems; they have been experienced, for instance, in France, where the *préfet* of a department plays much the same role as the Collector of a district. But whereas the rather elaborate compromises required for their solution are comparatively easy to make in a developed country, the demands they make on institution-building ingenuity in an underdeveloped country, such as India, are formidable indeed.

Having looked at the impact of panchayati raj on politics and administration, one must now ask whether it has had any effects on the process of economic and social development. First, one owes the reader some justification of the statement made on p. 189, to the effect that panchayati raj was not successful in achieving the purpose for which it was designed, viz. the rehabilitation of the Community Development Projects. That community development has not been conspicuously assisted by the introduction of panchayati raj seems now to be generally agreed. The Balvantray Mehta Committee was subject to the same illusions as the original protagonists of the community projects about the capacity of the village community to act as a community in social and economic matters. The commissioners seemed to imagine that the baleful influences of caste, class, community and faction could be banished by the waving of the democratic wand. Yet even at the time of their report, it was obvious to level-headed observers that the effect of introducing democratic institutions was more likely to exacerbate divisions in the village than to lessen them. This is indeed what has happened in most areas, with predictable effects on community development. The partial removal of the heavy bureaucratic hand and the new influence acquired by democratic representatives have combined to intensify the struggle over the allocation of the various inputs that the state and central governments have to offer – a struggle in which the dominant groups, both new and old, have often succeeded in giving 'democratic' sanction to the privileges they were already enjoying before panchayati raj was introduced. The result, in most cases that have been examined, has been a set-back for community development as originally conceived. As Dr Narain has said in his study of development administration in Rajasthan, the first of the states to introduce panchayati raj, 'the price of political interference at times is to be paid in terms of development.' The same author notes that there were allegations 'that the improved variety of seeds (made available through the CD programme) were distributed only to members of the dominant group and when the time for recovery of seeds came, seeds of inferior quality were returned, which resulted in a financial loss to the panchayati samiti.' He also alleges that, when it came to the spraying of crops with pesticides, the *total* area covered belonged to a few cultivators who happened to be panchayat members. Similar reports have come from elsewhere. In some areas, dominant vested interests have even used the panchayat bodies as a means of deceiving and misinforming the masses of ordinary villagers. The local moneylenders, for instance, are not likely to allow these institutions to be used to advertise the fact that the cooperative bank lends money at 2 per cent, when they themselves are charging 25 per cent or more. Admittedly, the patchiness of the evidence does not permit us to make reliable generalisations, but at least one conclusion appears to be firmly established: that there is no correlation, of the kind that the Balvantray Mehta Committee envisaged, between the liveliness of panchayati raj institutions and the progress of community development.

Nor is there any indication that panchayati raj has given a fillip to rural economic development in general. Dr Alice Ilchman, who attempted to find a causal relationship, completely failed to do so, and her conclusions have been supported rather than undermined by subsequent studies. That wheat production, since the discovery and introduction of the high-yielding varieties of seeds, has been significantly improved in many areas is no longer open to doubt; but this, as far as can be discovered, has nothing to do either with panchayati raj or with the community development projects. Concentrated mainly in the areas of the Intensive Agricultural Development Projects (IADPs), it is mostly the product of the availability of new inputs to groups of comparatively substantial farmers who have learned to behave like 'economic men'. A final irony is that the community development projects themselves, which panchayati raj was intended to revive, have subsequently received decreasing emphasis as a means of rural development. Whatever the merits of panchayati raj may be, therefore, those putatively attributed to it by its originators have been the least to which it may actually lay claim.

Nevertheless, the *potential* impact of the new institutions on socio-economic development is still considerable, since they could conceivably be the means whereby the results of rural economic progress might become distributed more in accordance with the principles of justice and equality to which the Indian governments still pay lip-service. One rather optimistic observer, Sadiq Ali, has found that as a result of participation in electoral processes 'the people in the village are definitely more alert and conscious towards their betterment'. If such alertness and consciousness becomes more widespread, and it can be 'contained' within the limits set by democratic procedures, panchayati raj could be the means of adding a measure of *social* democracy in the village to the measure of political democracy already achieved. In some cases, the ordinary villager, while still electing his 'betters' to office, will insist on a material return for his vote; in others, he may organise to secure the election of people of his own kind, thereby bringing about a minor social revolution, the consequences of which are difficult to foresee. Much depends on the ability of the poor and deprived to use the panchayati raj for their own purposes, and the readiness of the relatively rich and privileged to permit them to do so. Much also depends on the availability of resources to satisfy rising expectations. Optimism on either count would be extremely foolish.

What is important, if panchayati raj institutions are to develop healthily, is that they should not be burdened with duties that are beyond their capacity. In the past, and to some extent even at present, they have suffered from the sheer multifariousness of the responsibilities which have been imposed upon them. In particular, they have been expected to 'plan' – a duty which they have been as unwilling to undertake as incapable of undertaking. The result has been a plethora of 'Plans from below', usually the product of the imaginations of officials and rarely taken seriously by anyone. Where participation in such planning has been genuine, unrealism has reached even further heights, particularly as the ambitions of the participants have never been held in check by a consciousness that they might conceivably have to raise some of the resources required. Of the Plan produced by one panchayat samiti in Rajasthan, the Chief Secretary to the state government said that its cost would exceed the funds available for the implementation of the entire state Plan. The fact is that the panchayati raj bodies, as might be expected, are 'more concerned with immediate need fulfilment than with long-term goals' and 'emphasise consumption-oriented activities in preference to production-oriented schemes'. In a poor and predominantly illiterate country, this is inevitable. It has to be accepted and cannot be just wished away. At the basic level of the village panchayat, moreover, the problem at present is not to persuade the organisation to undertake more sophisticated functions, but to give it the will and to provide it with the resources to perform the most elementary of its 'obligatory' ones. In the great majority of cases, as a recent report emphasises, 'even the basic civil amenities like safe drinking water supply, sanitation and conservancy' are 'not being provided to the community'.

Another essential precondition for the healthy growth of these institutions is the strengthening of democracy at the genuinely grass roots level. At present the panchayati samitis and zilla parishads, largely staffed by 'notables', are often lively institutions, possessing real political significance; but the village panchayat and its gram sabha (village assembly), which are supposed to provide the foundation for the whole system, are as often lacking in vitality. In particular, the gram sabha rarely has much more than a purely formal existence. Even the Union Minister for Community Development, Panchayati Raj and Cooperation, who was not likely to underestimate the achievements of the institutions under his care, said (1964): 'We know that in spite of statutory provisions, members of the gram sabha are not taking an interest in the deliberations of this body. This is the experience all over the country.' More specific evidence comes from West Bengal, a state where political consciousness runs high. There a survey revealed that in all but one or two of twenty-five villages the gram sabhas had not met for lack of a quorum, even though that had been fixed at the deliberately low level of one-tenth of those qualified to attend.

It would be too easy simply to attribute this apparent lack of interest to apathy. The reasons for such apathy need to be sought. Some of them are obvious and familiar. The implicit egalitarianism of the public meeting runs counter to a whole complex of traditional beliefs and attitudes associated with caste. Ordinary villagers often feel that decision-taking is the prerogative of their natural leaders or of those among them who have acquired prestige through education, material success, or contact with the mysterious, power-laden world of the city. Women are still, for the most part, house-bound and tongue-tied. Democratic procedures are poorly understood, with the result, for instance, that a defeated faction will boycott subsequent gram sabha meetings. All this might be held sufficient to account for the weakness of panchayati raj at its village foundations. But there are also other factors which should not be neglected. Often, for instance, the gram sabha fails to meet for lack of a suitable meeting-place or convenient meeting-time. Sometimes the local political bosses deliberately discourage it from meeting, either because they despise the villagers to whom they are supposed to be responsible or because they wish to avoid giving unnecessary publicity to the things they have done in the name of democracy. Perhaps most important of all is the prevalence of a feeling that the gram sabha enjoys no effective power and meets simply to give *ex post facto* approval to decisions made elsewhere.

However, even if a more deliberate effort were made to strengthen the gram sabhas than is being made anywhere at present, the process of 'democratising' the village would still be a long and painful one. For those who believe that it can and should be undertaken, the question arises of what style of politics is most appropriate at this level, where traditional ways of life are so strongly entrenched. As we have seen, the inventors of panchayati raj were of the view that party politics should be excluded from the new institutions, which were to operate on a neo-traditionalist 'consensus' bias. We have also seen how soon the political parties, eager for local spoils and local support, succeeded in falsifying this expectation. It would be too early to say, however, that the concept of 'consensus democracy' is dead. It has deep roots in India's traditions and able contemporary exponents; and although it may appear to be on the way out, with the advances of modernisation and sophistication, circumstances could conceivably arise in which a further attempt to give practical expression to it might be made. For the present situation is extremely unsatisfactory, by any democratic criteria that one might choose to apply. The invasion of the villages by the political parties, and their attempts to find local bases in village factions, have all the appearance of artificiality, and it can be cogently argued that, far from cultivating the democratic spirit, party politics in the panchayati raj institutions, and particularly in the lower-level ones, have merely produced a caricature of it. For it is rare to find a village that is prepared to abide by the rules of the democratic game, as conceived in party-political terms. In most cases, the taking of a majority decision is not accepted by those who have lost the day as a legitimate way of settling the issue. Such a decision tends to be regarded merely as a registration of an irreconcilable division, and the defeated faction will do all in its power, by means stretching from non-violent non-cooperation to physical violence, to obstruct its implementation. Jayaprakash Narayan has put his finger unerringly on this contradiction in panchayati raj, as at present operated, when he says: 'The sad thing is that there should be persons with such split minds as to ask villagers in one breath to make a common endeavour to better their lives and in the second breath to ask them to fight among themselves for power to achieve that very end.'

Even today there is a widespread view that party politics at the village level is harmful and even shameful. In many states villagers are encouraged to select their representatives to the panchayati raj institutions by unanimous acclaim, and in some their success in doing so is rewarded, as we have noted, by a cash prize. Given the social structure of most villages, however, the 'consensus' thereby achieved is fictitious rather than real, since the process of open voting is replaced by one of backstairs manoeuvring. Moreover, the implicit identification of consensus with agreement, made by Narayan and his fellow thinkers, is entirely fallacious. Consensus may mean a whole number of things – apathy, weariness with long discussions, or – as Professor Retzlaff has pointed out – a decision on the part of the minority to accept a predictable winner, in order to avoid the loss of face involved in being identified as a defeated group. It is also most easy to come by, not in the more advanced rural areas but in the more backward ones, where the god-given dominance of a caste or of a traditional landowning group is passively accepted. In short, as Professor Morris-Jones has said, 'Consensus is a fair name for what may be an ugly reality'.

One may, therefore, recognise the artificiality of party conflict at the village level and yet claim that the alternative offered to it is likely to be worse. Even if, as is conceivable, national and regional parties were abolished by a stroke of the presidential pen, the class, caste and factional divisions in the village would remain, because they are part of the social order, and would express themselves in naked forms, unmediated by the modicum of ideology which now provides them with a little respectability. Perhaps unfortunately, conflict is of the essence of democracy in a society experiencing the strains of modernisation; the advantage of institutionalising it is that the disadvantaged groups may acquire both new material benefits and a new dignity without reducing the society in which they live to a bloody shambles. Hence, although competitive party politics might receive its quietus in India, as it did – temporarily – in Pakistan, and a renewed attempt be made to go back to the original conception of panchayati raj, consensus-type decision-making, as understood by Narayan, is unlikely to become a reality. Indeed, if it did, the effect might well be to stifle change in the village rather than to promote it.

The invasion of the village by political parties has not *created* class, caste and factional disputes, as some have tended to suggest. Rather, it has reflected them and given them new forms of institutional expression, bringing them into some kind of relationship, however ill-defined, with the wider political issues. To this extent, it may be regarded as playing a socialising role. This, it would seem to us, has to be recognised in any appraisal of the role of panchayati raj. It was introduced for reasons which one can now clearly recognise as fallacious or irrelevant; it was expected to work in a manner that was contrary to its very nature; it failed to achieve the things it was expected to achieve. But all this does not mean that it should be written off as a futile experiment in institution-building. Certainly, if the Indian political system collapses, panchayati raj will collapse with it, although perhaps after some delay. But as long as the system remains viable, panchayati raj will continue to be an important component of it; for through the 'rule of the panchayats' the masses of the Indian people are beginning, for the first time in their history, to experience the realities of democracy, in however contradictory and distorted a form. For this reason, panchayati raj must be regarded as the most important political invention of independent India.

10 Conclusion

To attempt to describe the condition of India's political life in 1971 is a difficult exercise, because the unexpected has happened and as yet one is unable to assess its significance. Commentators on the 1971 election campaign were divided into those who thought Mrs Gandhi would be defeated, those who thought that she would return at the head of a minority or coalition government, and those who gave her an absolute but small majority. No-one expected that she would sweep the polls and reduce the opposition to a rump, and few would have dared predict that her rivals who still claimed the 'Congress' label, possessed more political experience than she could ever lay claim to, and appeared to have at their disposal a considerable part of the old political machine, would muster a force of no more than sixteen in the new Lok Sabha.

What does it all mean? At first sight, one might well conclude that Congress (which is now to all intents and purposes Mrs Gandhi's Congress) has achieved what most students of Indian politics regarded as the impossible: the restoration and indeed reinforcement of its former dominance. Such a conclusion, however, would be premature for several reasons. First, the circumstances of the election were unusual. Never before had there been a 'mid-term' election to the Central Parliament and never before had a Union election been 'de-linked' from elections in most of the states. Secondly, the results of those state elections that *did* coincide with the Union election provided little evidence to suggest that, if there had been a *general* coincidence of elections at the two levels, Congress would have achieved a success in the state capitals equal to its success in New Delhi. In West Bengal, despite a massive improvement in the Congress position, the CPI(M) emerged, as was expected, the largest party in the state assembly. In Orissa, although Congress outpaced all its rivals, it found itself with considerably fewer seats than the

Swatantrists and 'Utkal' Congressmen combined. (Tamil Nadu provided no evidence of any kind, in view of the standing down of Mrs Gandhi's Congressmen in favour of the DMK's candidates). Thirdly, it is a matter for conjecture how far the re-achieved 'dominance' was Congress's collectively and how far Mrs Gandhi's personally. To all appearances, she made an appeal to the people over the heads of the machine politicians and won a personal vote of confidence. If this is the case, one would expect her huge majority to disintegrate as soon as her own popularity wears thin – as it is bound to do – and as sectional, regional and local pressures begin to bring themselves to bear on the members she has brought back with her to the Lok Sabha.

Much depends on the satisfactions she is able to supply to the people who voted for her, and in this respect she has given hostages to fortune. 'Indira versus the politicians' worked wonders – but Indira is herself a politician and subject to much the same constraints as the rest of her breed. One may well wonder, therefore, how successfully she will succeed in coping with the enormous tasks she has set herself, and how solid her impregnable majority will prove when the euphoria is over and the problems seem as untractable as ever. For these reasons, it would be foolish, at this stage, to speak in terms of the restoration of Congress dominance.

Nevertheless, the results of the 1971 election do compel serious students to think again about the characteristics of political behaviour in India. Hitherto, most of the analysis has been in terms of caste, community, region, factions and 'brokerage', and the possibility of a successful direct appeal to the people, without benefit of the mediation that the various intermediate groupings and vote-grubbing techniques provide, has been largely discounted. It now looks as though the Indian electorate has learnt, or is learning, to understand politics in national terms. If this is so – and as yet it is by no means certain – then something in the nature of a breakthrough has been achieved which could augur well for the future of Indian democracy.

Furthermore, for the present, certain political possibilities, until recently widely canvassed, seem to have been ruled out.

In our first version of this 'Conclusion', written well before the elections of March 1971, we characterised them as follows:

1 A type of political polarisation which could bring into existence something broadly equivalent to a two-party system. This would involve the creation of reasonably stable left-of-centre and right-of-centre alliances. One of these would be a grouping of 'leftist' parties, Communist and Socialist, around Mrs Gandhi's Congress; the other a corresponding grouping of 'rightist', neo-traditionalist and communalist parties around the 'old' Congress. Depending on the fortunes of successive elections, the two groups would alternate in the exercise of political power at the Centre and in the states.

2 A political polarisation of a different variety. Governmental office would be held, at least temporarily, by a 'centrist' group of some kind. This could be one of the existing Congress parties, or a reunited Congress party, in coalition with or supported by a number of other parties brought together by – if by nothing else – their determination to maintain constitutional forms of government. On their flanks, and making the political pace, would be the enemies of constitutional government, both right and left, now strong enough to squeeze the moderate and constitutionalist centre into a very narrow manoeuvring space indeed. Clearly, this would be a very unstable political situation which would lead almost inevitably to a show-down probably taking the form of the imposition of Presidential rule, with army support.

3 Complete political fragmentation. This, which already exists in some of the states, might well extend itself to the Centre. In New Delhi there would be a series of unstable minority or coalition governments, incapable of pursuing any consistent policies or of making their wills effective in any of the significant areas of administration. This situation would also be extremely unstable, and might likewise lead to the imposition of Presidential rule.

4 A situation in which the political life of the country becomes more variegated and decentralised without losing all elements of coherence. A comparatively weak but also comparatively stable central government, supported by a single party or firm coalition of major parties, would perform coordinating and conciliating functions for the benefit of a series of state governments which would largely monopolise such political interest as the people chose to display. Some of these might be chronically unstable, like so many of the present state governments, but many would be dominated, like Maharashtra, Mysore or Madras, by a single party, or, like Punjab, by a firm party coalition. In this respect the situation in the states would be analogous to that at the centre, but there would

be no necessary or even probable correspondence between the party composition of the various ruling groups (nor, indeed, between the party composition of the various oppositions) either vertically or horizontally.

These are not now immediate options, yet in the long run they all remain open, some of them being obviously much better candidates than others. Perhaps the vital question is whether the tendency, so strongly marked in the late 1950s and the 1960s, for the political centre of gravity to shift away from New Delhi and towards the state capitals will continue, and with it the growth of regional parties, the regionalisation of national parties, and the creation of specifically regional coalitions and alliances. If so the preservation of democratic forms of rule will demand of India's politicians the frequent striking of new balances, each capable of displaying a relative stability, and the penalty of failure to perform this exercise successfully will be the fragmentation envisaged by the third option.

On past showing, the difficulties will be very great, and one must therefore hesitate before giving India a clean democratic bill of health on the strength of Mrs Gandhi's recent success in restoring what appears to be coherent government at the centre. The elections of 1971 may have given India's democracy no more than a respite, and one is still justified in registering surprise that it has enjoyed so long a life. Indeed, one may also legitimately ask whether, over the long term, democracy is capable of providing the most appropriate political environment for the accomplishment of the huge developmental tasks which the country inevitably faces.

Nevertheless, on the assumption that democracy is desirable *per se,* or that there is no practicable alternative, it is well worth while enquiring whether, given greater wisdom on the part of India's governments, the present prospects for democratic politics might not have been considerably better than they are, and what could conceivably be done, from now on, to improve them. Any discourse on these themes, of course, presupposes that there both were and are alternative courses of action available; but such a presupposition has necessarily to be made in any political discussion which goes beyond the mere

explanation of past events and attempts to rise to the level of
the prescriptive.

Criticism may possibly be directed most cogently at the
economic policies that successive governments have pursued. In
placing the emphasis here we are not arguing in favour of a
deterministic relationship between economics and politics, but
rather suggesting that the area of choice available to the government of a developing country depends to a very considerable
extent on the success of its efforts to increase the production
of material goods and to arrange for their distribution on
principles that prove to be widely acceptable.

Looked at from this point of view, India's political crisis can
at least partly be explained by the fact that the economic
development of the country has been fast enough to exacerbate
existing group antagonisms and to create new ones but not
fast enough to facilitate the containment of these antagonisms
within a democratic framework, through the judicious distribution of benefits of adequate size. There has, of course, been
some degree of inevitability about this, since the pace of
economic development has been limited both by the shortage
of indigenous resources and by the insufficiency of foreign
assistance. Nevertheless, it can be argued that the political
situation might have evolved more favourably if different
methods of *utilising* the available resources had been adopted.
In fact, one can make a case to the effect that, in certain crucial
respects, India has chosen the *wrong* kind of economic
development.

As we have indicated in the chapter on planning, there has
been a considerable emphasis on the creation of a heavy
industrial base. Here the vital decisions were taken at the
beginning of the Second Five Year Plan, by Nehru under the
influence of Mahalanobis. Once taken, they acquired a
momentum of their own. Although the initial over-confidence
about agriculture which stimulated them underwent very rapid
evaporation, it was long before the government developed a
reasonably coherent and realistic policy for the rural sector; for
in this sphere too 'bigness' proved fatally attractive, with the
result that far too much attention was paid to the construction
of massive irrigation dams (the benefits of which were both
problematical and long-term) and too little to the sinking of

tube-wells. Excessive faith was also placed in the developmental potential of the Community Projects and in the virtues of rural cooperative institutions. Whether the distribution of expenditure as between agriculture and heavy industry was right or wrong is a matter for dispute – and the answer partly depends on what one counts as 'agricultural' expenditure; what is certain is that the concentration of attention and of skills on heavy industry inhibited the devotion of careful thought and institutional inventiveness to the problem of agricultural productivity that it demanded. One of the more obvious results of this inter-sectoral disproportion was rapid inflation, which brought with it the usual discontents and tensions, finding plenty of opportunities for expression through the facilities provided by a democratic political system. The heavy industry emphasis, combined with the increasing shortage of foreign exchange, also meant that the development of industries producing consumer goods was slower than it might have been, as a result both of a lack of resources and a lack of that buoyant demand which might have come from a prospering rural sector. Rising expectations, therefore, went relatively unsatisfied. If India had possessed a Soviet-type political system, whereby such expectations could have been suppressed, partly by force, partly by dint of a severing of all but official communications with affluent societies, the political repercussions could have been minimised. As it was, her democracy gave them full rein.

An even more serious result of the adoption of the 'heavy industry' pattern was the rapid growth of unemployment. This indeed soon became the despair of the planners, who periodically expressed pious hopes that it could be halted but were forced to recognise an ever-increasing 'back-log' as one of the facts of life. That it *could* have been halted is not open to doubt; but this would have required a policy-reorientation which was not among the options ever seriously considered. If the creation of new employment opportunities had been given higher priority, much more attention and resources would have been devoted to labour-intensive improvements in agriculture and to the expansion of small-scale industries (using intermediate technology) in a large number of provincial towns. As it was, the planners hoped that unemployment would be looked after by the 'spread effect' of large industrial centres and by the development of Gandhi's favourite cottage and handicraft industries; but 'spread' was inevitably weak, while the cottage and handicraft industries, whose promotion really represented an attempt both to provide employment and to fill the 'wage-goods gap' on the cheap, proved disappointingly uneconomic. As a result, the employment situation got right out of control. Moreover, through the emigration of labour from the countryside to the big towns, in search of largely mythical employment opportunities, there was a steady flow of jobless people from a rural environment to an urban one, where the behavioural restraints characteristic of village life were absent. As is well known, urban unemployment is politically far more explosive, at least in the short run, than rural unemployment. The consequences of this rural-urban transfer of unemployment may be witnessed at any time in Calcutta – preferably by observers who are not over-sensitive and are used to living dangerously. While it may be admitted that the politically disorderly elements in this distressing city are 'natives' rather than immigrants, the sheer congestion of jobless, homeless and hopeless people in its filthy streets has provided the extremist with an ideal *casus belli.*

This growth of unemployment has combined with the ineffectiveness of the state governments' land reforms, and the central government's lack of seriousness about the 'socialistic' philosophy it so frequently proclaims, to exacerbate the inequalities which are the inevitable product of almost any known pattern of economic development. No-one can claim that India is a more egalitarian country than she was when she commenced her Five Year Plans. Inequalities between employed and unemployed, between rich and poor, and between region and region are increasing rather than diminishing, and very little is being done to mitigate them. It might be suggested, of course, that all that has happened is that new forms of inequality have superseded, or been superimposed upon, the old; but this, if it is true, by no means diminishes the seriousness of the political consequences of the phenomenon – rather the reverse. For the new inequalities, being unhallowed by tradition, are less acceptable than the old, and tend to be regarded by their victims as having been deliberately created, or at least allowed to develop, through negligence on the part of the government. Hence the politicians, held to be responsible, lose the confidence of their clients and become regarded with a mixture of hatred and contempt, as people mainly occupied with feathering their own nests at a time when so many of their countrymen have no nests at all, even of the poorest quality. It is in this way that inequality, once it passes beyond a certain limit, breeds political violence.

One should add, for full measure, that both unemployment and inequality are vastly aggravated by the sheer rapidity with which the Indian population increases. At present some thirteen million children are born annually, while the expectation of life, despite poverty, has been enhanced by the great reduction in the incidence of communicable diseases, which has been achieved, comparatively inexpensively, by the application of modern medical knowledge. Currently, some eight million new job-seekers enter the labour market each year. One can only sympathise with a government confronted with such a problem, which with the best will in the world can be solved, or mitigated, only over a period of very many years. But one may also criticise India's government for not having taken earlier account of the country's population problem. If its seriousness had been fully realised in the early 1950s, not only would employment-creation have been given much higher priority in the Plans, but a greater proportion of India's scarce resources would have been devoted to research into the techniques of family limitation and to the diffusion and application of its findings. Birth control is now being given considerable attention, with results which, although variously assessed, cannot be regarded as very promising. Its lack of immediate impact is hardly surprising, for a birth control campaign, particularly in a very poor country with low levels of literacy, is a long haul. If, however, it had been regarded, in the 1950s, as having an importance at least equal to that of steel mills and irrigation dams, India might by now have acquired an experience which was beginning to pay off, rather than still being in the comparatively early stages of her population control effort.

When all this has been said, it remains true, as we have suggested, that a serious rethinking of approaches to economic development is now proceeding and that important changes of aim and technique are under way. The question, however, is whether these have not come too late to have any political impact that could strengthen the forces of constitutionalism and democracy. This we will not attempt to answer, except by way of suggesting that 'lateness', in this context, may be used in two senses, which are generally complementary. New policies may be late in the sense that their political impact is likely to be insufficient in the time available; they may also be late in the sense that certain vested interests, the product of the old policies, have consolidated themselves to such an extent that they cannot be shifted by any methods available to a democratic polity. In the latter case the 'new' is unlikely to be sufficiently radical to meet the needs of the situation, or, if radical enough, is doomed to ineffectiveness.

Much of the blame for present difficulties must therefore be attributed to Indian governments' sins of omission and commission. But a great deal, too, must be laid at the doors of those countries which have failed to assist to the best of their ability what, after all, has been one of the most promising experiments ever undertaken by a poor country. India, one must remember, has been most grossly under-assisted. While the total sums made available by the Consortium and the Comecon countries look considerable they are almost derisory when expressed in per capita terms. On the average, India has been only half as well assisted as her neighbour, Pakistan, and has been scandalously neglected by the principal aid-giver, the United States, in comparison with those countries, such as Israel, South Korea, South Vietnam and Taiwan, where the Americans have an immediate military or strategic interest. Given the world as it is, this is perhaps inevitable; and, given the world as it is, there seems little likelihood that the rate of assistance will be stepped up.

That India's experiment in combining political democracy with economic development may conceivably be running into the sands is a tragedy, on any showing. It is not only sad for the Indian people, who have had more than their measure of sadness, but of deep concern for the Third World as a whole, and particularly for the Asiatic part of it. There was a time, hardly more than ten years ago, when India was the hope of well-informed and progressive people throughout the world. It seemed that, contrary to ideas that had gained wide currency, there was at least one underdeveloped country – and a very large and important one – that was making a go of social-democracy. This was the period when India was identified with Nehru, and when Nehru himself was making what seemed likely to be a successful bid for Third World leadership, based not on military power but on moral persuasion and practical example. That period came to an end with the Chinese border conflict, Indian rearmament, and the virtual collapse of the Third Five Year Plan. Today India looks much more like a sick man than a pioneer; and, in the manner of sick men, directs attention inwards rather than outwards. This change in her self-image, admittedly, is primarily a reflection of a change in the world situation; but even if, inconceivably, that situation had not changed to the extent that it has, India would still have reason enough to be preoccupied with her internal condition.

It is because of this introspectiveness that we have been able to get away without intention of writing a book about Indian politics which deals no more than peripherally and incidentally with the country's international relations; and indeed India is fortunate that these relations are now such that, at least for the moment, she can *afford* to adopt an introspective posture. For she is assisted, inadequately, by both of the great world powers and threatened by neither. Admittedly, she possesses 'foreign problems' which occupy a good deal of ministerial attention and which can provoke angry debates in the Lok Sabha. The dispute with Pakistan, for instance, rumbles on ominously, without much hope of a settlement, and since 1962 there has been a messy no-peace-no-war relationship with China, the former brother who has become the most feared of antagonists. But neither country presents India with a clear and present danger. Pakistan is now militarily weaker than India, and perhaps even more preoccupied than India herself with internal problems. Moreover, these are not even of a kind that will yield to the adoption of an aggressive stance towards India, since the people of East Pakistan, who are more numerous than those of the West Wing, have very little interest in the main cause of dispute, Kashmir; and might, if pushed sufficiently hard, even begin to think in terms of some kind of reunion, however loose, with their fellow-Bengalis on the other side of the lunatic frontier. As for China, it is now generally realised, even in India itself, that her foreign policies are far more cautious than the stereotyped hymns of hate she so persistently intones would suggest. She is suspected of giving military support to the tribal rebels of India's periphery, pursues the time-honoured policy of trying to draw Nepal, Sikkim and Bhutan into her sphere of influence, and looks with conspicuous favour on the activities of the Naxalites and the Communist Party (Marxist-Leninist); but it seems unlikely that she would choose to renew her assault on India (particularly now that India is so much better-armed than she was in 1962) except in the unlikely event of India's again attempting to interfere with her vital communications through the inhospitable and disputed territory of Aksai Chin – unlikely, because for India one bloody nose is more than enough. For the present, therefore, these 'problems' are serious only in so far as they cause India to spend more on defence than she would otherwise spend, to the detriment of her Five Year Plans, and to toy with the possibility of rivalling China as a minor nuclear power.

What has changed, and changed decisively, is the international status of India. The non-alignment to which she was committed by Nehru received a deadly blow in the early 1960s and has now lost most of its positive content. The Third World bloc which India aimed to lead has now disintegrated, except to the extent that its members make common cause in debate at the United Nations on some of the bigger issues, such as South Africa and Vietnam, through which the cause of anti-colonialism is kept alive. The path, through democracy to socialism, which India was hopefully treading now appears bestrewn with formidable obstacles, and there are few other countries that wish to follow her trail. From social-democratic brown hope to sick man – such is the tale, and no Indian can tell it and retain the fullness of the national pride he once felt. It is no wonder that Indians today would appear to be acquiring a reputation for hypersensitivity, and should even be providing some evidence of xenophobia. Before they can aspire again to the heights where Nehru briefly lifted them, they will need to cure their sickness. Whether they can or not is one of the unanswered and unanswerable questions, for no-one can as yet say whether it is a severe attack of something comparatively trivial or a wasting disease.

What is certain is that, irrespective of her self-image and international status, India remains one of the most important countries in the world, if for no other reason than that of size. The effect of what happens to India, economically and politically, cannot be confined to India. If the country remains viable, it will again have a powerful influence on South Asian and world politics. If a political vacuum appears where there was once a federal democracy, a vast area of chronic political instability will have been created. Hence, although we in this book have devoted almost all our attention to the country's internal problems, we must end by asserting, yet again, that India concerns everyone.

Table I

Lok Sabha Elections 1952–71

Parties	Number of candidates	Number of seats won	% of seats	% of votes
1952				
Congress	472	364	74.4	45.00
Indian Communist Party	49	16	3.3	3.30
Socialist Party	256	12	2.5	10.60
Kisan Mazdoor Praja Party	145	9	1.8	5.80
Hindu Mahasabha	31	4	0·8	0.95
Jan Sangh	93	3	0.6	3.10
Ram Rajya Parishad	55	3	0.6	2.03
Republican Party	27	2	0.4	2.36
Other Parties	215	35	7.2	11.10
Independents	521	41	8.4	15.80
Total		489		
1957				
Congress	490	371	75.1	47.78
Indian Communist Party	108	27	5.4	8.92
Praja Socialist Party	189	19	3.8	10.41
Jan Sangh	130	4	0.8	5.93
Republican Party	19	4	0.8	1.50
Hindu Mahasabha	19	1	0.2	0.86
Ram Rajya Parishad	15	—	—	0.38
Other Parties	73	29	5.9	4.81
Independents	475	39	7.9	19.39
Total		494		

Table 1

Parties	Number of candidates	Number of seats won	% of seats	% of votes
1962				
Congress	488	361	73.11	46.02
Indian Communist Party	137	29	5.9	9.96
Swatantra	172	18	3.6	6.80
Jan Sangh	198	14	2.8	6.44
Praja Socialist Party	166	12	2.4	6.84
DMK (Tamil Nadu only)	18	7	1.4	2.02
Socialist Party	107	6	1.2	2.49
Republican Party	69	3	0.6	2.78
Ram Rajya Parishad	35	2	0.4	0.55
Hindu Mahasabha	32	1	0.2	0.44
Other Parties	64	14	2.9	4.31
Independents	497	27	5.5	12.27
Total		494		
1967				
Congress	516	283	54.42	40.73
Swatantra	179	44	8.46	8.68
Jan Sangh	250	35	6.73	9.41
DMK (Tamil Nadu only)	25	25	4.80	3.90
CPI	109	23	4.42	5.19
Samyukta Socialist Party	122	23	4.42	4.92
CPI (M)	59	19	3.65	4.21
Praja Socialist Party	109	13	2.50	3.06
Republican Party	70	1	0.19	2.48
Other Parties	65	19	3.65	3.67
Independents	865	35	6.73	13.75
Total		520		

Adapted from W. H. Morris-Jones, *Government and Politics of India*, Hutchinson University Library, 3rd edn. 1971.

Parties	Number of candidates	Number of seats gained	% of seats
1971			
Congress (R)	439	350	67.5
Congress (O)	238	16	3.1
CPI (M)	85	25	4.8
CPI	86	23	4.4
Samyukta Socialist Party	91	3	0.6
Praja Socialist Party	62	2	0.4
Jan Sangh	154	22	4.2
Swatantra	58	8	1.5
DMK (Tamil Nadu only)	24	23	4.4
Republican Party	46	0	0.0
Other parties and independents	1,481	43	8.3
Total		515	

1) Polling postponed in 3 constituencies, in 2 cases owing to inclement weather and in the remaining constituency because of the death of a candidate.
Adapted from *The Indian Election Results: 1967, 1969 and 1971* by B. D. Graham, M. Johnson and J. White.
South Asian Review 4, No. 3, April 1971.

Table 2

THE DISTRIBUTION OF CANDIDATES, SEATS, AND VOTES
IN STATE ASSEMBLY ELECTIONS, 1952–67

Parties	Number of candidates	Number of seats won	% of seats	% of votes
1952				
Congress	3,153	2,246	68.4	42.20
Socialist Party	1,799	125	3.8	9.70
Indian Communist Party	465	106	3.2	4.38
Kisan Mazdoor Praja Party	1,005	77	2.3	5.11
Jan Sangh	717	35	1.1	2.76
Ram Rajya Parishad	314	31	0.9	1.21
Hindu Mahasabha	194	14	0.4	0.82
Republican Party	171	3	0 1	1.68
Other parties and independents	7,492	635	19.3	32.14
Total		3,272		
1957				
Congress	3,027	2,012	64.9	44.97
Praja Socialist Party	1,154	208	6.7	9.75
Indian Communist Party	812	176	5.7	9.36
Jan Sangh	584	46	1.5	3.60
Ram Rajya Parishad	146	22	0.7	0.69
Republican Party	99	21	0.7	1.31
Hindu Mahasabha	87	6	0.2	0.50
Other parties and independents	4,863	611	19.7	29.81
Total		3,102		

Table 2

Parties	Number of candidates	Number of seats won	% of seats	% of seats
1962				
Congress	3,062	1,984	60.2	43.53
Indian Communist Party	975	197	6.0	10.42
Praja Socialist Party	1,149	179	5.4	7.69
Swatantra	1,012	170	5.2	6.49
Jan Sangh	1,135	116	3.5	5.40
Socialist Party	632	64	1.9	2.38
DMK (Tamil Nadu only)	142	50	—	—
Ram Rajya Parishad	99	13	0.4	0.29
Republican Party	99	11	0.3	0.56
Hindu Mahasabha	75	8	0.2	0.24
Other parties and independents	5,313	555	16.8	23.00
Total		3,347		
1967				
Congress	3,443	1,694	48.59	39.96
Jan Sangh	1,607	268	7.70	8.78
Swatantra	978	257	7.37	6.65
Samyukta Socialist Party	813	180	5.16	5.19
DMK (Tamil Nadu only)	174	138	3.96	4.34
CPI (M)	511	128	3.67	4.60
CPI	625	121	3.47	4.13
Praja Socialist Party	768	106	3.04	3.40
Republican Party	378	23	0.66	1.53
Other Parties	430	195	5.59	4.75
Independents	6,774	376	10.79	16.67
Total		3,486		

Adapted from W. H. Morris-Jones, *Government and Politics of India*, Hutchinson, London, 3rd edn. 1971.

Further Reading

This is not a bibliography, even 'select'. It is a list of some of the more obvious and readily accessible books through which the reader may follow up the subjects we have dealt with. The attachment of books to chapters follows rather rough-and-ready principles. Those that cannot be so attached appear under 'General'. There is also a short list for the benefit of the reader with a taste for the biographical and autobiographical approach to politics.

General

Reinhard Bendix, *Nation Building and Citizenship* (1964)
Charles Bettelheim, *India Independent* (1968)
Percival Griffiths, *Modern India* (fourth ed. 1965)
Beatrice Pitney Lamb, *India, A World in Transition* (1963)
Philip Mason (ed.), *India and Ceylon: Unity and Diversity* (167)
W. H. Morris-Jones, *The Government and Politics of India* (third ed. 1971)
Norman Palmer, *The Indian Political System* (1961)
K. M. Panikkar, *The Foundations of New India* (1963)
C. H. Philips (ed.), *Politics and Society in India* (1963)
Donald Eugene Smith (ed.), *South Asian Politics and Religion* (1966)
M. N. Srinivas, *Social Change in Modern India* (1964)
Hugh Tinker, *India and Pakistan, a Short Political Guide* (1962)
Taya Zinkin, *Challenges in India* (1966)

Chapter 1 Introduction

Nirad C. Chaudhuri, *The Continent of Circe* (1967)
Louis Dumont, *Homo Hierarchicus* (1970)
Gunnar Myrdal, *Asian Drama* (3 vols, 1968)
V. S. Naipaul, *An Area of Darkness* (1967)

India's Democracy

Jawaharlal Nehru, *The Discovery of India* (fourth ed. 1956)
O. H. K. Spate, *India and Pakistan* (1954)
M. N. Srinivas, *Caste in Modern India and Other Essays* (1962)
George Woodcock, *The Face of India* (1964)

Chapter 2   The British Legacy

Christine Dobbin, *Basic Documents in the Development of Modern India and Pakistan 1835–1947* (1970)
H. V. Hodson, *The Great Divide* (1969)
Martin Deming Lewis (ed.), *The British in India, Imperialism or Trusteeship* (1966)
V. P. Menon, *The Transfer of Power in India* (1957)
B. N. Pandey, *The Break-up of British India* (1969)
C. H. Philips (ed.), *The Evolution of India and Pakistan 1858–1947* (1962)
Percival Spear, *The Oxford History of Modern India 1740–1947* (1965)
E. Thompson and G. T. Garratt, *The Rise and Fulfilment of British Rule in India* (1934)
Philip Woodruff, *The Men Who Ruled India* (2 vols, 1953–54)

Chapter 3   The Constitution

C. H. Alexandrowicz, *Constitutional Developments in India* (1957)
Granville Austin, *The Indian Constitution, Cornerstone of a Nation* (1966)
A. Gledhill, *The Republic of India* (second ed. 1964)
M. V. Pylee, *Constitutional Government in India* (revised ed. 1965)
K. V. Rao, *Parliamentary Democracy in India* (1961)
D. E. Smith, *India as a Secular State* (1963)

Chapter 4   Elections, Parties and Pressure Groups

F. G. Bailey, *Politics and Social Change in Orissa in 1959* (1963)
Craig Baxter, *The Jan Sangh* (1969)
Paul Brass, *Factional Politics in an Indian State* (1966)
Howard L. Erdman, *The Swatantra Party and Indian Conservatism* (1967)
Robert Hargreaves, *The Dravidian Movement* (1965)
Selig Harrison, *India, the Most Dangerous Decades* (1960)
Stanley A. Kochanek, *The Congress Party of India* (1968)

Rajni Kothari (ed.), *The Party System and Election Studies* (1966)
Baldev Raj Nayar, *Minority Politics in the Punjab* (1966)
Gene Overstreet and Marshall Windmiller, *Communism in India* (1959)
Mohan Ram, *Indian Communism* (1969)
Myron Weiner, *Party Politics in India* (1957)
Myron Weiner, *The Politics of Scarcity* (1962)
Myron Weiner, *Party Building in a New Nation* (1966)
Myron Weiner and R. Kothari (eds.), *Indian Voting Behaviour* (1965)

Chapter 5 Parliamentary Government

A. B. Lal (ed.), *The Indian Parliament* (1956)
W. H. Morris-Jones, *Parliament in India* (1957)
A. R. Mukherjea, *Parliamentary Procedure in India* (1958)
A. Premchand, *The Control of Public Expenditure in India* (1963)
K. V. Rao, *Parliamentary Democracy in India* (1961)
R. J. Venkateswaran, *Cabinet Government in India* (1967)

Chapter 6 Centre and States

S. P. Aiyer and Ushu Mehta (eds), *Essays on Indian Federalism* (1965)
R. N. Bhargave, *Indian Public Finances* (1962)
Asok Chanda, *Federalism in India* (1965)
Marcus Franda, *West Bengal and the Federalising Process in India* (1968)
G. S. Halappa (ed.), *Studies in State Administration* (1963)
Amal Ray, *Intergovernmental Relations in India, a Study in Indian Federalism* (1966)
K. Ventakaraman, *States' Finances in India* (1967)
Myron Weiner (ed.), *State Politics in India* (1968)

Chapter 7 Administration

David H. Bayley, *The Police and Political Development in India* (1969)
Ralph Braibanti (ed.), *Asian Bureaucratic Systems Emergent from the British Imperial Tradition* (1966)
Ralph Braibanti and J. J. Spengler (eds.), *Administration and Economic Development in India* (1963)

Asok Chanda, *Indian Administration* (second ed. 1967)
S. S. Khera, *District Administration in India* (1964)
Shanti Kothari and Ramarshray Roy, *Relations between Politicians and Administrators* (1969)
V. V. Ramanadham, *The Structure of Public Enterprise in India* (1961)
N. C. Roy, *The Civil Service in India* (second ed. 1960)
R. Singh, *Aspects of Indian Defence* (1965)
Richard P. Taub, *Bureaucrats under Stress* (1969)
Richard Symonds, *The British and their Successors* (1966)

Chapter 8   Planning the Economy

D. R. Gadgil, *Planning and Economic Policy* (1961)
A. H. Hanson, *The Process of Planning* (1966)
V. T. Krishnamachari, *Fundamentals of Planning* (1962)
H. K. Paranjape, *The Planning Commission, a Descriptive Account* (1964)
H. K. Paranjape, *The Reorganised Planning Commission* (1970)
George Rosen, *Democracy and Economic Change in India* (1966)
Paul Streeten and Michael Lipton (eds.), *The Crisis of Indian Planning* (1968)
H. Venkatasubbiah, *Indian Economy since Independence* (second ed. 1961)

Chapter 9   Local Government

S. C. Dube, *India's Changing Villages* (1958)
G. Jacobs (ed.), *Readings in Panchayati Raj in India* (1967)
Henry Maddick, *Democracy, Decentralisation and Development* (1963)
Henry Maddick, *Panchayati Raj* (1970)
M. V. Mathur and I. Narain, *Panchayati Raj, Planning and Democracy* (1969)
Kusum Nair, *Blossoms in the Dust* (1961)
D. C. Potter, *Government in Rural India* (1963)
Report of the Team for the Study of Community Projects and National Extension Service (1957)
R. Retzlaff, *Village Government in India* (1962)
Hugh Tinker, *Foundations of Local Self-Government in India, Pakistan and Burma* (1954)

Chapter 10   Conclusion

J. P. Narayan, *Socialism, Sarvodaya and Democracy* (1964)
Lloyd I. Rudolph and Susanne Hoeber Rudolph, *The Modernity of Tradition* (1967)
Ronald Segal, *The Crisis of India* (1965)
Patwant Singh, *India and the Future of Asia* (1966)
Barbara Ward, *India and the West* (1961)
Maurice and Taya Zinkin, *Requiem for Empire* (1964)

Biography and Autobiography

Michael Brecher, *Nehru, a Political Biography* (1959)
Nirad C. Chaudhuri, *The Autobiography of an Unknown Indian* (1951)
Walter Crocker, *Nehru, a Contemporary's Estimate* (1966)
Durga Das, *India from Curzon to Nehru and After* (1969)
Louis Fischer, *The Life of Mahatma Gandhi* (1951)
Sudir Ghosh, *Gandhi's Emissary* (1967)
James Halliday, *A Special India* (1968)
J. Nehru, *An Autobiography* (new ed. 1949)
P. Tandon, *Punjabi Century* (1961)

Index

Gandhi, Mahatma, 19, 21–2, 25, 27, 28, 30, 37–8, 39, 65, 82, 88–9, 183
Gandhian Social Service Groups, 88
Germany, 156
Ghose, Aurobindo, 13, 21
Ghosh, Ajoy, 80
Ghosh, Atulya, 57, 72, 73, 74, 119, 121
Giri, President N. V., 47, 76, 157, 179
Gokhale, Gopal Krishna, 20–1
Gorwala, A. D., 143, 190
Gujerat, 55, 58, 61, 66, 82, 126, 155, 160, 161, 187, 199
Gupta, C. B., 121

Hargraves, Robert L., *The Nadars of Tamilnad*, 89
Harrison, Selig, 62, 112, 130; *India, the Most Dangerous Decades*, 62, 126
Hart, Henry C., 103
Haryana (formerly part of Punjab), 44, 83, 84, 86, 109, 126
Haryana Congress Party, 109
Hatch, Spencer, 184
Hazelhurst, Peter, 110
Health, Ministry of, 118
Hill Cultivators' Union, 90
Himachal Pradesh, 127
Hindi language, 2, 79, 123–4
Hindu Mahasabha Party, 48, 82, 104
Hinduism, Hindus, 2–3, 4, 20, 27–9, 88; communalist parties, 49, 82–4
Hindustan Aeronautics Ltd., 153
Hodson, H. V., *The Great Divide*, 31
Home Ministry, 159; Central Bureau of Investigation (CBI), 159; Central Reserve, 158–9
Hume, Allan Octavian, 30
Hussain, Dr Zahir, 108

IAS *see* Indian Civil Service
ICS *see* Indian Civil Service
Ilchman, Dr Alice, 201
Imports, Chief Comptroller of, 142
Indian Chamber of Commerce, Calcutta, 91
Indian Civil Service/Indian Administrative Service (ICS/IAS), 17, 18, 19, 23–4, 133–7, 144, 145–50, 154, 158; Collector, 181, 189, 197, 199–200; District Officer, (DO), 134, 135–6, 184; Secretariat, 134, 135–6, 140–1
Indian Federation of Labour, 165
Indian Institute of Public Opinion, 62
Indian Mutiny (1857), 18, 27
Indian National Army (INA), 154; *see also* Army

Indian Police Service (IPS), 137, 158–9; *see also* Home Ministry
Indian Union, 44, 48
Indonesia, 7
Industrial Finance Corporation, 167
Industrial Management Pool, 144
Industrial Policy Resolutions: First (1948), 167; Second (1956), 170
Intensive Agricultural Development Projects (IADPS), 201
International Bank, 144; Mission, 142

Jaipur, Maharani of, 82
Jan Kranti Dal Party, 87
Jan Sangh *see* Bharatiya Jan Sangh
Janata Party, 86
Jharkhand Party (Orissa), 56, 85
Jinnah, Ali, 28, 29
Justice Party, 85

Kairon, P. S., 73, 121
Kamaraj, Nadar K., 57, 71
Kamma caste, 82, 86
Kashmir dispute, 32, 112, 154, 217
Katju episode, 121
Kaul, General B. M., 155
Kerala, 35, 56, 57, 58, 80–1, 84, 86, 90, 121–2, 160, 175, 177, 182
Khilafat (Muslim) movement, 28
Kisan Mazdoor Praja Party, 79
Kochanek, Stanley, *The Congress Party of India*, 71
Kothari, Rajni, 104, 134
Kripalani, Archarya, 70
Kripalani, Mrs Sucheta, 119
Krishnamachari, T. T., 133
Kumar, Dr Ravinder, 17

languages, linguistic groups, 2, 84, 90, 123–7
'law and order', 159–62
Local Government *see* Community Development Programme; Panchayati Raj; under British Imperial rule
Lohia, Dr R., 79
Lok Sabha (Lower House of Parliament), 39–40, 44, 55, 57, 59–60, 69, 76, 77, 96–101, 102, 107, 109–10, 127, 139, 208, 217; Chief Whip, 97; Leader of the House, 98; Rules of Procedure, 97; Speaker, 97, 98, 99; Committees: Business Advisory Committee, 97, 99; Committee on Government Assurances, 101; Committee on Petitions, 99; Committee on Private

233